10 THINGS YOU MIGHT NOT KNOW

ABOUT NEARLY EVERYTHING

10 THINGS YOU MIGHT NOT KNOW

ABOUT NEARLY EVERYTHING

A Collection of Fascinating Historical, Scientific and Cultural Facts about People, Places and Things

Mark Jacob and Stephan Benzkofer

Chicago Tribune

MIDWAY

AN AGATE IMPRINT

CHICAGO

Chicago Tribune

Tony W. Hunter, Publisher

Gerould W. Kern, Editor

R. Bruce Dold, Editorial Page Editor

Bill Adee, Vice President/Digital

Jane Hirt, Managing Editor

Joycelyn Winnecke, Associate Editor

Peter Kendall, Deputy Managing Editor

This book was created from the Chicago Tribune's popular feature "10 Things You Might Not Know" by Mark Jacob and Stephan Benzkofer.

Printed in the United States of America

Library of Congress Cataloging in Publication Data on file at the Library of Congress

10 9 8 7 6 5 4 2 1

Midway is an imprint of Agate Publishing. Agate books are available in bulk at discount prices. For more information, go to agatepublishing.com.

For Marjorie

—Stephan Benzkofer

For Malcolm and Brendan

—Mark Jacob

CONTENTS

10 Things You Might Not Know About...

10 THINGS YOU MIGHT NOT KNOW ABOUT
ARTS/CULTURE

BEST-SELLERS

1 In "The Da Vinci Code" and other Dan Brown novels, characters are compelled to unravel mysteries at a frenetic pace. The same thing happened to Brown as a child. On Christmas and his birthdays, his parents hid his gifts, requiring him to solve puzzles and riddles to find the presents.

2 Matt Latimer, a former speechwriter for George W. Bush, wrote recently that unidentified "people in the White House ... objected to giving author J.K. Rowling a presidential medal because the Harry Potter books encouraged witchcraft."

3 The Oxford English Dictionary credits the Kansas City Times & Star with the first use of the term "best sellers" — with no hyphen — in 1889. Since then, various book-sales rankings have appeared — from The New York Times to Publishers Weekly to Amazon. They use different criteria, which means there is no strict definition of a best-seller. For purposes of this article, it's simply a book that sells well. Some best-seller lists are quite exclusive. Publishers Weekly's analysis of its own 2005 lists found that of the estimated 200,000 books published that year, only 0.2 percent were best-sellers.

4 Richard Wright's 1940 novel "Native Son" was the first work by an African-American to be a Book of the Month Club selection, guaranteeing the novel a wide audience. But before agreeing to the sponsorship, the Book of the Month Club asked Wright to tone down the book's sexual content — and he agreed. Despite Wright's notoriety, he often struggled financially. Near the end of his life as an expatriate in Paris, he earned money by writing liner notes for record albums.

5 Cormac McCarthy's post-apocalyptic page-turner, "The Road," may be the ultimate dark novel. In fact, the word "dark" appears in the book 95 times, with an additional 42 variants such as "darkness" and "darkly." References to "black" (68) and "gray" (78) far outstrip those to "green" (10) and "white" (18).

6 Dr. Seuss' editor, Bennett Cerf, bet him $50 that he could not write a book with a vocabulary of only 50 words. Seuss won by penning "Green Eggs and Ham."

7 The first printing of Barack Obama's book "Dreams From My Father" in 1995 sold about 10,000 copies. At the time, Obama had not yet been elected a state senator. Now he's president, and more than 3 million copies are in print. Signed first editions have carried an asking price of up to $13,500.

8 Where did Chicagoan L. Frank Baum come up with the name of the magical land in "The Wonderful Wizard of Oz"? Baum said he was looking at his alphabetically arranged file cabinets and was inspired by the one labeled "O-Z." But there are other theories, according to the debunking website Snopes.com. Perhaps it's a tribute to Percy Shelley's poem "Ozymandias." Or it's a nod to the Land of Uz in the Bible's book of Job. Or it's related to Charles Dickens' pseudonym "Boz." Or it's a letter-shifting code for Baum's native state of New York in which N has moved up one place in the alphabet to become O, and Y has done the same to become Z.

9 Jack Canfield, who co-authored "Chicken Soup for the Soul" with Mark Victor Hansen, said their manuscript was rejected by about 140 publishers, whose criticism included the assertion "It's a stupid title." Well, that stupid title has appeared on more than 112 million books, including nearly 200 spinoffs such as "Chicken Soup for the Soul in Menopause" and "Chicken Soup for the Soul: What I Learned from the Cat."

10 "Staying Dry: A Practical Guide to Bladder Control" had trouble finding a publisher. And even when Johns Hopkins University Press released the work by Kathryn L. Burgio, K. Lynette Pearce and Angelo J. Lucco in 1989, major bookstore chains took a pass. But when the Chicago Tribune's Ann Landers mentioned the book in her column, the dam broke. "Staying Dry" sold more than 100,000 copies in a year.

SOURCES: *"Why We Read What We Read" by Lisa Adams and John Heath; "Casanova Was a Book Love"" by John Maxwell Hamilton; "Richard Wright: The Life and Times" by Hazel Rowley; "Dr. Seuss: American Icon" by Philip Nel; New York Daily News; Sydney Morning Herald; GQ magazine; snopes.com; chickensoup.com; voanews.com; abebooks.com; common-place.org; publishersweekly.com.*

BLONDS

1   People have gone to great lengths to achieve blondness. In ancient Rome, people used pigeon poop; in Renaissance Venice, horse urine. Throughout history, nonblonds have also tried white wine, olive oil, ivy bark, soap and saffron.

2   Alfred Hitchcock cast so many blondes in his movies that film critics now write of "Hitchcock blondes:" beautiful, aloof, smart leading ladies. Think Grace Kelly, Tippi Hedren and Kim Novak. Hitchcock offered myriad reasons for his preference for light-haired actresses, including that they film better in black and white, but one quote seems to sum it up: "Blondes make the best victims," Hitchcock said. "They're like virgin snow that shows up the bloody footprints."

3   According to Victoria Sherrow's "Encyclopedia of Hair," there was an original "dumb blonde." An 18th century French actress and prostitute named Rosalie Duthe was known for being very beautiful but incapable of intelligent conversation. She was satirized in a play called "Les Curiosites de la Foire" in 1775. But dumb is relative: Duthe was extremely wealthy as a mistress of royalty.

4   If the director yells "Kill the blonde!" on a movie set, he's probably ordering the crew to shut off an open-face, 2,000-watt spotlight.

5   Actress Marilyn Monroe colored her hair using a shade of blond called dirty pillow slip.

6   In junior high, Kurt Cobain was profiled in his school newspaper, the Puppy Press: "Kurt is a seventh-grader at our school. He has blond hair and blue eyes. He thinks school is alright. ... His favorite saying is 'Excuse you.' "

7 Actress Veronica Lake's peekaboo hairdo, with long blond hair over one eye, was a 1940s sensation. According to Life magazine, she had about 150,000 hairs on her head, with her tresses 17 inches long in front and 24 inches long in back. The downsides: "Her hair catches fire fairly often when she is smoking" and "it has a bad habit of snagging on men's buttons." About the buttons, Life wrote: "If Miss Lake were in fact the kind of girl she portrays on the screen, this might lead to all kinds of fascinating complications..."

8 Only one in 20 white American adults is naturally blond.

9 In the early '80s, Brad Pitt dropped out of the University of Missouri two credits short of graduating and went to Hollywood. But before his light-haired good looks became famous, Pitt worked a variety of odd jobs in California — delivering refrigerators, serving as a chauffeur for strippers and dressing as a chicken to promote El Pollo Loco "flame-grilled" chicken.

10 Former members of the '70s rock group Stilettos were searching for a name for their new group and settled on Blondie. Lead singer Debbie Harry said the name came from truck drivers who would pass her and shout, "Hey, Blondie!" In 1997, the band performed on an Iggy Pop tribute album using the pseudonym Adolph's Dog. It's probably not a coincidence that Adolf Hitler had a pet dog named Blondi.

SOURCES: *"Strike the Baby and Kill the Blonde: An Insider's Guide to Film Slang" by Dave Knox; "Encyclopedia of Hair: A Cultural History" by Victoria Sherrow; "Encyclopedia of Prostitution and Sex Work, Vol. 1" by Melissa Hope Ditmore; "On Blondes" by Joanna Pitman; "Peekaboo: The Story of Veronica Lake" by Jeff Lenburg; "Alfred Hitchcock: A Life in Darkness and Light" by Patrick McGilligan; "Punk: The Definitive Record of a Revolution" by Stephen Colegrave and Chris Sullivan; "Heavier Than Heaven: A Biography of Kurt Cobain" by Charles R. Cross; "The Rolling Stone Film Reader," article by Chris Mundy; Life magazine; Boston Herald.*

BRIDGES

1 A remarkable photo of Korean refugees on a bridge near Pyongyang helped The Associated Press' Max Desfor win a Pulitzer Prize in 1951. The bridge was bombed by American planes to slow the Chinese advance in December 1950, and refugees had to climb over the wreckage to reach the other side of the Taedong River. Desfor told the Tribune: "For a long time I thought, 'I'd like to meet some of the people who were on that bridge.' That idea haunted me for a long time." Visiting South Korea in 2000, he said, "I got to meet one man who had crossed over.... He may be in that picture somewhere."

2 Almost 500 soldiers were marching across a suspension bridge over the Maine River in Angers, France, when it collapsed in 1850, killing 226. Experts theorized that the vibration of the men marching in step had caused the disaster. Thus the catastrophe helped establish the tradition of armies "breaking step" (marching out of step) over bridges.

3 A lawyer named Abraham Lincoln defended a bridge in the 1850s. Lincoln represented the owner of a new railroad bridge across the Mississippi River that was hit by a steamboat. The boat sank, and the owner sued, declaring the bridge a hazard to navigation. Arguing in federal court — located in the Saloon Building on Chicago's Lake Street — Lincoln suggested that the accident was staged to challenge Chicago's railroad interests. The jury deadlocked, and the suit was dismissed, effectively establishing the railroads' right to expand westward.

4 Chicago has long boasted that it has more movable bridges than any other city in the world, but several of them have been removed in recent years. The city replaced a nearly century-old trunnion bascule bridge with a suspension and cable-stay bridge at North Avenue and the Chicago River.

5 Since San Francisco's Golden Gate Bridge opened 70 years ago, more than 1,300 people have jumped from the span. One leaper left a note reading: "Absolutely no reason except I have a toothache." Some Bay-area residents have become jaded. As the 1,000th fatality approached in the 1990s, a radio disc jockey promised to give the victim's family a free case of Snapple. One of the very few to survive the jump, Ken Baldwin, told The New Yorker about his thoughts after he leaped: "I instantly realized that everything in my life that I'd thought was unfixable was totally fixable — except for having just jumped."

6 Chicago had its own suicide-beckoning bridge but tore it down in 1919. Known as High Bridge, it rose 75 feet over the Lincoln Park lagoon and was designed for sightseers. But it became a macabre mecca. People not only jumped off of it but also went there to shoot themselves or take poison. A postcard of the time featured the common name for the span: "Suicide Bridge."

7 Osama bin Laden's half brother, Sheikh Tarek Mohammed bin Laden, said in 2007 he would try to raise about $20 billion to build a 17-mile bridge off the Horn of Africa, between Djibouti and Yemen. A source close to the Saudi-based businessman told the Times of London that one motivation for the project was to rehabilitate the bin Laden family's name.

8 In 2006, Italy scrapped 30-year-old plans to build a bridge across the Strait of Messina, linking Sicily with the mainland. Lawmakers wanted the $5.5 billion spent elsewhere, environmentalists feared the bridge would disrupt the migration of birds and fish, and prosecutors worried that the Mafia would skim the construction money.

9 Despite impassioned backing from then-Sen. Ted Stevens (R-Alaska), Congress rejected in 2005 a Stevens-backed "earmark" to spend about $200 million on a "bridge to nowhere" that would connect Ketchikan, Alaska (population 8,900), with Gravina Island (population 50). The proposed bridge became a symbol of government excess and an issue in presidential campaigns, with both Sarah Palin and Rick Santorum criticized for their past support.

10 A bridge across the Arkansas River opened in 2006 in Little Rock. It's for pedestrians and bicycles only — the nation's longest bridge built for that purpose. Because the span is over the Murray Lock and Dam, naming it was easy. It's called the Big Dam Bridge.

SOURCES: *Village Voice; The New Yorker; San Francisco Chronicle; Times of London; "A Court That Shaped America" by Richard Cahan; "Challenging Chicago" by Perry Duis; Tribune news services and staff reports.*

FICTIONAL FATHERS

1   Among the most admired fictional fathers is Atticus Finch, the widower lawyer in Harper Lee's novel "To Kill a Mockingbird." The character, played by Gregory Peck in the film, was based on Lee's father, Amasa Lee. One day on the set, Peck saw the novelist crying as she watched a scene. Thinking "we just got to her something terrific," Peck stopped to talk. She told him: "Oh, Gregory, you've got a little potbelly just like my daddy!"

2   Chevy Chase plays Clark Griswold in four "Vacation" feature films, but Clark's two kids are played by different actors in each. In the fourth movie, "Vegas Vacation," Griswold declares: "You guys are growing up so fast, I hardly recognize you anymore!"

3   Imagine Gene Hackman as the father in "The Brady Bunch." Impossible? Lucky for him, he lacked celebrity, so he was passed over for the role. In stepped Robert Reed, who considered himself a real actor and feared being typecast as a sitcom dad. The show was so silly, Reed said, "I do not want it on my tombstone."

4   Pat Conroy's abusive character Lt. Col. "Bull" Meecham in the novel "The Great Santini" was based on his own fighter-pilot father. But Conroy said the truth was even worse — he toned down the depiction because he was afraid readers would find it incredible. Yet when the book came out, Don Conroy reformed himself. "My father may be the only person in the history of the world who changed himself because he despised a character in literature who struck chords of horror in himself that he could not face," the novelist wrote.

5   One of the most popular TV dads was Dr. Heathcliff Huxtable, better known as Cliff. He was played by a philosopher of fatherhood, Bill Cosby, whose advice included: "Always end the name of your child with a vowel, so that when you yell, the name will carry."

6 Some commonly quoted movie lines never really appeared in films. Among them is "Luke, I am your father," supposedly said by the evil Darth Vader in "The Empire Strikes Back." The actual line is "No, I am your father."

7 Laurence Fishburne and Cuba Gooding Jr. played father and son in the 1991 film "Boyz N the Hood" even though they're only six and a half years apart.

8 Before he was Howard Cunningham, everybody's favorite dad on "Happy Days," Tom Bosley acted with Paul Newman at the Woodstock Opera House in Woodstock, Ill. Bosley, who was born in Chicago and grew up in Glencoe, served in the Navy during World War II.

9 In John Irving's novel "The World According to Garp," the protagonist is conceived when his mother, a nurse, has sex with a dying, brain-damaged patient named Technical Sergeant Garp. In real life, Irving did not know his biological father and told his mother that if she did not tell him the circumstances of his conception, he would make them up. "Go ahead, dear," she said.

10 "Father Knows Best" started as a radio sitcom in 1949 as "Father Knows Best?" When it moved to TV in 1954, the producers were apparently more confident in dad's wisdom and the question mark was left behind.

SOURCES: *"My Losing Season: A Memoir" by Pat Conroy; "Glued to the Set: The 60 Television Shows and Events that Made Us Who We are Today" by Steven D. Stark; "Gregory Peck: A Biography" by Gary Fishgall; "Fatherhood" by Bill Cosby; "Television Characters" by Vincent Terrace; "Encyclopedia of Television" by Horace Newcomb; timesonline.co.uk; imdb.com; Tribune archives.*

MODERN ART

1 There were plenty of people in early 20th Century Paris who thought they were doing Amedeo Modigliani a favor. They accepted the charming but poverty-stricken artist's work in exchange for food. But they didn't realize what they had. A restaurateur stored Modigliani's paintings in his basement, where rats chewed them up. The operator of a potato stall used Modigliani's drawings to wrap her fried chips. In 2006, more than eight decades after Modigliani's death, one of his works sold for $30 million.

2 Georgia O'Keeffe's flower paintings have fascinated many people, but the fuss over them annoyed the artist. She once told art critic Emily Genauer: "I hate flowers — I paint them because they're cheaper than models and they don't move."

3 When the Picasso sculpture was installed in Chicago's Daley Plaza in 1967, then-Ald. John Hoellen (47th) called on the city to "deport" the artwork to France and replace it with a statue of Cubs slugger Ernie Banks. (Pop quiz: What's the title of the sculpture? Answer: It doesn't have one.)

4 Robert Rauschenberg produced a 1953 work titled "Erased de Kooning Drawing" by using rubber erasers to rub out a drawing that artist Willem de Kooning had given him for that purpose.

5 Chicago painter Ivan Albright was so meticulous that during a typical five-hour workday, he would paint about a half of a square inch.

6 You've heard of op art and pop art — but "plop art"? It's a term for public art that bears no relation to its environment, as if it was plopped down in its location without any thought.

7 Andy Warhol's paintings of Campbell's soup cans were the ultimate pop art. But not everyone was impressed. When Warhol's first soup-can exhibit opened in New York City in 1962, a competing gallery put actual Campbell's cans in its windows with a sign reading, "Buy them cheaper here — sixty cents for three cans."

8 Edward Hopper's wife, Jo, once bit his hand to the bone.

9 Max Ernst's embrace of surrealism seems more understandable when you understand that his father, an amateur weekend painter, had a problem with plain old reality. The senior Ernst, painting a picture of his garden but struggling with how to depict a tree in the scene, solved the problem by grabbing an ax and chopping down the tree.

10 Chris Burden, a California performance artist in the '70s, stuffed himself into a school locker for five days, nailed himself to the roof of a Volkswagen Beetle in a mock crucifixion, arranged for an assistant to shoot him in the arm and fired a gunshot at a plane passing overhead. If he did any of those things today, he'd get his own reality TV show.

SOURCES: *"Anecdotes of Modern Art" by Donald Hall and Pat Corrington Wykes; "The Life and Death of Andy Warhol" by Victor Bockris; "Pop Art" by Tilman Osterwold; "Retailing," edited by Anne M. Findlay and Leigh Sparks; "Lives of Great 20th Century Artists" by Edward Lucie-Smith;"Shock of the New" by Robert Hughes; Art in America magazine; Grove Art Online; artforum.com; artinfo.com; Tribune archives and news services.*

MUSIC FESTIVALS

1 Creedence Clearwater Revival was the first big-name band lined up for Woodstock. The group's signing encouraged others to appear at the 1969 event, but Creedence ended up with a lousy time slot: about 1:30 a.m., after the Grateful Dead. Said Creedence frontman John Fogerty: "Wow, we got to follow the band that put a half a million people to sleep."

2 The name of the Bonnaroo festival in Manchester, Tenn., came from Dr. John's album "Desitively Bonnaroo," a title based on New Orleans slang. "Desitively" is a combination of "definitely" and "positively"; bonnaroo is an amalgam of two French words, "bon" and "rue," meaning the best on the streets.

3 The end of the Franco-Prussian War was celebrated with a music fest in Boston, of all places. Composer Johann Strauss conducted about 17,000 singers and an orchestra of 1,500 at the World's Peace Jubilee and International Musical Festival of 1872.

4 Kris Kristofferson's 1969 appearance at the Newport Folk Festival, one of his first breaks as a performer, was arranged by the late country legend Johnny Cash. Kristofferson made an impression on Cash by landing a helicopter on his lawn and handing him a demo tape.

5 Live Aid begat Farm Aid. Bob Dylan was performing at the Philadelphia portion of the huge 1985 festival, which was intended to benefit the starving peoples of Ethiopia, when he said he hoped some of the money could go to help the American farmer. Live Aid organizer Bob Geldof said Dylan's plea "was crass, stupid and nationalistic." Two months later, the first Farm Aid concert took place in Champaign.

6 U2's legendary performance at Live Aid is widely credited with launching the Irish band to superstardom. But at the time, it was a disaster. After Bono left the stage for more than two minutes during an unplanned 13-minute rendition of "Bad" and danced with fans, U2 didn't have time to play their third song. The rest of the band was so angry they asked Bono to quit. "I thought I'd made a big mistake," Bono said. "I went out and drove for days. ... And when I got back, I found people were saying the bit they remembered was U2."

7 Supermodel Kate Moss booted up the popularity of Hunter Wellies when she sported the rugged footwear at the muddy Glastonbury music festival in Britain in 2005. Fashionistas interviewed by Canada's Globe and Mail said the 2011 fest faves included feathers, scarves and floppy hats.

8 Our nomination for best fest name: Blistered Fingers, a bluegrass event in Maine. Possibly the worst-named: a Kansas festival called Kanrocksas

9 Milwaukee's Summerfest was nearly silenced on opening day in 2006. An electrocuted falcon caused a three-hour power failure, rendering numerous electric guitars useless. That didn't stop the University of Wisconsin-Madison marching band, which required no artificial amplification. The students played an impromptu show that included "Roll Out the Barrel."

10 Britain's tallest teen girl, Jessica Pardoe, who was described by the Sunday Mirror as "6 foot 9 inches in bare feet," told the newspaper earlier this month: "I love going to music festivals, and it's great to be able to see over everyone's heads."

SOURCES: *"Music of the Gilded Age" by John Ogasapian and N. Lee Orr; "Woodstock: Three Days That Rocked the World" by Mike Evans and Paul Kingsbury; "Alternative Rock" by Dave Thompson; "Back to the Garden: The Story of Woodstock and How It Changed a Generation" by Pete Fornatale; "Hollywood Songsters, Volume 2" by James Robert Parish and Michael R. Pitts; "Chicago Neighborhoods and Suburbs" by Ann Durkin Keating; New York Times; Milwaukee Journal Sentinel; Sunday Mirror; Globe and Mail; newportfolkfest.net.*

SCREENWRITERS

1 Joseph Farnham was a "title writer" in silent-era Hollywood, fashioning the words that appeared between scenes in films. In the first-ever Academy Awards, for 1927-28, Farnham won the Oscar for Best Title Writing. By the next year, talkies were in vogue and the "title writer" award was dropped, leaving Farnham as the only winner of that prize. After suffering a heart attack in 1931, Farnham added another distinction: the first Oscar winner to die.

2 Ben Hecht, the Chicago Daily News reporter and playwright who served as a script doctor on "Gone With the Wind," won the first Academy Award for original screenplay (for "Underworld"). Hecht used his statuette as a doorstop.

3 "The Dick Van Dyke Show" was the quintessential television program about television writers. Since the show carried Van Dyke's name, you might think it was designed around him. But you would be wrong. Carl Reiner envisioned himself as Rob Petrie when he wrote and starred in a pilot called "Head of the Family." When the pilot was rejected, other leading men were considered. Even then Van Dyke wasn't a shoo-in. He had to beat out a guy named Johnny Carson.

4 Paul Schrader, who wrote the screenplay for "Taxi Driver," was raised in an ultraconservative Christian household and didn't see a single movie until age 18.

5 Robert Towne, screenwriter of "Chinatown" and "Shampoo," was so annoyed with the movie based on his script for "Greystoke: The Legend of Tarzan, Lord of the Apes" that he wouldn't allow his name to be used in the credits. Instead, the screenplay was credited to P.H. Vazak — Towne's sheepdog.

6   Some famous writer-directors, such as David Mamet and John Sayles, have worked as script doctors on other people's movies. Mamet was brought in on "Ronin" and shared writing credit under the pseudonym Richard Weisz. Sayles wrote the final draft of "Apollo 13" but got no screen credit. Sayles complained that credits were unfairly based on how much of a script a writer changed: "It's this funny thing where you can make the movie 20 percent better and you won't get credit, but if you make it 60 percent worse ... you'll get credit," he told the Tribune's Mark Caro.

7   The film version of "The Flintstones" (1994) may have set the record for the number of screenwriters. Reports range from 30 to 60.

8   Spike Lee, the writer-director whose screenplay for "Do the Right Thing" received an Oscar nomination, has never learned how to drive a car.

9   Chevy Chase was first hired for "Saturday Night Live" as a writer, but later became a performer. Two decades later, the same thing happened to Tina Fey. Chase's real name is Cornelius Crane Chase. Fey's is Elizabeth Stamatina Fey.

10   One of the funniest endings of a TV series wasn't conceived by a screenwriter. Bob Newhart portrayed a Chicago psychologist in "The Bob Newhart Show," and later played a Vermont innkeeper in "Newhart." In the last scene of "Newhart," he was shown in bed with Suzanne Pleshette, who played his wife in the earlier show. He told her he had had a dream about a weird Vermont town — thereby relegating the show's 182 episodes to a dream sequence. The ending was suggested by Newhart's real wife, Virginia, at a Christmas party.

SOURCES: *imdb.com; Tribune news services and archives.*

STANLEYS

1 In honor of the Chicago Blackhawks' 2010 Stanley Cup run, we honor the name Stanley. Its popularity as a boy's name in the United States peaked in 1915-1917, when it was the 34th most popular name three years running, as tracked by the Social Security Administration. It has been downhill ever since. In 2009, it was No. 676.

2 President Barack Obama's grandfather was Stanley Dunham, and — far more unusually — Obama's mother was named Stanley too. A childhood friend recalled Stanley Ann Dunham explaining that "my dad wanted a boy and he got me. And the name Stanley made him feel better, I guess." After high school, Obama's mother stopped introducing herself as Stanley and switched to Ann.

3 "Stanley" is Chicago slang for a Pole or Polish-American.

4 Actor Marlon Brando beat out John Garfield and Burt Lancaster to play the brutish Stanley Kowalski in Tennessee Williams' play "A Streetcar Named Desire." Brando won the part by visiting Williams' home in Provincetown, Mass., in 1947 and performing three virtuoso acts: reading the script well, repairing Williams' overflowing toilet, and fixing a blown fuse that had forced the playwright to read by candlelight.

5 A young Welshman named John Rowlands immigrated to New Orleans, where he was befriended by merchant Henry Morton Stanley and adopted the man's name as his own. The new Stanley joined Confederate forces, was captured at Shiloh and was imprisoned in Chicago. At war's end, things got even more interesting. Stanley became a newspaper correspondent in Spain, Crete, Ethiopia and what is now Tanzania, where he found missing Scottish missionary David Livingstone and uttered the famous line, "Dr. Livingstone, I presume." Though they were in what Stanley called "darkest Africa," they drank champagne in silver goblets to celebrate the meeting.

6   Among the secret Stanleys in show business are Bobby Vinton (Stanley Robert Vinton Jr.) and M.C. Hammer (Stanley Kirk Burrell). But KISS co-founder Paul Stanley merely moved the "Stanley" in his name. At birth, he was Stanley Eisen.

7   The Stanley Steamer was the most famous of the steam-powered cars, which had their heyday in the early 1900s. As crazy as it sounds, driving around on top of a boiler was surprisingly safe. That said, the internal-combustion engine eventually won the day. But some Stanley enthusiasts wouldn't let it go. So in 1951, the Museum of Science and Industry and Popular Mechanics magazine staged a race from Chicago to New York between a 1913 Stanley Steamer and a 1911 gas-powered Stoddard-Dayton to settle which car was better. The Stanley won.

8   For decades, Flat Stanley was just a 2D character from Jeff Brown's 1964 book and series. But in 1995, Canadian third-grade teacher Dale Hubert gave him a whole new dimension when he used him as part of a letter-writing project. It went viral, to say the least. Today, the Flat Stanley Project is worldwide. Its website features photos of Flat Stanley with, among others, President Obama and Clint Eastwood.

9   According to NHL.com, in 2010 there were no active NHL players named Stanley, Stan — or Stanislaus for that matter. But Stanleys have had some success playing hockey. Allan Stanley played on a powerhouse Toronto Maple Leafs team that won four of Lord Stanley's cups in the 1960s. But for Chicagoans, you need look no further than Stan Mikita, who helped the Blackhawks win it all in 1961, for the most famous hockey-playing Stan.

10   A low point for the Stanley Cup came in 1924. The triumphant Montreal Canadiens put the trophy in their car trunk to drive to the victory party. But their car got a flat, and they took the trophy out and perched it on a snowbank so they could take out the spare tire. After changing the tire, they arrived at the party, only to realize they had misplaced the Stanley Cup. They found it where they had left it: on the snowbank.

SOURCES: *"Somebody: The Reckless Life and Remarkable Career of Marlon Brando" by Stefan Kanfer; snopes.com; nhl.com; Tribune archives.*

TEACHERS

1　Pink Floyd's 1979 song "Another Brick in the Wall, Part II" — with lyrics such as "We don't need no education" and "Hey, teacher, leave them kids alone" — put an unwelcome spotlight on a maverick London high school instructor known for chain-smoking in class. Music teacher Alun Renshaw brought 23 students to a studio to record the song's chorus for Pink Floyd, but failed to secure his boss' permission. The school got lots of criticism, the music department got 1,000 pounds, and Renshaw got out of the country, moving to Australia.

2　When Americans are asked which occupations contribute the most to society's well-being, they answer teachers, second only to military personnel, according to a 2009 Pew Research survey. (Scientists were third and medical doctors fourth.) That esteem for educators appears to be even higher among Generation Next, those born from 1981 to 1988, who are twice as likely as older generations to name a teacher or mentor when asked to list people they admire.

3　Teenage outlaw John Wesley Hardin, wanted for killing four men, hid from authorities for three months in the late 1860s by working as a teacher at his aunt's school in Texas. "John Wesley Hardin prayed before class every morning," a schoolgirl recalled.

4　Educators in 19 states, including Indiana and Missouri, can still discipline a student by paddling. While most of the states that allow corporal punishment are in the South, it is also legal in Idaho and Wyoming. New Mexico became in 2011 the most recent state to ban the practice. At the time, Vernon Asbill, a Republican state senator and retired educator, argued, "The threat of it keeps many of our kids in line so they can learn." A 2010 bill in the U.S. House to ban corporal punishment in schools died in committee.

5　When future president Lyndon Johnson taught speech at Sam Houston High School in Houston, he drove the debate team relentlessly, putting them through 50 practice competitions. The team charged through city and district competition but lost in the state finals, upsetting Johnson so badly that he ran to the bathroom and threw up.

6 Famed educator Maria Montessori left Italy and went into exile because of philosophical clashes with a former teacher — Italian dictator Benito Mussolini, whose students once nicknamed him il tiranno (the tyrant).

7 Teachers are heroes every day, but especially when violence erupts. Shannon Wright shielded a student and was fatally shot during a school massacre in Jonesboro, Ark., in 1998. Dave Sanders was killed while helping scores of students to safety at Columbine High School outside Denver in 1999. When a student started setting off pipe bombs at a school in San Mateo, Calif., in 2009, Kennet Santana tackled him. "I just thought to myself, 'If I'm wrong, I'll apologize to his parents later,' " he explained.

8 Some guidebooks for teachers encourage them to use euphemisms to avoid offending students and parents. A student is not described as lazy — instead, he's "a reluctant scholar." A student isn't spoiled — instead, she "only responds positively to very firm handling." Those dice you're using in math class aren't really dice — they're called "probability cubes" to avoid upsetting parents opposed to gambling.

9 Kiss bassist Gene Simmons, the rocker known for his heavy makeup and long tongue, was once a teacher. "I used to be a sixth-grade teacher in Spanish Harlem," he said. "I did it for six months, and I wanted to kill every single kid." But in a separate interview, he said: "Children need to learn to be selfish, to put themselves first and not care what other people think."

10 Female instructors in Chicago became more active in the women's suffrage movement in the 1890s after school board member William Rainey Harper (also president of the University of Chicago) rejected the idea of raises for teachers, noting that they already made more money than his wife's maid. He also suggested a compromise: raises for male teachers only.

SOURCES: *"The Ultimate Teachers' Handbook" by Hazel Bennett; "John Wesley Hardin: Dark Angel of Texas" by Leon Claire Metz; "Lone Star Rising: Lyndon Johnson and his Times, 1908-1960" by Robert Dallek; " 'Everybody's Paid but the Teacher': The Teaching Profession and the Women's Movement" by Patricia Anne Carter; "The Montessori Method" by Maria Montessori, edited by Gerald Lee Gutek; "Mussolini" by Peter Neville; "Unusually Stupid Americans" by Kathryn Petras and Ross Petras; govtrack.us; U.S. Department of Education; Pew Research Center; The New York Times; Newsday; spinner.com; cbs.com; cnn.com; news.bbc.co.uk.*

TV ADS

1 The first legal television commercial was pretty simple: A picture of a clock on a U.S. map, with a voice-over saying, "America runs on Bulova time." The 10-second spot on July 1, 1941, aired on the New York NBC station and cost the watch company $9.

2 Your favorite hourlong, prime-time show is closer to 40 minutes, once you subtract commercials and network promotions. From 1991 to 2003, the total time viewers spent not watching the show jumped to 17.5 minutes from about 13 minutes per prime-time hour. Many countries regulate the amount of advertising per hour, but a similar industry agreement in the U.S. was ruled illegal in the 1980s.

3 As of December 2011, a law now requires a TV ad to be aired at the same volume as the program it's running in. The two-page bill took two years to pass.

4 The longest-running TV commercial appears to be for Discount Tire. The 10-second spot, which first aired in 1975, shows an old lady throwing a tire through a store window as the announcer says, "If you're not satisfied with one of our tires, please feel free to bring it back." But that's no granny tossing a tire. The woman hired to play the disgruntled customer wasn't strong enough, so a man on the production crew named John Staub stood in for the stunt. "I'm an old lady with a mustache in the window reflection, but you can't really see it because it edits so fast," he said.

5 Sometimes the commercials bleed into the shows. In 1959, the script for a "Playhouse 90" about the Nuremberg war crimes trials included the word "gas" in reference to the Nazi death chambers. But that word was edited out of the script at the insistence of the show's sponsor, a natural gas industry group. Despite that, some references to "gas ovens" made it through, so they were removed during the live broadcast. Actors' lips moved, but viewers heard "(silence) ovens."

6 Counter to conventional wisdom that says people use DVRs to skip ads, Nielsen reported in January 2011 that 45 percent of all recorded commercials are still viewed.

7 Public service announcements were first created by the Ad Council during World War II to get Rosie to work and to tighten loose lips. In 1971, on the second Earth Day, the world met "the crying Indian," played by Iron Eyes Cody. The famous anti-pollution ad, which showed Cody paddling a canoe and watching motorists litter, effectively gave the new ecology movement a huge boost. As it turns out, Cody was of Italian descent (real name Espera DeCorti), but he appeared in hundreds of movies and TV shows as a Native American and denied his European ancestry until his death in 1999.

8 The "I'd like to buy the world a Coke" commercial in the early 1970s was so popular that people called local TV stations to request it. It was reprised with the original singers and their children for a 1990 Super Bowl ad.

9 In 1989, Pepsi ran a TV commercial that advertised a TV commercial. An ad during the Grammy Awards revealed that a Pepsi commercial featuring Madonna and her hit, "Like a Prayer," would debut a week and a half later. Indeed it did, but the impact was ruined amid the outrage over the song's racy video.

10 For a time, "The Flintstones" was sponsored by Winston cigarettes, and commercials showed prehistoric puffing by Fred, Barney and Wilma.

SOURCES: *"Encyclopedia of Television" by Horace Newcomb; "Connecting with Consumers: Marketing for New Marketplace Realities"by Allan J. Kimmel; "Television's Strangest Moments" by Quentin Falk and Ben Falk; "Truth and Rumors: The Reality Behind TV's Most Famous Myths" by Bill Brioux; "What Were They Thinking: The 100 Dumbest Events in Television History" by David Hofstede; "Madonna: An Intimate Biography" by J. Randy Taraborrelli; "Fifties Television" by William Boddy; "Invasion of the Mind Snatchers: Television's Conquest of America in the Fifties" by Eric Burns; "The New Icons?: The Art of Television Advertising" by Paul Rutherford; U.S. House; White House; Arizona Republic; vintageTVcommercials.com; bulova.com; snopes. com; adcouncil.org; tvacres.com; Nielsen Media Research.*

UNDERWEAR

1 People have been wearing things under there for a long time. The Otzi Man, found in 1991 in the Italian Alps, lived 5,300 years ago and was wearing a loincloth. In 1352 B.C., Pharaoh Tutankhamun was buried with myriad priceless objects — including 145 loincloths.

2 There's no Otto Titzling, and he did not invent the bra. The fictional character in Wallace Reyburn's 1971 novel "Bust-Up: The Uplifting Tale of Otto Titzling and the Development of the Bra" has been taken for real in various places, including Trivial Pursuit.

3 Minnesota Gov. Jesse Ventura announced in a 1999 autobiography that he was a commando in more ways than one. The former Navy SEAL and professional wrestler wrote that he didn't wear underwear. Fruit of the Loom promptly sent 12,000 pairs.

4 Madonna wasn't the first to cause a scandal by wearing underwear for outerwear. Marie Antoinette reportedly shocked France by wearing a chemise to court. Prior to that, it was considered an undergarment.

5 There's a huge market for used underwear — of the famous. John Kennedy's GI boxers, Jackie Kennedy's slip, Queen Victoria's massive bloomers (50-inch waist!), as well as underwear once owned by Madonna, Michael Bolton, members of ZZ Top and Arnold Schwarzenegger have been sold for profit or to benefit charities. In 2000, Greek opera star Maria Callas' belongings, including underwear, were auctioned off. A buyer identified only as a former Greek diva bought all of the underwear and promised to burn it to "preserve the honor and dignity" of the legend.

6 While governor of Arkansas, Bill Clinton donated his used underwear to charity, valued it at $2 a piece and deducted it from his federal income taxes.

7 In 1856, some belles wore as many as 16 petticoats, a not inconsiderable weight. So the cage crinoline, an undergarment made of a series of light-weight steel or cane hoops that provided the same bell shape, was a boon. Though easier to wear, it wasn't without its own problems. On windy days it could blow inside out like an umbrella. And when a woman leaned forward, she had to be wary of how much her dress tipped up in back. And just moving around was tricky. Consider: The hoops could be nearly 6 feet in diameter.

8 What's with King Henry VIII's codpiece? The need for that piece of cloth-ing came about because men's hose at the time was actually two separate stockings with no crotch. As the tunic hemline rose, the chance for embar-rassing viewings rose with it, thus the introduction of the codpiece. But by the early 1500s, it was the fashion to wear grossly oversized and bejeweled codpieces to flaunt one's masculinity. They also doubled as pockets to carry valuables or even small weapons.

9 Just because a woman became pregnant didn't mean she gave up her cor-set. Special pregnancy and nursing corsets were available.

10 Maidenform had a long-running ad slogan in the 1950s and '60s that used the line, "I dreamed I (fill in the blank) in my Maidenform bra." Some examples: "I dreamed I stopped traffic ...," "I dreamed I grabbed a bull by the horns ..." and "I dreamed I was a social butterfly ..." One pictured a woman in a boxing ring, wearing gloves, shorts and bra with the line, "I dreamed I was a knockout in my Maidenform bra."

SOURCES: *"How Underwear Got Under There: A Brief History" by Kathy Shaskan; "Unmentionables: A Brief History of Underwear" by Elaine Benson and John Esten; "Origins of the Specious: Myths and Misconceptions of the English Language" by Patricia T. O'Conner and Stewart Kellerman; "The Book of Answers" by Barbara Berliner with Melinda Corey and George Ochoa; "Underwear: A Fashion History" by Alison Carter; fashionencyclopedia.com; vintagead-sandstuff.com; snopes.com; Los Angeles Times; New York Times; Dallas Morning News; New York Post; Tribune archives.*

THE UNHINGED

1 In medieval times, cases of mass hysteria were reported in Europe after cool, wet weather. Among the symptoms were hallucinations, writhing in agony and barking like a dog. Many experts believe that the affliction, known as St. Anthony's Fire, was ergot poisoning, caused by a fungus growing on rye and other grains.

2 Jack Nicholson attacked another motorist's car in 1994 with a golf club because he was furious over being cut off in traffic. In a 2007 Golf Digest interview, he said he was "out of his mind," but he admitted he was clearheaded enough to grab his 2-iron, which he never used on the course.

3 Daniel Sickles, a New York congressman, may have been the first American to claim "temporary insanity" as a defense. In 1859, he fatally shot his wife's lover, Philip Barton Key, son of "Star Spangled Banner" composer Francis Scott Key. Then Sickles hired eight lawyers to argue that his wife's infidelity had caused his "mental unsoundness." The jury bought it. Sickles went on serve as a general in the Civil War, losing his right leg at Gettysburg and donating it to a museum, where he would visit it on the anniversary of the battle.

4 The word "berserk" comes from the Old Norse "berserkr," which means "bear shirt" and refers to a frenzied warrior wearing a bearskin shirt. The phrase "running amok" comes from the Malay word "amok," which means a furious attack.

5 Remember astronaut Lisa Nowak, who drove 1,000 miles in 2007 to confront a romantic rival while equipped with diapers and pepper spray? She was charged with attempted kidnapping and burglary — both felonies — as well as misdemeanor battery. But she was convicted of third-degree felony burglary and misdemeanor battery, and she got off with two days in jail (time served) and a year's probation, later reduced to nine months. In March 2011, she asked a judge to seal her criminal record because "it could impair her ability to obtain employment and support for her family." (By the way, Nowak's ex-boyfriend and her rival are now married.)

6   Agatha Christie had a steel trap for a mind, coming up with complicated plots for her murder mysteries. But for 11 days in 1926, she may have come unhinged. Christie learned that her husband was having an affair, and she disappeared for 11 days. After her car was found abandoned, authorities dredged a nearby lake, and the British newspapers reported on every clue. She eventually was found in a Yorkshire hotel, claiming amnesia. But others speculated that she was simply trying to embarrass her husband.

7   It can be difficult to separate substance abuse from mental shakiness, because each can lead to the other. In 1974, a drunken and disturbed John Lennon stuck a Kotex on his forehead and wore it in Los Angeles' Troubadour nightclub. The joke didn't go over well. When Lennon asked a waitress, "Don't you know who I am?" she replied: "Yeah, you're some (expletive) with a Kotex on his forehead."

8   Tennis legend John McEnroe was infamous for losing it over bad calls, but his antics in 1984 at the Stockholm Open were particularly embarrassing. After his usual rude remark to the umpire, he cleared a table of soda and water with a swipe of his racket, and in the process showered the king of Sweden, who was watching the match.

9   In 1994, Roseanne Barr accused husband Tom Arnold in a divorce filing of abusing her. Days later, she recanted and apologized, saying, "I just lost it completely and found myself camping in the sequoias."

10   During a baseball game in 1996, Roberto Alomar was called out, and he freaked out. The Baltimore Orioles star spit in the face of umpire John Hirschbeck, and said after the game that the ump had been bitter ever since his son died of a degenerative nerve disease. When Hirschbeck heard about that remark, he had to be restrained from attacking Alomar. The makings of a lifelong feud, right? Wrong. Alomar apologized, and the two are now friends. When Alomar was picked for the Hall of Fame this year, Hirschbeck said: "I'm very, very happy for him."

SOURCES: *"Poisons of the Past: Molds, Epidemics, and History" by Mary Kilbourne Matossian; "Cuisine and Culture" by Linda Civitello; "Lethal Imagination: Violence and Brutality in American History" by Michael A. Bellesiles; "Sickles at Gettysburg" by James A. Hessler; "The Merriam-Webster New Book of Word Histories"; "Lennon Revealed" by Larry Kane; "From Agatha Christie to Ruth Rendell" by Susan Rowland; London Daily Telegraph; Los Angeles Time; Washington Post; CNN; Time magazine; espn.com; golfdigest.com; Orlando Sentinel, Tribune news services.*

LEAKS

1 Lewis "Scooter" Libby, chief of staff to Vice President Dick Cheney, divulged the fact that Valerie Plame, wife of a White House critic, worked for the CIA. Libby wasn't the only leaker, and in fact the original news report came from a different source, Richard Armitage. But Libby got in big trouble, jailed for perjury until his sentence was commuted by President George W. Bush. Also jailed was New York Times reporter Judith Miller, who refused to identify Libby as a source. Though Libby leaked badly, he wrote well, freeing Miller from her confidentiality pledge in a letter that included these words: "You went to jail in the summer. It is fall now...Out West, where you vacation, the aspens will already be turning. They turn in clusters, because their roots connect them. Come back to work — and life."

2 Some key pieces of evidence against Army Pfc. Bradley Manning, arraigned in 2012 on charges of leaking U.S. diplomatic documents to WikiLeaks, are purported copies of his online chats with former hacker Adrian Lamo. According to the chats, Manning erased Lady Gaga songs from CD-RWs and loaded them up with secret U.S. communications. One alleged Manning entry: "listened and lip-synced to Lady Gaga's 'Telephone' while exfiltratrating (sic) possibly the largest data spillage in american history."

3 "Loose lips might sink ships" was a World War II slogan to remind citizens back home and soldiers in the theater to keep their mouths shut to avoid inadvertent leaks — and yes, original posters included the "might." The pamphlet given to soldiers included warnings like this: "A harmful letter can be nullified by censorship; loose talk is direct delivery to the enemy."

4 One of the least known yet most amazing leaks in history occurred in Boston on Jan. 15, 1919. A huge steel tank gave way, unleashing more than 2 million gallons of molasses that covered two city blocks, killing 21 people and injuring 150.

5 "The Family Jewels" was the nickname of a secret CIA report detailing the unsavory and illegal activities of the U.S. spy agency in the 1950s and '60s, including domestic spying and foreign assassination plots. Its leak led to President Gerald Ford's executive order in 1976 banning political assassinations.

6 The Nixon White House formed a shadowy group called the Plumbers to prevent news leaks. But instead, an illegal break-in by the Plumbers inspired a source nicknamed Deep Throat to help The Washington Post. Three decades later, Deep Throat was identified as FBI No. 2 man Mark Felt. Before that, speculation pointed to a dozen or more people, including Pat Buchanan, Henry Kissinger, President George H.W. Bush, Gerald Ford, Gen. Alexander Haig, Sen. Lowell Weicker, Diane Sawyer and even comedian Ben Stein.

7 The famous children's story about the little Dutch boy who plugs a leaking dike with his finger is really more of an American tale. Author Mary Mapes Dodge included it in her best-selling "Hans Brinker, or the Silver Skates" in 1865, popularizing a story that had been around in England and America since at least 1850. While there are statues in the Netherlands that try to capitalize on the tale, the story is much more famous in the United States. Trivia buffs take note: The boy at the dike is unnamed or the "Hero of Harlaam," not Hans Brinker.

8 Space flight is notoriously unforgiving. The space shuttle Challenger explosion in 1986 that killed seven astronauts was caused by a leak. An O-ring failed to seal properly, allowing pressurized hot gas to escape. And in 1971, three cosmonauts aboard the Soyuz 11 died after a then-record 24 days in space when their spacecraft's airtight hatch proved to be not so airtight. The men, who weren't wearing spacesuits, were found dead in their seats when the capsule was opened on Earth.

9 When the development of an atomic bomb was top secret, a comic strip called "The Science of Superman" caused FBI agents to worry about a leak in the Manhattan Project. The comic ran in April 1945 — four months before the bomb was a public fact. It featured a professor testing the powers of Superman and explaining: "The strange object before you is the cyclotron, popularly known as an 'atom smasher.' " The FBI tried to persuade DC Comics to pull the strip, but most newspapers had already delivered it.

Apparently, the leak was unintentional. The comic's ghostwriter said he had read the word "cyclotron" in Popular Mechanics magazine 10 years earlier.

10   The massive oil leak at the Deepwater Horizon well in 2010 allowed many strange terms to spill into the language: The failure of a "blow-out preventer" was blamed for the disaster. Officials considered using a "top hat," tried a "junk shot" and a "top kill," and finally succeeded with a "containment cap."

SOURCES: *"FBI 100 Years: An Unofficial History" by Henry M. Holden; "Dark Tide: The Great Boston Molasses Flood of 1919" by Stephen Puleo; "Encyclopedia of Cold War Espionage, Spies, and Secret Operations" by Richard C.S. Trahair; "Encyclopedia of the Central Intelligence Agency" by W. Thomas Smith Jr.; npr.org; theweek.com; thespeedingbullet.com; eyewitnesstohistory.com; The Australian; Encyclopedia Mythica; Tribune archives and news services.*

10 THINGS YOU MIGHT NOT KNOW ABOUT

SPORTS

CHICAGO'S BALLPARKS

1 The Chicago Cubs played from 1893 to 1915 at the West Side Grounds, which now is the site of the Near West Side's medical campus. The origin of the phrase "out of left field" is not known for certain, but some people believe it comes from the fact that a psychiatric facility stood beyond the West Side Grounds' left field.

2 When the Chicago White Sox left South Side Park in 1910 and moved a few blocks north to Comiskey Park, the old site was taken over by the Chicago American Giants, a founding member of the Negro Leagues. The Giants were run by black player-manager Andrew "Rube" Foster and white tavern owner John Schorling, who was the son-in-law of Sox owner Charles Comiskey. The Sox boss tried and failed to persuade Schorling to keep the black team from playing at home when the Sox also were at home. Historian Robert Charles Cottrell cites one Sunday afternoon in 1911 when the Giants drew 11,000 fans, versus 9,000 for the Sox and 6,000 for the Cubs.

3 The green scoreboard that towers over Wrigley Field's center-field bleachers was reddish brown from 1937 until the mid-'40s. The red marquee at the corner of Clark and Addison Streets originally was fern green.

4 Speaking of color schemes, U.S. Cellular Field has completed the transformation of its seats from blue to forest green. But two seats remain blue: the places where home runs by Paul Konerko and Scott Podsednik landed in Game 2 of the 2005 World Series. Why the change to green? As a throwback to the color at old Comiskey.

5 Wrigley Field has a long tradition of non-baseball events, including concerts by the Police and Paul McCartney. Wrigley has been the scene of a circus, a Harlem Globetrotters basketball game, five decades of Bears games, Jehovah's Witness conventions, a boxing match featuring Jake LaMotta, rodeos and even a ski-jumping contest.

6 U.S. Cellular Field has a pet-check area where fans can board their animal friends while they're watching the game.

7 Hillary Rodham Clinton, who grew up as a Cubs fan, was invited to throw the first pitch of the 1994 opener at Wrigley Field. Tribune columnist Mike Downey, then of the Los Angeles Times, wrote: "Knowing the Cubs, she'll probably hurt her arm."

8 The foul lines at old Comiskey were made of water hoses painted white and pressed flat.

9 The tradition of singing "The Star-Spangled Banner" at ballgames began at Comiskey during the 1918 World Series between the Boston Red Sox and the Cubs. (Yes, we mean the Cubs at Comiskey. The Cubs played their World Series home games at the Sox park that year because it had more seats.) Another singalong popularized at Comiskey was "Take Me Out to the Ballgame." Harry Caray led the crooning as a Sox announcer before he moved to the Cubs.

10 WGN-TV pioneered the use of a center-field camera to capture baseball action. But the innovation didn't start at Wrigley Field. It began at Thillens Stadium, at Kedzie and Devon Avenues, when WGN was televising a Little League game in the mid-'50s. Thillens' stands were too close to the field to allow a camera behind the plate.

SOURCES: *"The Best Pitcher in Baseball: The Life of Rube Foster, Negro League Giant" by Robert Charles Cottrell; whitesox.mlb.com; ballparks.com;Los Angeles Times; and Tribune archives.*

THE CHICAGO BEARS

1 The Bears were called the Decatur Staleys — sponsored by a downstate agri-businessman — when they helped organize pro football in 1920. The Staleys' first victory was against the Moline Tractors; their first loss was to a Chicago team, the Cardinals. In 1922, the Staleys became the Chicago Bears.

2 If 20-year-old George Halas had arrived on time to a work outing in 1915, his Bears might never have been established. Halas and other Western Electric employees were invited to ride a steamship across Lake Michigan for a picnic. But Halas showed up late, possibly because he overslept. By the time Halas arrived, the ship — the Eastland — had overturned in the Chicago River, sending more than 800 people to their deaths.

3 "Monsters of the Midway" first referred to the fearsome University of Chicago Maroons. Back in the 1930s, when professional football could only hope for the same prominence as college programs, the team fielded by the University of Chicago was the gridiron giant, and Midway was a reference to the campus' Midway Plaisance. But the U. of C. dropped its football program in 1939, and the Bears gobbled up the "Monster" title in 1940 with a championship season.

4 During World War II, many players quit to serve in the armed forces. For the 1944 season, 19 of 28 men from the 1943 championship team went to war. That included star quarterback Sid Luckman, who participated in the Normandy invasion. Midway through the 1942 season, Coach Halas left for the Pacific theater. There, as Lt. Cmdr. Halas, he was the welfare and recreation officer for the 7th Fleet. He reportedly still kept track of the Bears' progress and telegrammed orders from overseas.

5 In 1925, President Calvin Coolidge was introduced to Red Grange, who was "with the Chicago Bears." Coolidge replied, "I'm glad to know you. I always did like animal acts."

6 The Bears sit atop the NFL record books in a number of categories, thanks in no small part to the powerhouse teams of the 1930s and 1940s. As of 2010, the team led the league in more seasons than any other team in: scoring, touchdowns, first downs, rushing and fewest rushing yards allowed. And for a team started by Halas, who coached a rough-and-tumble style of football, maybe it's no surprise it also leads in the penalties category.

7 Famed columnist Irv Kupcinet refereed Bears games in the '40s while writing about the team for the Chicago Times.

8 Walter Payton stunk up the joint — at first. In his debut regular-season NFL game, he gained zero yards on eight carries. And he missed a game due to injury that season. Granted, he wouldn't miss another one through his entire 13-season career. The brilliant and versatile Payton so believed in consistency that he sat in the same seat on the team's charter flights all 13 years.

9 In 1968, the Bears defeated the Green Bay Packers on a "fair-catch kick" — a rare play that's still in the NFL rulebook. When a team makes a fair catch of a kick, it has the option of attempting a field goal from that very spot, with defenders kept 10 yards away. The Bears defeated the Packers 13-10 on Nov. 3, 1968, when Mac Percival booted a 43 yard field goal in the last minute. The next morning's Tribune described the fair-catch kick as a "very rare stratagem."

10 Bears quarterback Jay Cutler was born in Santa Claus, Ind., has Type 1 diabetes and was lampooned on TV's "South Park" when he was a Denver Bronco. In a 2007 "South Park" episode, Stan and Kyle attend a pool party with "all the biggest stars in Colorado," and Stan tells Cutler that "you kind of suck but my dad says you might be good someday." Jay Cutler is also the name of a bodybuilder who was Mr. Olympia — but that Jay Cutler is an entirely different guy who's 10 years older and hails from Sterling, Mass.

SOURCES: *"The Bears: A 75-Year Celebration" by Richard Whittingham; "Papa Bear: The Life and Legacy of George Halas" by Jeff Davis; "Rivals, the 10 Greatest American Sports Rivalries in the 20th Century" by Richard O. Davies; "The Galloping Ghost: Red Grange, An American Football Legend" by Gary Andrew Poole; "Bearers: Webster's Quotations, Facts and Phrases"; "The Pro Football Historical Abstract" by Sean Lahman; "Baseball and the Media" by George Castle; National Football League; southparkstudios.com; quirkyresearch.blogspot.com; chicagobears.com; mrolympia.com; Tribune archives.*

COLLEGE FOOTBALL

1   The first college football game west of the Allegheny Mountains took place in 1879 at the Chicago White Stockings' baseball park in what is now Millennium Park. The University of Michigan defeated Racine (Wis.) College.

2   The first all-America quarterback, chosen in 1889, was Princeton's Edgar Allan Poe, grandnephew of the famed writer of the same name. (No, he wasn't drafted by the Ravens.) Two literary giants who played college football were poet Archibald MacLeish of Yale and novelist F. Scott Fitzgerald of Princeton.

3   In 1916, Georgia Tech led Cumberland College at halftime 126-0. Even so, Tech coach John Heisman (the guy they named the trophy after) wasn't satisfied. "Men, don't let up," he exhorted in his halftime speech. "You never know what those Cumberland players have up their sleeves." Not much, as it turned out. Tech won 222-0.

4   A 1920s football player at the University of Southern California named Marion Morrison lost his athletic scholarship because of an injury and dropped out of school. He went into the movie business and became known by another name: John Wayne. Other notables who played college football include former Detroit Mayor Kwame Kilpatrick (Florida A&M), comic actor Kevin James (State University of New York at Cortland) and Hillary Clinton's father, Hugh Rodham (Penn State).

5   The Rose Bowl is held in Pasadena, Calif., right? Except in 1942, when fears of a Japanese attack on the West Coast forced a move. Chicago's Soldier Field offered to stage the game, but it was shifted to Durham, N.C., where Duke welcomed Oregon State and lost 20-16.

6   Soldier Field has hosted such famous tilts as the 1926 Army-Navy game in front of 110,000 fans. Less famous as a college football venue is Wrigley Field, where DePaul played before dumping football as a varsity sport in the late 1930s. (DePaul's team nickname, Blue Demons, came from the fact that athletes were known as "D-men" because they wore sweaters with D's on them.)

7 Once glorious, now defunct: The Oil Bowl in Houston, the Refrigerator Bowl in Evansville, Ind., and the Salad Bowl in Phoenix, Ariz.

8 Before the 2004 Rose Bowl game against Michigan, USC coach Pete Carroll invited comedian Will Ferrell to practice with the team. Ferrell, a USC alumnus who was a kicker in high school, showed up in full uniform, with his last name on his jersey, and caught a pass for a gain of about 40 yards. Other celebrities who have visited USC practices: George Lucas, Kirsten Dunst, Jessica Simpson, Snoop Dogg, Spike Lee, Alyssa Milano, Anthony Kiedis, Wilmer Valderrama, Jake Gyllenhaal and Andre 3000.

9 As part of a Cuban sports festival in 1937, two American football teams, Auburn and Villanova, were invited to play in the Bacardi Bowl in Havana. But Cuban military dictator Fulgencio Batista flew into a rage because his photo was omitted from the game program. Only a quick trip to the printer averted the game's cancellation.

10 In the Texas-Texas A&M game in 2004, Texas scored a touchdown, but its point-after kick was blocked, and an A&M defender picked up the ball. If he had managed to run all the way down the field, it would have been worth 2 points for A&M. But instead he fumbled backward into the end zone where Texas had just scored its touchdown, and another A&M player jumped on the ball. It was ruled a "1-point safety," giving Texas its extra point in a very strange way.

SOURCES: *"Rites of Autumn" by Richard Whittingham; Sarasota Herald-Tribune; Marin Independent Journal; Evansville Courier & Press; Detroit Free Press; Columbus Dispatch; Auburn University.*

SPORTS GAMBLING

1   The University of Chicago boasts about its connection to 25 winners of the Nobel Prize in economics, but little is heard about a U. of C. graduate named Charles McNeil who helped transform the economics of gambling. McNeil was an early proponent of the point spread and indeed may have invented the concept, in which the margin of victory is the key number. As one bookie put it: "The point spread was the greatest invention since the zipper."

2   A bookmaker's commission on a bet is called juice, or vigorish, or simply vig. Vigorish is Yiddish slang, from the Russian vyigrysh, meaning winnings.

3   History's most famous sports gambling scandal occurred when the Chicago White Sox threw the 1919 World Series to the Cincinnati Reds. Eight so-called Black Sox, including star outfielder "Shoeless" Joe Jackson, were banned from baseball for life. Eliot Asinof's book about the plot was called "Eight Men Out," but there was a ninth man out. St. Louis Browns second baseman Joe Gedeon, who didn't play in the series but heard about the fix from his Sox friends, was banned because he didn't tell authorities.

4   In soccer, an "own goal" occurs when a player accidentally knocks the ball into his own goal, giving the opposition a point. Colombia defender Andres Escobar did that in the 1994 World Cup against the United States, costing his team the game. When he returned to Medellin, he was shot to death. The motive has never been firmly established, but many observers believe disgruntled gamblers ordered his murder.

5   In the history of bookmaking, one particular incident is known as Black Sunday. Before Super Bowl XIII in 1979, Pittsburgh started out as a 2½-point favorite over the Cowboys. When most bettors picked Pittsburgh, the bookmakers moved their line to 4½ to attract balancing wagers on Dallas. But when Pittsburgh ended up winning by 4 points, the bookies were "middled" — they had to pay off the early bets on Pittsburgh and the late bets on Dallas.

6 In 1993, "The Wiz Kid" sold NFL predictions to bettors for $25 per phone call. Only later did the service's proprietor, David James, reveal that his 4-year-old son made the picks.

7 "Proposition bets," involving aspects of the game other than the final score, are wildly popular for Super Bowl bettors. When hockey star Wayne Gretzky's wife, Janet Jones, got caught up in a gambling scandal in 2006, it was reported that she bet $5,000 on the Super Bowl coin flip. People also wager on the length of the game's first punt, the number of penalties and which player will score the first touchdown. Bears star Devin Hester's touchdown on the opening kickoff of the 2007 Super Bowl earned bettors a ridiculous 25-1 payoff.

8 Some Super Bowl "prop bets" don't even involve the game. In 2007, wagers were taken on whether Billy Joel's national anthem would be longer or shorter than 1 minute and 44 seconds (it was shorter). One sports book gave 50-1 odds that Carmen Electra would make an unscheduled appearance with Prince at halftime (she didn't) and 2-1 odds that Prince would have a wardrobe malfunction (he didn't).

9 British bookmaking firm William Hill offers bets on sports but also features wacky non-sports bets, such as who will be the first celebrity to be arrested in a given year. Singer Amy Winehouse was the co-favorite for 2008, along with rocker Pete Doherty. Before the last Harry Potter novel came out, William Hill set odds on whether the saga would end with Harry's death (it didn't).

10 Las Vegas wastes no time. Sports books released odds on the 2009 Super Bowl before the 2008 Super Bowl had even been played. The Las Vegas Hilton listed the New England Patriots as a strong favorite. For the record, the Pittsburgh Steelers defeated the Arizona Cardinals, 27-23, and the Pats didn't even make the playoffs.

SOURCES: *Las Vegas Sun, Tribune news services, "Winning Is the Only Thing" by Randy Roberts and James Olson, "The Man With the $100,000 Breasts and Other Gambling Stories" by Michael Konik, American Heritage Dictionary, Times of London.*

THE OLYMPICS

1   Olympic sites are chosen by secret ballot, so we're not sure how London beat Paris for the 2012 Summer Olympics. But some blame French President Jacques Chirac, who insulted Britain before the vote by saying, "After Finland, it's the country with the worst food." France's bid wasn't getting British support anyway, but Finland had two IOC members, and some speculate that they were swing votes in the 54-50 outcome.

2   Tug-o-war made its last appearance as an Olympic sport in 1920.

3   Pierre de Coubertin, founder of the International Olympic Committee, decreed in his will that his heart be sent to the site of ancient Olympia in Greece, where it is kept in a monument. The rest of him was buried in Lausanne, Switzerland.

4   Chicago was supposed to host the 1904 Olympics, but St. Louis stole it away. The Games were a fiasco. Only 14 of 32 participants finished the marathon, which was held in 90-degree heat with a single water well at the 12-mile mark. Cuban marathoner Felix Carvajal, who lost his money in a craps game in New Orleans, hitchhiked to St. Louis and ran the race in street shoes. He stopped to chat with spectators and to steal apples from an orchard but still finished fourth. American Fred Lorz dropped out after nine miles, rode in a car for 11, then rejoined the race and crossed the finish line first, quickly admitting his hoax. The prize went to American Thomas Hicks, whose supporters gave him strychnine (a stimulant in low doses) and brandy — the first known use of performance-enhancing drugs in the Olympics.

5   French athletes bent the rules at the 1932 Los Angeles Olympics: Despite Prohibition, they were allowed wine with their meals.

6 George Patton, who would later become a famous U.S. general, competed in the 1912 Stockholm Olympics pentathlon, an event combining pistol shooting, swimming, fencing, cross country and steeplechase. Patton performed poorly in his best event — pistols — but shined in fencing, defeating the French army champion. Old Blood and Guts finished fifth overall, the only non-Swede to make the top seven.

7 The greatest star of the 1936 Berlin Olympics was the 10th child born to an Alabama sharecropper family named Owens. But he was not born with the name Jesse. He was called James Cleveland Owens, and as a child moved to his namesake city — Cleveland. A teacher asked his name, and he said "J.C." The teacher thought he said "Jesse," and the boy was too polite to disagree. (Former Mayor Richard M. Daley often cited Owens in pushing Chicago's failed bid, and indeed Owens was a Chicagoan, but only late in life. A dozen years after the Olympics, Owens settled in Chicago, and he is buried in Oak Woods Cemetery on the South Side.)

8 Another great Olympian with Chicago ties was Johnny Weissmuller, the winner of five gold medals in swimming who later starred as Tarzan in the movies. Weissmuller swam brilliantly in the 1924 and '28 Olympics — and also in the waters off Chicago's North Avenue Beach on a stormy day in July 1927. Weissmuller was training on the lakefront with his brother Peter when a sudden storm swamped the pleasure boat Favorite. The disaster killed 27 of the 71 people aboard — mostly women and children — but the Weissmuller brothers rescued 11 people.

9 No boxing was held at the 1912 Stockholm Olympics because the sport was illegal in Sweden.

10 A study of the 2004 Athens Olympics found that athletes who wore red while competing in "combat sports" such as wrestling scored higher than opponents wearing blue.

SOURCES: "Historical Dictionary of the Modern Olympic Movement," edited by John E. Findling and Kimberly D. Pelle; "The Complete Book of the Olympics" by David Wallechinsky; "General Patton: A Soldier's Life" by Stanley Hirshson; "Johnny Weissmuller: Twice the Hero" by David Fury; "Jesse Owens: An American Life" by William J. Baker; The Wall Street Journal; Tribune news services.

THE OLYMPIC TORCH

1   The Nazis invented the Olympic torch relay. Fire was an Olympic symbol in ancient Greece, and torch relays were conducted apart from the Olympics. But the Nazis first combined those elements to create pageantry and propaganda before the 1936 Berlin Games. On its way to Germany, the torch went through Greece, Bulgaria, Yugoslavia, Hungary, Austria and Czechoslovakia. Within six years, Nazi Germany had annexed or occupied all of those countries.

2   The torch has been transported by canoe, steamboat, parachute, camel and Concorde. Before the 1976 Montreal Games, it traveled by satellite, sort of. A sensor in Greece detected the "ionized particles" of the torch and transmitted coded impulses by satellite to Canada, where they activated a laser beam that "re-created" the Olympic flame.

3   Before the 1956 Melbourne Games, a group of Australian students pulled off the greatest hoax in torch relay history. They fashioned a torch out of a plum pudding can, part of a chair leg and a pair of underpants set aflame. Then one of them joined the relay route, presented the contraption to the mayor of Sydney and slipped into the crowd before anyone realized he was an impostor.

4   The torch was transported under water at the Great Barrier Reef before the 2000 Sydney Games. The specially designed solid-fuel torch operated like a distress flare.

5   The identity of the final torch bearer, who lights the caldron, is kept secret until the opening ceremonies. At the Los Angeles Olympics in 1984, many thought Romanian gymnast Nadia Comaneci would be chosen because her nation was the only East Bloc member that didn't boycott the event. But U.S. Olympic hero Rafer Johnson won out. Far less attention was paid to the man who later doused the flame. Gas company worker Marv Wig, 59, put it this way: "There are two switches that both essentially cut the fuel to the flame. I haven't decided which one I'll flip. One needs to build a little suspense."

6 Critics complained that the red-and-yellow caldron at the 1996 Atlanta Games resembled the french-fry containers used by McDonald's, an Olympic sponsor.

7 Antonio Rebollo, a disabled archer who shot a flaming arrow to light the caldron at the 1992 Barcelona Games, complained days later that he wasn't given tickets to any competitions, not even archery. A local Olympic committee spokesman responded that Rebollo had been sent a thank-you letter and, "I can only assume he hasn't gotten the letter yet."

8 Olympic officials always keep an extra "pure" flame on standby in case a torch goes out. During the 1976 Montreal Olympics, a downpour doused the flame, and an official relit it with a cigarette lighter. Olympic purists were appalled. They extinguished the unclean flame and relit it the proper way.

9 Yoshinori Sakai, the torch relay runner who lit the caldron for the 1964 Tokyo Games, was born near Hiroshima two hours after the atomic bomb was dropped there.

10 As Chinese philosopher Lao-tzu said, "A journey of 1,000 miles must begin with a single step." For the 2008 Summer Games in Beijing, the journey created one heck of a carbon footprint. According to calculations by wired.com, the Air China A330 jet transporting the Olympic torch burned 462,400 gallons of jet fuel, emitting 11 million pounds of carbon dioxide. Let the Games begin, if only for the sake of the environment.

SOURCES: *"Hitler's Olympics" by Christopher Hilton; bbc.com; olympic.org; National Geographic; "My Olympic Journey" by James Worrall;wired.com; Tribune news services.*

RUNNING

1   The verb "run" has 645 meanings, more than any other word in the Oxford English Dictionary. In addition to putting one foot in front of the other rapidly, there's "running an idea up the flagpole," "the days running into weeks," "running the numbers," "running a fever," "running with the wrong crowd" and "running your mouth." When early 20th century Australians said they were "running the rabbit," that meant they were bringing home liquor.

2   A cheetah runs faster than a sand gazelle, which is speedier than a zebra, which is faster than a kangaroo, which outruns a human, which can outleg a rhino. (This is based on estimated maximum running speeds; do not try at your local zoo.)

3   Dr. Gabe Mirkin, author of "The Sports Medicine Book," asked more than 100 elite runners if they would be willing to take a magic pill that would make them an Olympic champion but would kill them within a year. More than half said yes.

4   The Chicago marathon was called the Mayor Daley Marathon in its first two years. Its first running in 1977 got off to a rocky start: Three people were sent to the hospital with powder burns when the starter's cannon misfired.

5   "Freak races" were a favorite form of entertainment in 17th and 18th century England. In one race witnessed by the king, two runners were evenly matched: Each had a wooden leg. In another race, a man on stilts faced off against an accomplished runner on foot. In yet another contest, a man was given an hour to run seven miles while carrying 56 pounds of fish on his head.

6   Haitian runner Dieudonne Lamothe was 78th — the final finisher — in the 1984 Los Angeles Olympics marathon. And it's a good thing for Lamothe that he finished. He later revealed that dictator "Baby Doc" Duvalier's henchman had threatened to kill him if he did not complete the race.

7 Until 1950, a major league baseball player who was on base could be replaced by a "courtesy runner" without having to leave the lineup. In modern times, a pinch runner is allowed, but the player being replaced is out of the game for good. Perhaps the most unusual pinch runner was Oakland's Herb Washington, who played in 105 games over two seasons in the 1970s and never came to bat or played the field. A track star, Washington was strictly a pinch-runner.

8 Two great American runners overcame potentially crippling illnesses. Sprinter Gail Devers suffered from Graves' disease, and doctors were close to amputating her feet before her condition improved and she went on to win Olympic gold in 1992. Decades earlier, sprinter Wilma Rudolph became the first American woman to win three track-and-field gold medals in a single Olympics — a glorious fate for a woman who was sickly as a child and wore a leg brace. "My doctor told me I would never walk again. My mother told me I would," said Rudolph. "I believed my mother."

9 University of Oregon track coach Bill Bowerman was trying to develop a new athletic shoe, and one day in 1971 he used the family's waffle iron to meld urethane into a wafflelike tread pattern. The idea caught on for the company he started with Phil Knight. First known as Blue Ribbon Sports, it was renamed Nike. Today, a life-size statue of Bowerman at the university stands on a base of waffle irons.

10 GOP presidential candidate Ron Paul likes to run. He has run for political office for most of the last 37 years, and as a high school junior in Pennsylvania, he raced to a state title in the 220-yard dash.

SOURCES: *"Cassell's Dictionary of Slang" by Jonathon Green; "Running Through the Ages" by Edward Seldon Sears; "The Olympic Odyssey" by Phil Cousineau; "The Complete Book of the Summer Olympics" by David Wallechinsky; "The Dickson Baseball Dictionary" by Paul Dickson; "African-American Sports Greats" by David L. Porter; "Only in Oregon" by Christine Barnes; Oxford English Dictionary; baseball-reference.com; espn.go.com; nike.com; npr.org; The Oregonian; The New York Times; Christian Science Monitor.*

STADIUMS

1 Because of frigid conditions in December 1932, the Chicago Bears played the NFL title game indoors at Chicago Stadium. The circus had performed the week before, leaving a layer of dirt — and some droppings that created an unpleasant scent by game time. The field was only 80 yards long, including end zones. The teams adjusted by kicking off at the 10-yard line and banning field goals. The Bears, led by Bronko Nagurski and Red Grange, defeated the Portsmouth (Ohio) Spartans 9-0.

2 Wrigley Field was knocked down in 1966. We're not talking about the landmark ballpark at Clark and Addison — we mean the stadium of the same name in Los Angeles. The California park hosted minor league ball for many years and had a single year of major league glory as the home of the Los Angeles Angels in 1961. In that year, 248 home runs were hit there, setting a major league record.

3 In the Indian city of Mumbai (aka Bombay), "stadium" is slang for a man who is bald on the top of his head, with a fringe of hair all around.

4 Brainiac students at Caltech hacked into the electric scoreboard during the 1984 Rose Bowl in Pasadena, Calif., and changed the UCLA-Illinois score to read Caltech 38, MIT 9.

5 When the San Diego Padres moved to the new Petco Park in 2004, they sold bricks on which sponsors inscribed messages. People for the Ethical Treatment of Animals bought a brick reading "Break open your cold ones! Toast the Padres! Enjoy this champion organization!" The subliminal message, based on the first letter of each word, was "Boycott Petco."

6 During halftime of a Jets-Patriots game at New York's Shea Stadium in 1979, a show by a model airplane group went bizarrely wrong. A radio-controlled model plane shaped like a lawnmower flew out of control and plunged into the stands, killing a 20-year-old New Hampshire man.

7 Freak accidents also happen on the field. During the 1951 World Series at Yankee Stadium, Mickey Mantle tripped on a water sprinkler, leading to the first of his knee surgeries. But no stadium-infrastructure accident was weirder than that suffered by the St. Louis Cardinals' Vince Coleman during the 1985 National League Championship Series. The Busch Stadium grounds crew turned on a machine to roll out the tarp, not realizing that Coleman was warming up nearby. The tarp rolled over his left leg. He missed the rest of the NLCS and the World Series.

8 The Roman Coliseum was not only an architectural wonder, but also a marvel in crowd control. The ancient stadium could seat 50,000 ticketed customers and many thousands more standing. But even packed with 70,000 people, the stadium could empty in as little as 10 minutes.

9 Wilbur Snapp, organist at minor league baseball's Jack Russell Stadium at Clearwater, Fla., in 1985, objected to an umpire's call and played "Three Blind Mice." The umps ejected him from the ballpark.

10 Four different New York arenas have been called Madison Square Garden. Among the significant historical events there: the first Muhammad Ali-Joe Frazier boxing match in 1971; the murder of the building's architect, Stanford White, in a love triangle in 1906; and the least wholesome performance of the song "Happy Birthday" ever, delivered to President John Kennedy in 1962 by Marilyn Monroe, whose dress was so tight she had to be sewn into it.

SOURCES: *"The World Series' Most Wanted" by John Snyder; "Mickey Mantle's Greatest Hits" by David S. Nuttall; "Amazing But True Sports Stories" by Steve Riach; "Red Grange and the Rise of Modern Football" by John M. Carroll; "Architecture of Italy" by Jean Castex; ballparks.com; ballparktour.com; doubletongued.org; snopes.com; Sports Illustrated; Christian Science Monitor; Tribune news services.*

10 THINGS YOU MIGHT NOT KNOW ABOUT

CHICAGO

CHICAGO AUTHORS

1   Ben Hecht, who co-wrote the play "The Front Page" and was a script doctor for the movie "Gone With the Wind," got his start in Chicago journalism in 1910 as a "picture chaser" for the Chicago Journal. The job required him to find pictures of murder victims and other newsmakers — and to swipe the pictures if necessary. According to a friend, Hecht would climb into people's windows or pose as a gas meter reader in order to gain entry to a home and nab the picture.

2   Saul Bellow was once discouraged from pursuing a doctorate in English because, he was told, as a Jew he would never have the right "feel" for the language. Bellow won the Nobel Prize for Literature and the Pulitzer Prize and was given the National Book Award three times.

3   Ray Bradbury says he remembers being born. The beloved author of "The Martian Chronicles" and "Fahrenheit 451" admits it sounds preposterous, but the Waukegan native says he recalls emerging from the womb, the taste of his mother's breast milk and the pain of being circumcised.

4   Richard Wright based aspects of his novel "Native Son" on a 1938 Chicago case in which black suspect Robert Nixon was executed by electric chair for fatally beating a white woman with a brick. Wright said he studied Tribune articles that reflected the racism of the times, featuring headlines such as "Brick Slayer is Likened to Jungle Beast."

5   Hyde Park resident Blue Balliett rocketed onto the young adult literary scene in 2004 with "Chasing Vermeer" and has since sold more than 2 million copies of her four books. And yes, she has always been called Blue, though she says the name on her birth certificate is Elizabeth. As she told The New York Times: "I was named after the color of the sky. I don't really associate it with the color anymore."

6 Sherwood Anderson, an Ohio native who gained his fame in Chicago with such fictional works as "Winesburg, Ohio" (1919), died of peritonitis, an abdominal infection, after accidentally swallowing a toothpick at a cocktail party.

7 Dorothy, the Scarecrow, the Tin Man and the Cowardly Lion were not born at Oz Park on Chicago's North Side. Instead the "Wonderful Wizard of Oz" characters were created a few miles west of there at L. Frank Baum's home in Humboldt Park circa 1898. According to a family story, Baum's Emerald City got its name when a child asked where his story was set and he saw O-Z on a file cabinet and replied "Oz." But many believe that story is as fanciful as Baum's fairy tale.

8 Oak Park looms large in the literary world as the birthplace of Ernest Hemingway and the onetime home of Edgar Rice Burroughs, but the list doesn't stop there. Among those born in the near-west suburb: Pulitzer Prize-winner Carol Shields, Richard Bach, Jane Hamilton and the amazingly prolific Rev. Andrew Greeley. And those who call it home now: Elizabeth Berg, Alex Kotlowitz and graphic novelist Chris Ware. Finally, Barbara Mertz, who writes the Amelia Peabody mystery series as Elizabeth Peters, attended high school there.

9 In May of 1997, Sandra Cisneros, Chicago native and author of "The House on Mango Street," sparked an uproar when she painted her San Antonio home a vivid purple. Critics said it violated the law protecting the integrity of the historic district. Cisneros argued that it was a valid color for the area if city officials acknowledged Mexican culture and influences in the rules. In the end, Cisneros told The Philadelphia Inquirer, "My house faded to work-shirt blue. The sun resolved the issue."

10 Audrey Niffenegger, author of "The Time Traveler's Wife," is working on a novel called "The Chinchilla Girl in Exile," the story of a 9-year-old girl who has hypertrichosis–she's covered with hair.

SOURCES: *"L. Frank Baum, Creator of Oz," by Katharine M. Rogers; "Tarzan Forever," by John Taliaferro; "Richard Wright: The Life and Times," by Hazel Rowley; "Sherwood Anderson Remembered," by Welford Dunaway Taylor; "Ben Hecht: The Man Behind the Legend," by William MacAdams; "Dictionary of Midwestern Literature," by Philip A. Greasley; "Bellow: A Biography," by James Atlas; "The Bradbury Chronicles: The Life of Ray Bradbury," by Sam Weller; audreyniffenegger.com; blueballiettbooks.com; New York Times; Texas Monthly; Houston Chronicle; Philadelphia Inquirer.*

THE CHICAGO CITY COUNCIL

1   The council's activism on lifestyle issues in recent years inspired The Washington Post to label Chicago "That Meddlin' Town." But lest you think such social engineering is a modern trend, consider the Lager Beer Riot of 1855. The council, led by Mayor Levi Boone, cracked down on beer halls frequented by German and Irish immigrants, while overlooking the whiskey consumed by more established Americans. The newcomers rioted, then voted en masse in the next election, making Chicago safe again for beer drinkers.

2   A century ago, when Chicago had two aldermen per ward, the 1st Ward was led by corrupt characters named "Bathhouse John" Coughlin and Michael "Hinky Dink" Kenna. They held an annual 1st Ward Ball at the Coliseum on South Wabash Avenue, and the 1907 event featured two bands, 200 waiters, 100 police officers, 35,000 quarts of beer and 10,000 quarts of champagne "before they sent for reinforcements," according to one report. Facing pressure the next year to tone down the affair, Coughlin said, "All right, we'll compromise. We won't let parents bring their children. There!" After the 1908 event, Mayor Fred Busse ordered the balls stopped.

3   A special aldermanic "beauty committee" was appointed in 1904 by Mayor Carter Harrison II to choose a young woman to represent Chicago at the St. Louis world's fair. But the aldermen were overenthusiastic, drawing up a list of nine requirements, including, "She must be a brunette, to typify the city's atmosphere, dark with the smoke of commerce." The mayor labeled the list "foolish" and disbanded the committee.

4   Mayor William "Big Bill" Thompson arranged to have rodeo performers ride their horses into the City Council chamber and perform tricks with a whip in 1931.

5   Ald. Seymour Simon was so frozen out by the first Mayor Richard Daley's machine that when he wanted an alley cleaned in his ward in 1972, he contacted the Chicago Daily News' help line, and the Daily News arranged for the city to do the cleanup.

6   In 1999, the federal prison in Oxford, Wis., was home to four aldermen, a water reclamation commissioner and a state representative. When they would pass in the halls, they would sometimes yell, "Quorum call!"

7   The only murder of a Chicago alderman occurred in 1963 when the West Side's most powerful black politician, Ald. Ben Lewis, was handcuffed and shot in the head in his ward office a day after he won an election. The killing was never solved.

8   Chicago has 50 aldermen, more than almost any other American city. New York, in a typical case of one-upmanship, has 51 council members. Los Angeles has only 15, Houston 16 and Philadelphia 17. A century ago, Chicago had 70 aldermen — two in each of its 35 wards.

9   Aldermen are allowed to carry concealed handguns and act as "conservators of the peace" under an 1872 state law. In 1991, Ald. Dorothy Tillman waved a nickel plated, .38-caliber snub-nosed revolver at a raucous community meeting at Kennedy-King College on the South Side, according to witnesses. No one was hurt, and Tillman, who lost her seat in 2007, refused to discuss the incident. Ballard Powell, a supervisor at the Joliet Correctional Center who was at the meeting, told the Tribune at the time: "It's safer walking through a maximum-security prison with your eyes closed ... than being in a room with a wild alderman."

10   Though aldermen can brandish firearms, they can no longer sell booze. Ald. Tom Tunney (44th), owner of Ann Sather restaurants, had to surrender his liquor licenses when he was elected in 2003.

SOURCES: *"Lords of the Last Machine" by Bill and Lori Granger; "Don't Make No Waves — Don't Back No Losers" by Milton Rakove; "Grafters and Goo Goos" by James L. Merriner; "Fabulous Chicago" by Emmett Dedmon; Tribune archives.*

CHICAGO ELECTIONS

1   A Tribune story on April 8, 1896, reported an "unusually peaceable" Election Day with the remarkable headline "Only Two Politicians Are Shot." What the Tribune meant was that two political activists at the polls were wounded, one in the wrist and one in the ankle.

2   A variety of slang terms described Chicago election hijinks of the past. A "four-legged voter" was a person who was joined in the voting booth by an unscrupulous election judge who made sure the right candidates were picked. A person known as a "repeater" voted more than once at the same location; a "floater" went from one polling place to the next. The system of carting around vagrants as voters was given a faux Latin name: "Hobo floto voto."

3   When notoriously corrupt William Hale "Big Bill" Thompson was elected mayor in 1927, jubilant supporters flocked to his Fish Fans Club boat, well known as a floating speakeasy in Belmont Harbor. So many people climbed aboard that the boat sank into the mud, inspiring a joke that so much gin was spilled into Belmont Harbor that it became the world's largest martini.

4   The 1928 Republican primary in Chicago was so violent it was called the "Pineapple Primary," named for the grenade-like devices thrown around. But the general election that November was the city's cleanest in years. Who deserved credit? Al Capone, whose henchmen were involved in the earlier violence. After the bloody primary, Chicago Crime Commission founder Frank Loesch visited Capone and demanded he stop the violence. Capone's response? "All right. I'll have the cops send over squad cars the night before the election and jug all the hoodlums and keep 'em in the cooler until the polls close."

5   A Tribune story on Nov. 6, 1940, reported the separate heart-attack deaths of a man on his way to the polls, two women waiting to vote, and a cop guarding ballot counting. The headline: "Four Chicagoans Die in Election Day Excitement."

6   When machine stalwart Vito Marzullo ran against reform candidate Fred Hilbruner for the City Council in 1953, Marzullo got his foe kicked off the ballot. Hilbruner then ran a futile write-in race, winning only one precinct.

According to independent Ald. Leon Despres, Marzullo grumbled for years about the loss of that single precinct. "Somebody lied to me," he said.

7 In March 1972, the Tribune teamed with the Better Government Association to send 30 people undercover as election judges and poll watchers. They found widespread fraud. The newspaper didn't stop there. Reporter William Mullen was hired as an election board clerk and worked covertly for three months. At one point, board chairman Stanley Kusper Jr. held a staff meeting and demanded loyalty: "Come November, there aren't going to be any cracks in the wall of this office. Nobody has cracked this office from the outside." Mullen was standing 15 feet away. The stories won a Pulitzer Prize.

8 A 20-year-old Southwest Side man showed up at the polls in 1976 wearing pajamas and slippers and holding a shoebox, which he said contained flowers. Election judges, fearing the box held a bomb, summoned police. A responding officer found the young man smoking marijuana, with more of the "flowers" in the shoebox. He was arrested.

9 Longtime congressman Luis Gutierrez reached political prominence in a wild 1986 aldermanic race against Manuel Torres featuring a libel suit, street fighting, ghost-voter allegations, a gunshot fired in Torres' direction, a suspected pipe bomb, and accusations of communism and cocaine use. Gutierrez beat Torres by 20 votes, 5,245 to 5,225, while a crossing guard named Jim Blasinski received 11 write-in votes — which grew to 21 when more write-ins were found in a Chicago Board of Election warehouse. That meant Gutierrez was two votes shy of a majority, which meant a runoff was necessary. The second vote in the Near Northwest Side ward was anticlimactic, with Gutierrez winning handily.

10 In 1987, a dirty trickster altered a photo of Southwest Side Ald. William Krystyniak with Pope John Paul II, removing the pope and adding Mayor Harold Washington and former Israeli Prime Minister Shimon Peres. But Krystyniak won anyway. And it didn't seem to hurt Washington or Peres either.

SOURCES: *"Chicago Politics, Ward by Ward," by David K. Fremon; "Strange but True: Chicago," by Thomas J. O'Gorman and Lisa Montanarelli; "Grafters and Goo Goos: Corruption and Reform in Chicago, 1833-2003," by James L. Merriner; "Capone," by John Kobler; "The Mafia Encyclopedia," by Carl Sifakis; "Challenging the Daley Machine: A Chicago Alderman's Memoir," by Leon M. Despres with Kenan Heise; and Tribune archives.*

CHICAGO MAYORS NOT NAMED DALEY

1 Nine of the last ten Chicago mayors were born in Illinois, with the exception being Alabama native Eugene Sawyer. But early in city history, New Yorkers dominated. Fifteen people born in New York state have been mayor, while only 12 native Illinoisans have. Two mayors have been foreign-born: Joseph Medill in Canada and Anton Cermak in Bohemia.

2 Jane Byrne, Chicago's only female mayor, battled sexism as she rose to political power. The first Mayor Daley named her co-chairman of the Cook County Democratic Central Committee, but she didn't last long in the old boys network. After she quit in 1977, party chairman George Dunne promised that women would still have a role. "Women's card parties, fashion shows and the like will be continued," he said.

3 Big Bill Thompson, who deserves consideration as Chicago's most crooked mayor, threatened to punch Britain's King George V in the nose and once staged a "debate" in which he appeared onstage with two caged rats meant to represent his opponents.

4 Justice was in a hurry after Giuseppe Zangara mortally wounded Chicago Mayor Anton Cermak during an appearance with President-elect Franklin Roosevelt in Miami on Feb. 15, 1933. Within five days, Zangara was sentenced to 80 years in prison. On March 6, Cermak died of his wounds, and three days later, Zangara pleaded guilty to murder. He went to the electric chair March 20–just two weeks after Cermak's death.

5 The Chicago Marathon was called the Mayor Daley Marathon when it debuted in 1977, and the mayor at the time, Michael Bilandic, ran in the race.

6 Fred Busse was elected mayor in 1907 without giving a single speech or making any campaign appearances. Busse, who was postmaster of Chicago and had served as a state legislator and state treasurer, spent the campaign season recovering from a near-fatal train wreck. The Chicago Tribune did his campaigning for him, running Page 1 headlines like "Busse a fighter; credit to city" while ridiculing incumbent Mayor Edward Dunne.

7 During the Civil War, two former Chicago mayors were imprisoned at Camp Douglas on the South Side, suspected of being "Copperheads," or Southern sympathizers. Both were freed–Levi Boone after 37 days and Buckner Morris after about six months.

8 "Long John" Wentworth was a hard-drinking, heavy-eating, 6-foot-6 autocrat. When a state law shifted control of Chicago police from the mayor to an independent board in the 1860s, Wentworth fired the entire force, leaving a city of 100,000 people without a single officer for a few hours until the board could convene.

9 The Daleys weren't the first father-son dynasty in Chicago. Carter Harrison I served for 10 years in the 1880s and '90s. Carter Harrison II ran the city for 14 years at the turn of the last century. A survey of experts conducted in 1985 rated the father-son duo No. 2 and No. 3 behind Richard J. Daley as the city's best mayors.

10 Harold Washington's parents divorced when he was quite young, and he lived with his father, Roy, whom he adored. Washington had a way with words. Case in point: "I was very fortunate. My father was my role model. He was a real man. He was a good man. For many years, he was not only my father, he was my mother. And so I knew who Santa Claus was. He came home every night, put his feet under the table and had dinner with me."

SOURCES: *"The Making of the Mayor," edited by Melvin G. Holli and Paul M. Green; "The Chicago City Manual," (1911); "Political History of Chicago (Covering the period from 1837 to 1887)," by M.L. Ahern; "Fifty Years' Recollections," by Jeriah Bonham; "Big Bill Thompson, Chicago, and the Politics of Image," by Douglas Bukowski; "Capone: The Man and the Era," by Laurence Bergreen; "Fabulous Chicago," by Emmett Dedmon; "The Mayors: The Chicago Political Tradition," edited by Paul M. Green and Melvin G. Holli; "The Hoofs and Guns of the Storm: Chicago's Civil War Connections," by Arnie Bernstein; "American Bastille," by John A. Marshall; "To Die in Chicago: Confederate Prisoners at Camp Douglas, 1862-65," by George Levy; and Tribune archives.*

CHICAGO MURDERS

1 The first murder conviction based on fingerprint evidence occurred in Chicago. When Thomas Jennings broke into a South Side house in 1910 and was confronted, he killed the owner and fled. But his fingerprints remained — on a freshly painted railing outside the house.

2 Henry Spencer, who bilked and murdered a tango teacher near west suburban Wheaton, was hanged in August 1914, just as World War I began. Chicago Daily News reporter Ben Hecht, covering the hanging, got a wire from his editor: "Omit all gruesome details.... The world has just gone to war." The acerbic Hecht wired back: "Will try to make hanging as cheerful and optimistic as possible." LoL

3 In 1919-1933, more than 160 Chicago police officers died in the line of duty, an average of nearly one a month.

4 Mob-connected race track operator Ed O'Hare cut a deal with federal authorities in the 1930s: If he informed on organized crime, his son Butch would be appointed to the Naval Academy. When the mob learned of the father's treachery, he was shot to death. The son became a Navy flier, won the Congressional Medal of Honor during World War II, and disappeared in the Pacific during a mission. O'Hare International Airport is named for the son, but it owes something to his crooked but loyal father as well.

5 Over a century ago, only men were allowed on juries. That changed for several reasons. One was the desire to extend rights to women. Another was the need to prevent women from getting away with murder. The musical "Chicago" highlighted two cases in the 1920s in which female killers escaped justice. Before that came Nellie Higgs, who was seen boarding an Illinois Central train in 1914 and shooting her lover in the back, but evaded punishment by declaring, "My mind is a blank." She became the 17th female murder suspect acquitted in a decade. A prosecutor complained that any female killer could "shed a few tears and cast a few wistful glances at the jury, and she will be acquitted."

6 Richard Speck's murder of eight nurses wasn't the Sun-Times' lead story the next day. The July 15, 1966, paper featured another breaking story: West Side rioting in which several police officers were wounded. The Tribune led with the nurse murders but was similarly conflicted. Its lead headline was "SEARCH FOR MASS KILLER," and underneath was the headline "Six Policemen Shot on West Side" — representing two stories that had nothing to do with each other.

7 Chicago's murder count is way down from the early 1990s, but there's increasing concern about the "clearance rate" — the percentage of cases in which charges are filed or the alleged perpetrator has died. In the crime-racked Englewood neighborhood, only 101 of 230 homicides were cleared in the last five years, according to statistics compiled in 2012.

8 After John Wayne Gacy was executed in 1994 for killing 33 boys and young men, his brain was given to psychiatrist Helen Morrison, who kept it in the basement of her Chicago home.

9 Near the corner of Cleveland Avenue and Oak Street, a 7-year-old named Dantrell Davis was shot to death on his way to school in 1992. Even before that, the area had a murderous history. In the 1910s, the intersection was known as Death Corner. In a 15-month period, 38 people were killed in the area by the Black Hand, extortionists who threatened kidnapping, arson and murder if they were not paid off.

10 The most famous murder in Chicago history was the killing of 14-year-old Bobby Franks by graduate students Nathan Leopold and Richard Loeb, who attempted the "perfect crime." The 1924 killing took place in the South Side's Kenwood neighborhood about a block from where President Barack Obama owns a home. Anti-Obama conspiracy bloggers, take note. For one thing, Obama has never denied involvement. And, sure, his birth certificate says he wasn't born until 37 years later, but who can trust that?

SOURCES: *"Fabulous Chicago" by Emmett Dedmon, "Return to the Scene of the Crime" by Richard Lindberg, "The Crime of the Century" by Hal Higdon, "Paddy Whacked" by T.J. English, chicagopolice.org, "State Trooper" by Marilyn Olsen and Tribune news services.*

THE OUTFIT

1 Al Capone was known as Scarface, but his friends called him Snorky, which was slang for elegant.

2 Ethnic stereotypers, beware. Mobsters' names don't always match their nationalities. Hymie Weiss was a Polish Catholic whose birth name was Earl Wojciechowski. "Machine Gun" Jack McGurn was a Sicilian originally named Vincenzo Gibaldi.

3 The mob often stifled African-American political aspirations. In 1928, black lawyer Octavius Granady ran for Republican committeeman against a mob-backed white candidate in the "Bloody 20th" Ward on the West Side. On Election Day, two cars of gunmen chased Granady's car, which crashed into a tree. Granady was then shot to death for the crime of participating in a democracy. Nine men, including five police officers, were charged, but none was convicted.

4 Sometimes mobsters did good turns to boost their public image. Mob historian Gus Russo notes that Capone's henchmen successfully pressured the Chicago City Council to require a date stamp on milk cartons and to establish guidelines for what could be sold as Grade A milk.

5 The mob wasn't always consumer-oriented. In the early '50s, the Outfit tricked Chicagoans into eating horsemeat. Since beef cost four times as much as horseflesh, mob-controlled processing plants created a mix of 40 percent horse and 60 percent cow and called it ground beef. Millions of pounds were sold while inspectors were bribed to look the other way in the "horseburger" scandal.

6 Rep. Roland Libonati (D-Ill.), who served in Congress from 1957 to 1965, was an unabashed friend of many mobsters, including Capone, Tony Accardo and Paul Ricca. But he was especially famous for crimes against the English language. He referred to Slavic voters as "Slavishes," called Chicago "the aviation crosswords of the world," and uttered a world-class malapropism: "I resent the insinuendoes."

7 One of the biggest men in 20th Century Chicago crime was a man of Welsh descent named Murray Humphreys, who masterminded the mob's legal strategies and union takeovers. The press called him The Camel, but he was Curly to his friends. When Humphreys' daughter needed a high school prom date, Frank Sinatra showed up.

8 The movie "Analyze This" depicted how police broke up the famous 1957 meeting of the nation's top mobsters in rural upstate New York. While many wiseguys were nabbed, Chicago delegates Accardo and Sam Giancana escaped — but not unscathed. "I tore up a $1,200 suit on some barbed wire and ruined a new pair of shoes," Giancana later said.

9 While FBI agents were tracking mobsters, the mobsters were tracking the FBI agents. The crooks knew, for example, that FBI agent Bill Roemer coached his son's baseball team, so they would arrange mob meetings during the boy's practices.

10 Desi Arnaz had some 'splaining to do when he began producing television's "The Untouchables" in 1959. Many Italians thought the show made them look bad, and Arnaz got a protesting phone call from an old high school friend: Sonny Capone, Al's son. But Arnaz refused to budge. According to reports, Chicago mob bosses considered a "hit" on Arnaz, but Capone's widow, Mae, vetoed any rough stuff against him.

SOURCES: *"The Outfit" by Gus Russo; "Capone" by John Kobler; Tribune archives.*

CHICAGO PROTESTS

1   Chicago has never landed an Olympics, but in 1932 it hosted a "counter-Olympics." The event was organized by American communists as a protest against racism and nationalism, which they found on display at that year's real Olympics in Los Angeles. The alternative event, held at the University of Chicago and officially called the International Workers Athletic Meet, featured competitors wearing signs such as "Free Tom Mooney," in support of a labor activist convicted in a fatal bombing.

2   When the Chicago Board Options Exchange instituted a dress code in 1977 that banned blue jeans, T-shirts and halter tops, some traders protested by wearing tuxedos. CBOE officials decided not to levy fines for the stunt, but some colleagues grumbled about the traders' "childish behavior."

3   In August 1966, the Rev. Martin Luther King Jr. led about 350 protesters on a march through the Southwest Side to advocate for open housing. They were met by a mob of more than 4,000 who threw rocks, bottles, firecrackers and curses. King himself was knocked to the ground when a rock hit him in the back of the head. "I have seen many demonstrations in the South, but I have never seen anything so hostile and so hateful as I've seen here today." (This national news story somehow didn't lead the next day's Tribune. The paper's editors opted for the College All-Star Game at Soldier Field.)

4   Remember the famous clashes between police and demonstrators at the 1968 Democratic National Convention? Didn't happen. At least they didn't happen anywhere near the convention. The Democrats met at the old International Amphitheatre at 42nd and Halsted while the major confrontations were around Grant Park (about four miles away) and Lincoln Park (more than seven miles away).

5 Chicago officials, who were determined that the 1996 Democratic Convention not be a repeat of 1968, set up "designated protest areas" and required activists to participate in a lottery for protest times. The Lesbian Avengers of Chicago were turned down when they sought permission to eat fire as part of their protest. City officials deemed it unsafe.

6 When Southwest Side residents protested in 1910 about the vile condition of Bubbly Creek and other nearby garbage dumps and demanded the city clean them up, the health commissioner blamed the protesters for living in such conditions. And while he conceded the local dumps were a problem, he insisted: "A typhoid germ could not live in Bubbly Creek. That unspeakable filth would strangle a typhoid germ."

7 For most of the last century, one group of people could be counted on to attend many Chicago protests: police spies. By one count in 1960, the Chicago Police Department's Red Squad had gathered information on about 117,000 Chicagoans and 141,000 people from out of town. Its illegal surveillance of dissidents was put to an end by a court ruling in 1985.

8 The aggrieved class of citizens known as North Shore teenagers staged a protest in July 1988 at the Lake Forest Mini-Mart, complaining that they were not permitted to hang out there or use the bathroom. One sign read: "Open the laboratory."

9 Chicago fluoridated its water in 1956. A small but voluble group of protesters argued it was mass medication and illegal. They picketed City Hall with signs that asked: "Is Mayor Daley our Pied Piper?" and "Why drink rat poison?"

10 When Elvis Presley was inducted into the Army in 1958, schoolgirls wore dog tags bearing Elvis' name, serial number and blood type. But Jones Commercial High School in downtown Chicago banned the practice, setting off a protest by schoolgirls, who held a large banner declaring that the school was "Unfair to Elvis Presley."

SOURCES: *"Red Chicago: American Communism at Its Grassroots, 1928-35" by Randi Storch; "A People's History of Sports in the United States" by Dave Zirin; "Encyclopedia of Chicago", Tribune archives.*

CHICAGO RADIO

1   On Nov. 8, 1921, soprano Mary Garden helped radio station KYW test its transmitter in preparation for its groundbreaking broadcasts of opera. Garden stood on the stage of the Auditorium Theatre, inside a tent set up to reduce echo, with a single light bulb for illumination. Which explains why the first words ever spoken on Chicago radio were Garden saying, "My God, but it's dark in here!"

2   In radio's early days, the science of broadcasting was poorly understood by the public and news media. Signals were believed to travel through an invisible ether. "Radio" and "ether" were synonyms in headlines, and the phrase "crash the ether" meant to make a radio broadcast. A 1930 Tribune article expressed surprise that as listeners increased, they didn't use up the signal, and that "there always seems to be sufficient energy in the ether for all."

3   The most famous radio news account ever? Chicago broadcaster Herb Morrison's description of the explosion of the airship Hindenburg in Lakehurst, N.J., for WLS in 1937. You've heard it, of course: "Oh, the humanity!" Most people assume Morrison's words were broadcast live, but they were first aired the next day when a recording disc was played. Another misimpression involves Morrison's voice, which seems excited and high-pitched. But experts believe the recording speed was off, masking the fact that Morrison had a rather low voice.

4   Jack L. Cooper, a pioneering black disc jockey with WSBC, earned six figures in the mid-1940s. Serving Chicago's growing black population, many of whom had arrived from the South, Cooper offered an on-air missing person's service to help people reconnect with family and friends.

5   The call letters of Chicago radio stations reflected their missions. The Tribune's outlet was and is WGN — "World's Greatest Newspaper." Sears Roebuck & Co. sponsored WLS — "World's Largest Store." WVON was once the "Voice of the Negro." The call letters of WBBM have various interpretations. When the station broadcast from the Broadmoor Hotel in 1925, its slogan was "We Broadcast Broadmoor Music." In the early '30s, the station billed itself as "World's Best Broadcast Medium." One sponsor was the World Storage Battery Co., and some said that WBBM stood for "World's Best Battery Maker."

6 Chicago once had a station called WJBT — "Where Jesus Blesses Thousands."

7 A WGN radio interview with Yankees outfielder Jake Powell in 1938 went sour when he used a racial epithet in telling broadcaster Bob Elson that he stayed in shape during the off-season by working as a police officer "cracking [blacks] over the head." Powell was suspended and performed penance by visiting Harlem taverns and making apologies. Turns out that Powell was lying about being a police officer. A decade after his controversial quote, he was arrested for passing bad checks. He got his hands on a gun in the police station, and shot himself to death.

8 Years before Ray Kroc founded the McDonald's hamburger chain, he was staff pianist at radio station WGES in Oak Park.

9 Many of Steve Dahl's Chicago antics are well known, such as Disco Demolition Night at Comiskey Park and the play-by-play of his own vasectomy. But the pre-Chicago hijinks of his youth are less publicized. They include the time in Detroit when police surrounded the studio because he had discussed his own suicide on the air as a comedy bit, and the episode in Bakersfield, Calif., when he announced the death of Col. Harland Sanders' wife: He reported that she had been dipped in extra-crispy batter.

10 The real name of Chicago-based radio icon Paul Harvey was Paul Harvey Aurandt. And that's the rest of the story.

SOURCES: *"Listening In," by Susan J. Douglas; "Blackout," by Chris Lamb; wvon.com; richsamuels.com; professor emeritus Michael Biel of Morehead State University; radio historian Chuck Schaden; "Grinding It Out: The Making of McDonald's" by Ray Kroc with Robert Anderson; "Cassell's Dictionary of Slang," by Jonathon Green; and Tribune news services.*

THE NORTH SIDE

1   Billy Caldwell and Sauganash are two names for the same person. A chief of the Potawatomi, he was a half-British, half-Native American man who often played the peacemaker between the Indians and early settlers. He famously interceded to save white families in the aftermath of the Battle of Fort Dearborn in 1812. Sauganash was held in such esteem that the government granted him 1,600 acres of land on the North Branch of the Chicago River, an area that includes Sauganash, Forest Glen and South Edgebrook.

2   Looking for small-town life in the big city? You could do worse than tiny Brynford Park. This Far North Side enclave has just 120 homes and sits immediately northwest of the intersection of Bryn Mawr Avenue and Pulaski Road (formerly Crawford Avenue–the combination of Bryn Mawr and Crawford is where Brynford Park got its name). It is surrounded by Montrose Cemetery, Bohemian National Cemetery, North Park Village Nature Center and an industrial park.

3   Early residents of a Far North Side community marketed their town as the first "electric suburb" because it sported cutting-edge electric streetlights. And they didn't stop there. In 1890, they asked for–and received–Thomas Edison's approval to name their village in his honor. Edison Park joined the city in 1910.

4   Where's the world-renowned Steppenwolf Theatre? If you said Ranch Triangle, give yourself a prize. Make that R.A.N.C.H. Triangle, a name derived from its borders: Racine, Armitage, North, the Chicago River and Halsted, according to ranchtriangle.org. And if you're wondering how five sides make a triangle, then you're just being too literal.

5   Old Town Triangle, which sits just north of Old Town, is another geography-challenged triangle. It is bounded by North Avenue, Clark Street and … well, what happened to Ogden Avenue? That street, which is named after Chicago's first mayor, was cut off at North Avenue in 1967. That urban planning decision not only severed a key connection between Lake Shore Drive and the interstate highway system, but also separated Cabrini-Green from its more upscale neighbors to the north.

6 Riverview Park, which billed itself as the largest amusement park in the world, took up 74 acres at Belmont and Western avenues, and entertained millions during its six-decade run. In May 1928, Chicago Mayor William "Big Bill" Thompson closed public schools, 10 to 20 each day, so kids could attend the park for free, despite protests from outraged teachers and parents groups. The park closed suddenly in 1967.

7 Streeterville is named after a whiskey-selling squatter and scamp who was despised by city fathers. In 1886, Capt. George Streeter ran his steamship aground on a sandbar about 400 feet off Superior Street, or smack dab in the middle of what is today Northwestern's law school campus. Streeter urged builders to dump their junk around his boat, then declared the newly created land to be a "District of Lake Michigan" separate from Chicago and Illinois. He defended this claim in court and with a shotgun that he wasn't afraid to use. The city fought back by extending Lake Shore Drive south, creating the curve at Oak Street to surround Streeter's ville. It took decades for officials to wrest control from the irascible captain.

8 In Lincoln Square, you'll find a lot of things (a library, a school, a glass company) with the name Budlong. Lyman and Joseph Budlong's 700-acre farm and pickle factory sat northwest of Western and Foster avenues. The city still designates the area as Budlong Woods.

9 Developer Jesse Bowman helped establish the village of Bowmanville in the late 1800s. Trouble was, he didn't own the land he was selling. He skipped town, but his name stayed–on the neighborhood nestled south of Rosehill Cemetery.

10 Towertown, named after the Water Tower, was the community of artists, writers and free-love advocates who settled on the Near North Side just west of Michigan Avenue in the early 20th century. The area's high property values drove them out, and the neighborhood no longer exists.

SOURCES: *"History of Chicago: From the Earliest Period to the Present Time" by Alfred Theodore Andreas; "Encyclopedia of Chicago";"Chicago Politics, Ward by Ward," by David K. Fremon; "Our Old Town," by Shirley Baugher; forgottenchicago.com; Roscoe Village Neighbors; Chicago Public Library; Brynford Park Community Association; Edison Park Chamber of Commerce; Northwest Chicago Historical Society, and Tribune archives.*

THE SOUTH SIDE

1   Why is the South Side neighborhood southeast of Pershing Road and Halsted Street called Canaryville? According to the "Encyclopedia of Chicago," the name may refer to "sparrows who populated the area at the end of the 19th century, feeding off stockyard refuse and grain from railroad cars." But the name may also relate to the neighborhood's tough youths, known as "wild canaries."

2   The World's Columbian Exposition of 1893, located along the lakefront from 56th to 67th streets, made the South Side home to many "firsts": the first Ferris wheel, the first sales of a treat later called Cracker Jack, and the debut of a fictional pancake maker named Aunt Jemima. A pancake mix company hired Chicagoan Nancy Green, a former Kentucky slave, to play Jemima at the fair. Political correctness was many decades away. Fairgoers got buttons with Green's likeness and the words "I'se in town, honey."

3   There's an East Side on the South Side. Near the far southeast corner of the city, the East Side neighborhood has had three previous names: Taylorville, Goosetown and Colehour.

4   Pill Hill was so named because so many doctors called it home. Today, the neighborhood nestled inside Calumet Heights is still the upscale home to many professionals. The area also gave its name to a play by Samuel Kelley. The work, about a group of friends growing up in Chicago from 1973 to 1983, is three hours plus and was called "ambitious" in a 1994 Tribune review but "interminable" in its 1999 revival.

5   One of the last suburbs to become a Chicago neighborhood was Morgan Park on the Far South Side. It wasn't love at first sight. The 20-year annexation battle started in 1894 with a street fight between a Methodist minister and a politician, and included fistfights at village meetings, accusations of vote fraud, a banking scandal, state legislation, an Illinois Supreme Court ruling and a prank attempt by Morgan Park to annex Chicago. Before they officially joined the city in 1914, residents had gone to the polls eight times (six times voting no and two times yes).

6   The neighborhood of Douglas, which the city's map now splits into Prairie Shores and Lake Meadows, includes land donated by the family of Sen. Stephen Douglas, Abraham Lincoln's rival. During the Civil War, Camp Douglas at 31st Street and Cottage Grove Avenue was a horrific prisoner of war camp where thousands of Confederates died of abuse and disease. The dead were eventually buried at Oak Woods Cemetery, and today these soldiers who fought against emancipation rest alongside such African-American legends as Harold Washington and Jesse Owens.

7   The first fingerprints used to convict an American of murder were found in what is now the Beverly neighborhood. Thomas Jennings was burglarizing a house in 1910 when the homeowner confronted him. Jennings killed him. He also left fingerprints on a freshly painted railing outside the house, and police later picked him up as a suspicious character. Based on the fingerprints, he was convicted and hanged.

8   The White City amusement park, billed as "the city of a million electric lights," opened around 1905 and operated until the late '30s at 63rd Street and South Park. Goodyear's first commercial blimp, the Wingfoot, was assembled and hangared there. While sailing from Grant Park toward White City in 1919, the Wingfoot plunged through the skylight of a downtown bank, killing 10 bank employees and three people on the blimp.

9   Many amazing South Side sites have disappeared, including Frank Lloyd Wright's Midway Gardens entertainment complex at 60th and Cottage Grove and the Washington Park Racetrack at 61st and Cottage Grove. A less regrettable loss was the Robert Taylor Homes, a row of high-rises along the Dan Ryan Expressway that was considered a public housing failure. The development was named for Chicago Housing Authority board member Robert Taylor, grandfather of White House adviser Valerie Jarrett.

10   The Levee was a vice district around 20th and State streets with houses of ill repute bearing such colorful names as Bucket of Blood, Why Not and the Library. (A husband could tell his wife he was going to the Library and would not be lying.) Do-gooders closed the Levee in 1912, dispersing prostitution elsewhere in the city and suburbs.

SOURCES: *"Encyclopedia of Chicago"; "Streetwise Chicago" by Don Hayner and Tom McNamee; "Chicago and its Suburbs" by Everett Chamberlin; "Chicago Sketches" by June Skinner Sawyers, "Chicago Politics, Ward by Ward" by David K. Fremon; "Slave in a Box: The Strange Career of Aunt Jemima" by M.M. Manring; "Peanuts" by Andrew F. Smith; "Chicago Neighborhoods and Suburbs: A Historical Guide," edited by Ann Durkin Keating; and Tribune archives.*

THE WEST SIDE

1   When a fire broke out in the O'Leary family's barn near DeKoven and Jefferson streets southwest of downtown in 1871, it spread east and north, jumping the Chicago River twice, killing at least 300 people and leveling 18,000 buildings. But the blaze spared a building within a few feet of where it started — the O'Learys' home.

2   The quiet Galewood neighborhood hugs the city's western border north of Oak Park. A famous current resident? Gov. Pat Quinn. A famous former resident? Hugh Hefner.

3   The last time the Chicago Cubs won the World Series (in 1908), their home was the West Side Grounds, where the Illinois Medical District is now located. Some people trace the phrase "out of left field" to a mental hospital located beyond the ballpark's left-field wall.

4   White flight was so pronounced in North Lawndale that the black population soared to 91 percent from 13 percent in the 1950s.

5   Are you from Jackowo or Waclawowo? Those are Polish-American names for sections of the Logan Square and Avondale neighborhoods on the Northwest Side. Waclawowo is the area around St. Wenceslaus, while Jackowo is the area around St. Hyacinth Basilica.

6   The Second City has a Fifth City. That's the name for a section of East Garfield Park.

7   What is now the Logan Square neighborhood used to be an area separate from the city called Jefferson. The Bucktown area was at one time called Holstein; it reportedly got the name Bucktown from the large number of goats kept there.

8   The 1963 murder of a West Side alderman has never been solved. Benjamin Lewis, 24th, a black politician whose relationship with the Democratic power structure was tenuous, was in his office at 3604 W. Roosevelt Road when gunmen burst in, handcuffed him in a chair and shot him in the head. A burned-down cigarette was resting between his fingers when the police found him.

9   Pilsen got its name in the late 1800s from a Bohemian restaurant there called At the City of Plzen, referring to a city now in the Czech Republic. Acclaimed writer Stuart Dybek, the son of a Polish immigrant, grew up in Pilsen. But now the neighborhood is predominantly Mexican, the home of beautiful murals, vibrant restaurants and the National Museum of Mexican Art.

10   After the Civil War, entrepreneur Andrew Dunning tried to start a village east of what is now O'Hare International Airport. But his land was next to a poor farm and an insane asylum, putting off prospective settlers. Patients were taken to the county facilities aboard the insensitively dubbed "crazy train." Because the train station was named for Dunning, the facilities themselves became known by that name, and parents used to warn their unruly children that they might be "going to Dunning." Today, Dunning is a perfectly nice neighborhood that includes Chicago-Read Mental Health Center.

SOURCES: *"Challenging Chicago" by Perry Duis; "Block by Block: Neighborhoods and Public Policy on Chicago's West Side" by Amanda J. Seligman; "The Great Chicago Fire" by Robert Cromie; "Encyclopedia of Chicago"; James L. Merriner in Illinois Issues; Richard C. Lindberg in Illinois Police and Sheriff's News; sthyacinthbasilica.org; Northwest Chicago Historical Society; chicagohistory.org; and Tribune archives.*

CHICAGO'S NORTHERN SUBURBS

1   The Glen View Club is not in Glenview — it's in Golf. The Evanston Golf Club is not in Evanston — it's in Skokie. The Skokie Country Club is not in Skokie — it's in Glencoe.

2   Sir Edmund Hillary, one of the conquerors of Mount Everest (elevation 29,035 feet), spent a year as a resident of Park Ridge (elevation about 640 feet). The New Zealander and his family moved into a Park Ridge home in 1963 while he was paid by Chicago-based Field Enterprises to travel around the country giving speeches.

3   Arlington Heights used to be called Dunton, Lincolnwood was formerly Tessville, Evanston was Ridgeville, Waukegan was Little Fort, Northbrook was Shermerville and Niles was Dutchman's Point.

4   The people of Niles Center grew tired of their town being confused with Niles, so in 1940 they formed a renaming commission and chose "Skokie," the Potawatomi word for "big swamp." The commission's vote tally was Skokie 15, Oakton 4, Woodridge 2, Ridgemoor 2 and Westridge 1. (The name Woodridge didn't go to waste: a west suburban town adopted it in 1959.)

5   When Ravinia first opened in Highland Park in 1904, it offered a theater, dining rooms, a dance floor — and a baseball field.

6   In 1850, the Germans who settled in the Wilmette area named their township New Trier after the German city of Trier. That city was settled by a Gaulish people called the Treveri and was also known as Treves — which is why New Trier High School athletes are called Trevians. Little did the Illinois settlers know that Trier would soon be known as the birthplace of communist icon Karl Marx.

7   John Robert Rietz, who played the father in "The Brady Bunch" under his stage name Robert Reed, was born in Highland Park and buried in Skokie.

8   One of Evanston's greatest citizens is little remembered today. Charles Gates Dawes was a banker and politician who won the Nobel Peace Prize for his World War I reparations plan and served as vice president under Calvin Coolidge. But Dawes and Coolidge didn't get along, especially after Coolidge's nominee for attorney general was rejected by the Senate because Dawes took a nap instead of casting the tie-breaking vote.

9   Actor Marlon Brando's memoir recalls rough times as a teen in Libertyville. Fired as a movie usher, he stuffed rotting broccoli and stinky Limburger into the intake pipe of the theater's air-conditioning system. He was held back in 10th grade at Libertyville High School because he was a "bad student, chronic truant and all-around incorrigible." His father sent him to a military school in Minnesota.

10   In Zion, it once was illegal to whistle on Sundays, gamble, put on plays, sell alcohol or tobacco, eat pork or oysters, swear, spit or wear tan-colored shoes.

SOURCES: *"Encyclopedia of Chicago"; "Arlington Heights, Illinois: Downtown Renaissance" by Janet Souter and Gerry Souter; "Evanston" by Mimi Rotorma; "Wilmette: A History" by George D. Bushnell; "American Heritage Dictionary of the English Language"; "View From the Summit" by Sir Edmund Hillary; "Skokie: 1888-1988: A Centennial History" by Richard Whittingham; "Graveyards of Chicago" by Matt Hucke and Ursula Bielski; "Brando: Songs My Mother Taught Me" by Marlon Brando with Robert Lindsey; Bulletin of the American Geographical Society; vah. com; ravinia.org; biography.com; "Unknown Chicago" blog by John R. Schmidt at chicagonow. com; and Tribune archives.*

CHICAGO'S SOUTH SUBURBS

1 Thornton goes way back. An 1840 map of the area shows Chicago, "Napierville" (Naperville), "Juliet" (Joliet) — and Thornton. And the nearby Hoxie Site offers proof that Native Americans lived — and fortified — the area as early as 1400.

2 Harry Caray's first radio job was at WCLS in Joliet. That's where he got rid of his original surname, Carabina, and took on Caray.

3 Even if you're not in the south suburbs, you're closer than you think. Lemont stone, a warm, yellow limestone, quarried in and around the south suburb, was used to build Chicago's Water Tower and Pumping Station, Holy Name Cathedral and thousands of houses and house foundations across the Chicago area.

4 The town of Matteson is pronounced Mat-te-son, not Matt-son, according to the suburb's official website.

5 Chicago Mayor Richard J. Daley is not buried in the city he loved. His final resting place is Holy Sepulchre Cemetery in Worth.

6 After being excluded from Blue Island, African-Americans started their own community in 1917. They called it Robbins. Bessie Coleman, an early aviation pioneer who had to go to France to escape racism and learn to fly, helped found an airport there. A portion of Mannheim Road near O'Hare is named after her.

7 Thousands of acres of the south suburbs are set aside as forest preserves and parks. One section near Hickory Hills was called Buffalo Woods. It was home to Cook County's very own buffalo herd. A gift of Yellowstone National Park in 1924, the eight beasts grew to a herd of 24. But by 1934 the number was back to eight, and the county decided to get rid of them. One commissioner suggested "making buffalo robes" and another preferred "buffalo steaks." The commissioners voted to have the beasts killed, but in the end, the buffalo were spared after the county was inundated by pleas from animal lovers who offered to find homes for the beasts.

8   If you believe in ghosts — or even if you don't — one of the most unsettling stories is surely about Resurrection Mary in Justice. Legend has it that a young woman was killed in the late 1930s on Archer Avenue by a hit-and-run driver and that she's been hitchhiking in the area ever since. In 1979, Suburban Trib columnist Bill Geist recounted numerous sightings, odd encounters and even conversations by various people with a striking, blond-haired beauty who was "very cold to the touch."

9   Chances are if you grew up in the south suburbs and came of age in the 1980s and '90s, you know Reilly's Daughter. This legendary pub, at 111th Street and Pulaski Road in Oak Lawn, is now closed but in its heyday was known for its live music, St. Paddy's Day celebrations and an annual visit by Notre Dame's football coach.

10   The best-selling Bible translation, the New International Version, was conceived in Palos Heights. It was there in 1965 that a group of scholars agreed on the need for a new translation in contemporary English. The idea was seconded a year later in Chicago at a larger gathering of religious leaders. The NIV was published in 1978.

SOURCES: *"I Remember Harry Caray," by Rich Wolfe and George Castle; "Harry Caray: Voice of the Fans," by Pat Hughes and Bruce Miles; Cook County Forest Preserve; "Encyclopedia of Chicago"; Biblica; Christian Booksellers Association; Palos Heights; "A Native's Guide to Chicago's South Suburbs," by Christina Bultinck and Christy Johnston-Czarnecki; villageofmatteson.org; "The Chicago River: A Natural and Unnatural History" by Libby Hill; village of Lemont; "Oddball Illinois," by Jerome Pohlen; ghostresearch.com; and Tribune archives.*

10 THINGS YOU MIGHT NOT KNOW ABOUT
CHICAGO TRANSIT

1 In the second half of the 19th Century, Chicago had horsecars — streetcars pulled on a track by horses. The building at 500 N. LaSalle St. that once held Michael Jordan's Restaurant was at one time a facility serving the horsecar industry, according to Perry Duis's book "Challenging Chicago."

2 John Luther Jones was a train engineer who ran Illinois Central shuttles from downtown Chicago to the 1893 Columbian Exposition in Jackson Park. Better known as Casey Jones, he was killed seven years later in a rail accident in Mississippi that inspired the folk song "The Ballad of Casey Jones" and made him the most famous train engineer in American history. (The Grateful Dead song "Casey Jones" borrowed his name but not much of his story.)

3 The jazz-rock group Chicago was once named Chicago Transit Authority. Despite reports that the band changed its name because City Hall threatened to sue, the band's former manager, James William Guercio, said it was a "quiet suggestion" by Mayor Richard J. Daley's office, not a "formal demand." He added: "I decided to do it in the interest of harmony with the city of our heritage." Later, the city awarded the band a medal of merit.

4 Over a century ago, the word commonly used to describe public transit was "traction." A typical Tribune headline: "Put Traction Issue Up to Straphangers."

5 Speaking of headlines ... for decades, Chicago's daily newspapers have been waiting for the CTA trains to break down on Christmas Day so they could print the headline "No 'L'" (as in "Noel"). Ha ha!

6 The worst transit accident in Chicago history: the Eastland disaster, in which a ship that was to carry picnickers to Michigan City, Ind., overturned in the Chicago River, killing more than 800 people. The deadliest rail accident: the 1972 collision of two Illinois Central Gulf trains at the 27th Street Station, killing 45. The CTA's worst: the Green Hornet streetcar disaster in 1950, in which a streetcar slammed into a gasoline truck at State and 63rd Streets, killing 33 people in a tremendous inferno.

7 Many of the horsecar tracks were converted to cable-car lines in the 1880s, and at one time Chicago had the most extensive cable-car system in the U.S., surpassing even San Francisco. But the last of Chicago's cable lines were converted to electricity in 1906.

8 Contrary to popular belief, the term "Loop" did not come from the elevated train track that has circled downtown Chicago south of the river since 1897. The name came from an earlier cable-car route.

9 The abbreviation for Chicago's elevated trains has always been "L" not "El," which is how New Yorkers abbreviate it.

10 Hollywood loves the CTA, but doesn't understand it. The Internet Movie Database (imdb.com) lists some of the film goofs: "The Fugitive" (1993) features a Balbo "L" stop, which doesn't exist. In "High Fidelity" (2000), the character played by John Cusack takes a Purple Line express to the Loop that goes underground, something the Purple Line doesn't do. "Risky Business" (1983), featuring the famed sex scene on an "L" car, depicts a single-car train on an underground route, which the CTA did not operate at that time.

SOURCES: *"Challenging Chicago" by Perry Duis; imdb.com; and Tribune archives.*

CHICAGO'S WESTERN SUBURBS

1 The rivalry between Naperville and Wheaton goes way back. In 1867, DuPage County residents voted to move the county seat to Wheaton. Naperville challenged the election and refused to give up many of the county's records. That's when it got interesting. On the morning of Dec. 21, 1868, about 80 armed men, led by the county sheriff, raided the courthouse in Naperville, seized the records and fled to Wheaton. County business ground to a halt — for years. The legal issues weren't resolved until 1872 when the state Supreme Court ruled for Wheaton.

2 Too bad for Cicero that it's more associated with Al Capone than with Katherine Stinson. The 21-year-old pioneer pilot earned her wings at Cicero Field, the Chicago-area's first airfield when it opened July 4, 1911. The field (bounded by 16th and 22nd streets and what are now Laramie and Cicero avenues) was state-of-the-art, including having its own wind tunnel, and became the aviation capital of the Midwest. Stinson, known as the "Flying Schoolgirl," was just the fourth woman in the U.S. to earn a license. In 1915, above Cicero, she became the first woman to perform a loop.

3 Have you heard about the Great Snake Escape of 1935? Over the course of a few months, 19 snakes went missing from Brookfield Zoo, including three cobras. One Australian bandy-bandy was on the lam for four months before it was captured on the zoo grounds, but not before news of its escape caused a minor panic. "Harmless snakes by the hundreds were killed in and around Chicago," the Tribune reported. Reptile house curator Grace Wiley was fired over the debacle, and she died 15 years later — of a cobra bite.

4   Replogle Globes, the world's largest manufacturer of globes, is head-quartered in Broadview — but that's not enough to get the village of about 8,000 on Replogle's maps. The company, which annually ships about 250,000 globes in more than 20 languages, moved to Broadview in 1987 from Chicago's Galewood neighborhood.

5   The 31-story Oakbrook Terrace Tower, at 418 feet, is the tallest building in the suburbs and Illinois (outside Chicago). It would also be the tallest build-ing in 15 states, including Kansas and South Carolina, according to a 2010 accounting. It is not, however, the tallest office building between Chicago and the Rocky Mountains, as claimed on the Oakbrook Terrace city website. Unless you don't count Des Moines. Or Omaha.

6   Washington Irving, author of "Legend of Sleepy Hollow" and "Rip Van Winkle," was one of America's first literary superstars, and Chicagoans were among his fans. The Kane County village of Sleepy Hollow sports the im-age of a headless rider on its website. Other Chicagoland locations honoring Irving: the southwest Chicago neighborhood of Sleepy Hollow (so named by its mailman back in 1913) and the North Side's Irving Park (which was supposed to be called Irvington until early residents found that name was already taken).

7   For the first three years of writer Ernest Hemingway's childhood in Oak Park, his mother dressed him as a girl and passed him off as a twin of his slightly older sister, Marcelline. ... *why?*

8   Golfers, head west. Six area golf courses made Golf Digest's 2010 ranking of the nation's top 100, and four of them — including the top three — are in the western suburbs. The list rates the Chicago Golf Club in Wheaton as the area's best and the 12th best in the country. Medinah Country Club, Butler National Golf Club in Oak Brook and Rich Harvest Links in Sugar Grove rounded out that list. Golflink.com asserted the dominance of the western suburbs even further: Nine of its top 10 Chicagoland courses were in the western suburbs in 2010.

9 The Marx Brothers once lived at a farm outside La Grange, in what is now Countryside. Their mother, Minnie, reportedly wanted her sons to be farmers and thus exempted from service in World War 1. Groucho later said the wayward brothers spent too much time at Wrigley Field to make the farm a go.

10 When former first lady Mary Todd Lincoln started hallucinating and carrying up to $57,000 in cash and bonds in her pocket, it was time to send her to west suburban Batavia. In 1875, she was committed for just under four months in Bellevue Place, a home for the mentally ill.

SOURCES: *"Cicero Flying Field: Origin, Operation, Obscurity and Legacy, 1891-1916" by Carroll Gray; "Monkey Business: The Lives and Legends of the Marx Brothers" by Simon Louvish; "The Insanity File: The Case of Mary Todd Lincoln" by Mark E. Neely and R. Gerald McMurtry; "Hemingway: A Biography" by Jeffrey Meyers; "The Madness of Mary Lincoln" by Jason Emerson; "Posterity: Letters of Great Americans to Their Children" by Dorie McCullough Lawson; Illinois Historical Journal, "To Hold the Prize" by Stephen J. Buck; Flying magazine; U.S. Centennial of Flight Commission; Replogle; Old Irving Park Association; Village of Sleepy Hollow; golfdigest. com; golflink.com; "Encyclopedia of Chicago"; and Tribune archives.*

10 THINGS YOU MIGHT NOT KNOW ABOUT

LIFESTYLE

DIVORCE

1 Singer Marvin Gaye titled one of his record albums "Here, My Dear" because the profits from it were supposed to pay off his ex-wife.

2 Philadelphia lawyer H. Beatty Chadwick and his wife, Bobbie, didn't get along. She complained that he would engage in sex only at 7:30 a.m. on Tuesdays and Thursdays, and rationed her toilet paper to six sheets per bathroom visit. He denied such tyrannies, but there was no denying that when they got a divorce, $2.5 million was missing. He said it went to pay a debt overseas; the judge said he was hiding marital assets and sent him to prison in 1995. Chadwick stayed there for 14 years, stubbornly serving the longest contempt term in U.S. history.

3 Adlai Stevenson of Illinois was the first major-party presidential candidate to be divorced, and some say it was a factor in his defeats. A Gallup Poll in 1952 found that 14 percent of respondents would not vote for a divorced candidate. Yet less than three decades later, Ronald Reagan's divorce was a virtual non-issue. And six men who ran for president in 2008 had been divorced: Rudy Giuliani, John McCain, Fred Thompson, Chris Dodd, Mike Gravel and Dennis Kucinich.

4 Tammy Wynette, who sang "D-I-V-O-R-C-E," was married five times, and blamed her splitup with hard-drinking singer George Jones on "my naggin' and his nippin'." Wynette also made famous an anthem for fidelity: "Stand by Your Man." During the 1992 presidential campaign, Hillary Clinton declared, "I'm not sitting here like some little woman standing by my man like Tammy Wynette." That ticked off Wynette, who said Clinton had "offended every true country music fan and every person who has made it on their own with no one to take them to a White House."

5 California minister Glynn "Scotty" Wolfe died in 1997, 10 days before he would have celebrated his first anniversary with his 29th wife, Linda Essex-Wolfe. It was her 23rd marriage. Both numbers may have set records for men and women who marry one person at a time, but Egyptian polygamist Mustafa Eid Samida had them both beat. As of 2001, he had been married and divorced 203 times.

6 When Albert Einstein divorced his wife Mileva in 1919, he promised to give her winnings "from an eventual Nobel Prize." Three years later, he indeed was honored. It's not clear whether he ever gave her the winnings, though he supported her in other ways.

7 The Japanese call the end of a short-lived marriage a "Narita divorce." That refers to the common situation in which barely acquainted newlyweds fly off on their honeymoon, and by the time they get back to Narita Airport, they are ready to split up.

8 The per-capita U.S. divorce rate is at its lowest level since 1969: 3.4 per 1,000, way down from its peak of 5.3 in 1981. But that doesn't necessarily mean that marriage is working; it means that marriage is being delayed or avoided by more and more Americans.

9 For Valentine's Day 2008, a Charleston, W.Va., radio station gave away a free divorce. "Sure, we can give away concert tickets, and we do," said WKLCFM Program Director Jay Nunley. "That's going to make you happy for a little while. This is the chance to make someone happy for the rest of their life."

10 Twice-married Robin Williams once observed, "Ah, yes, divorce...from the Latin word meaning to rip out a man's genitals through his wallet."

SOURCES: *Guardian, People magazine; Entertainment Weekly; Dallas Morning News; U.S. Census Bureau; Tribune news services.*

GAY RIGHTS

1   In 1924, Chicago postal clerk Henry Gerber formed the Society for Human Rights, considered the first American gay-rights group. Gerber was soon arrested for being gay. He was never convicted, but the publicity (including a newspaper headline reading "Strange Sex Cult Exposed") led to his firing for conduct unbecoming a postal worker. The group quickly disbanded.

2   Is an Illinois tollway named after a lesbian? Probably. Jane Addams, founder of Chicago's Hull House settlement for immigrants and the poor, won a Nobel Peace Prize in 1931 and was honored in 2007 when part of Interstate Highway 90 was renamed for her. Though some scholars view Addams' sexual orientation as unprovable and irrelevant, historian Lillian Faderman summed up the beliefs of many in writing that "Addams had no interest in heterosexual marriage and spent her adult years, almost until her death, with other women, in long-term relationships that we would describe as lesbian today."

3   A few years ago, a book made the dubious assertion that Abraham Lincoln was gay, noting that he slept with men — in an era in which many Americans shared beds for non-sexual reasons. Some historians make a stronger but still inconclusive case that Lincoln's predecessor, James Buchanan, was the first gay president. He was the only president who never married, and his live-in relationship with William Rufus King, vice president in the Pierce administration, was the subject of sexual innuendo from rival politicians. Also, there is evidence that the nieces of Buchanan and King destroyed their uncles' correspondence when Buchanan became president.

4   Alan Turing, the British mathematician who helped crack the German code during World War II and was one of the pioneers of computer science, was convicted in 1952 of "gross indecency" for being gay. Given the choice of entering prison or undergoing an experimental hormone therapy, Turing chose the latter, which caused ill effects such as breast enlargement. In 1954, he committed suicide at age 41.

5   The Royal Canadian Mounted Police briefly used a device nicknamed the "fruit machine" to test recruits for homosexuality in the 1960s. Subjects were required to look into a box containing sexually explicit images while their pupil size, palm sweat and blood flow were measured. The device was soon abandoned as useless.

6   The 1969 Stonewall riots in New York's Greenwich Village, which began when patrons at a gay bar violently resisted a police raid, are considered the flashpoint of the modern gay-rights movement. But most homosexuals in the United States didn't hear about Stonewall until long afterward because it received virtually no coverage outside New York City. The New York Times reported the initial rioting on Page 33.

7   "Friends of Dorothy" once was a common code phrase used by gay men to refer to each other. The reference likely came from Judy Garland's character in "The Wizard of Oz." Journalist Randy Shilts wrote that when naval investigators were hunting for gays at Great Lakes Naval Training Center in North Chicago in the early 1980s, they encountered the phrase "friends of Dorothy" and began asking around for a real Dorothy who they thought was at the center of a gay network in the Chicago area.

8   Before the medical community settled on the name AIDS (acquired immune deficiency syndrome), some people called it GRID (gay-related immunodeficiency).

9   A Naperville high school student went to a federal appeals court to win a ruling in April 2008 allowing him to appear in school wearing a T-shirt that read "Be Happy, Not Gay."

10   Can homosexuality cause hurricanes? Yes, according to some evangelists. Rev. John Hagee famously declared that New Orleans was hit by Hurricane Katrina "because it had a gay pride parade the week before." But Hagee's weather analysis wasn't original. Pat Robertson warned in 1998 that if gay pride events were allowed at Disney World, Florida risked a hurricane as well as "terrorist bombs ... earthquakes, tornadoes and possibly a meteor."

SOURCES: *"Before Stonewall,"* edited by Vern L. Bullough; *"Out in All Directions,"* edited by Lynn Witt, Sherry Thomas and Eric Marcus; *"The Other Side of Silence,"* by John Loughery; *"Encyclopedia of Chicago"*; *"James Buchanan,"* by Jean Baker; *"To Believe in Women,"* by Lillian Faderman; *"Conduct Unbecoming: Gays & Lesbians in the U.S. Military,"* by Randy Shilts; and Tribune news services.

LOVERS

1   When French desperado Michel Vaujour was imprisoned for armed robbery and attempted murder, wife Nadine showed her love in a special way: She learned how to fly a helicopter. In 1986, she and an accomplice hovered over Paris' La Sante prison in a copter and picked up her husband, who had forced his way onto the prison's roof by wielding nectarines that were painted to look like grenades. The fruit of their labor was a few months' freedom, before they were captured.

2   The word "osculation" comes from Latin and means the act of kissing. "Tryst" is a Middle English word that originally meant a place where hunters waited for game.

3   Were Al and Tipper Gore the inspiration for the 1970 blockbuster novel and movie "Love Story," about a preppy Harvard student and his free-spirit girlfriend? Not exactly. When Al Gore was vice president in 1997, media reports suggested it was so, and Gore seemed to confirm them. But the book's author, Erich Segal, who had met the Gores while on a sabbatical at Harvard, insisted the girlfriend was not modeled on Tipper. He allowed that some aspects of the boyfriend were based on Al, but said the main inspiration was Gore's Harvard roommate — actor Tommy Lee Jones.

4   Melvin Kaminsky was born in Brooklyn in 1926, and Anna Maria Louisa Italiano was born in the Bronx five years later. Before they ever knew each other, each had gone into show business, adopted a stage name, and been married and divorced. They met on the set of "The Perry Como Show," and he bribed a studio worker to tell him where she was dining so that he could run into her later. A few years later, the two performers — Mel Brooks and Anne Bancroft — married.

5   Humphrey Bogart and Lauren Bacall called each other Steve and Slim, the characters they played in their first film together, "To Have and Have Not" in 1944. Bacall's famous line in that movie was: "You know how to whistle, don't you, Steve? You just put your lips together and blow." For Christmas after the movie came out, Bogie gave Bacall a gold whistle. At his funeral in 1957, she placed the whistle on his coffin.

6 According to legend, French emperor Napoleon finished a military campaign and wrote a love letter to empress Josephine that read, "Ne te lave pa. Je reviens" (Don't bathe. I'm coming home).

7 President Barack Obama probably had some explaining to do with his wife, Michelle, over his misstatement in Moscow on a weighty issue: Where they first met. "I don't know if anybody else will meet their future wife or husband in class like I did, but I'm sure that you're all going to have wonderful careers," he told Russian economics students. He and Michelle both attended Harvard Law School, but she graduated in the spring before he showed up later that fall. Their first meeting occurred the next year when she was a full-time attorney at Sidley Austin law firm in Chicago and he was a summer intern. Neither was "in class."

8 In a recent online poll, the most popular celebrity couple was a wife and a wife: comedian Ellen DeGeneres and actress Portia de Rossi. Born in Australia and named Amanda Rogers, de Rossi adopted a more exotic moniker at age 15. For four years, she dated Francesca Gregorini, daughter of actress Barbara Bach and stepdaughter of Ringo Starr. But then de Rossi met DeGeneres backstage at an awards show, and they fell in love. They married in 2008.

9 A young Muslim woman named Admira Ismic fell in love with a young Serbian man named Bosko Brkic in the wrong place and time: Bosnia, 1993. Seeking to flee war-ravaged Sarajevo, they tried to cross a bridge to safety. Snipers' bullets cut them down, and they died in each other's arms. Their bodies lay on the bridge for eight days before the area was safe enough for them to be recovered.

10 Actress and writer Mae West was an expert at love. During her affair with boxer William Jones, her landlord barred him from her apartment building because he was African-American. She responded by buying the building. For the last quarter century of her life, her lover was a bodybuilder 30 years younger than her named Paul Novak. Shortly before the 87-year-old West died in 1980, she shared her philosophy: "Sex with love, that is the best thing in life. But sex without love isn't so bad either. It's very good for the skin and the circulation, and keeps everything moving."

SOURCES: *"How They Met" by Joey Green; "Love: A Century of Love and Passion" by Florence Montreynaud; "Marry Me!" by Wendy Goldberg and Betty Goodwin; "100 Words for Lovers" from the editors of American Heritage dictionaries; Times of London; advocate.com; politico. com; Tribune news services.*

MARRIAGE

1 Widowers in Britain once were banned from marrying their dead wives' sisters. The law was supported by the Anglican Church and many politicians to protect what Prime Minister William Gladstone called "the purity of sisterly love." Even after that ban was lifted in 1907, a widow could not marry her dead husband's brother until a similar ban was dropped in 1921. Britain's marriage laws also intruded into the classroom: Until 1944, a female teacher could be fired if she got married.

2 Beatle Paul McCartney said that when he was considering whether to pursue a relationship with Heather Mills, he heard the sound of an owl and took it as a sign from his late wife, Linda, that she approved. Today, nearly a year after the bitter Mills-McCartney divorce was finalized, the owl still has not been brought to justice.

3 About 3 percent of Americans marry three times or more.

4 The Mosuo ethnic group in the Himalayan foothills of southwestern China follows a custom called "walking marriage." The man visits the woman at night for sex but does not live with her and has no legal commitment to her. The woman is free to entertain a variety of men in her bedroom, and the children from these relationships are raised by the mother and her extended family.

5 At a hearing on same-sex marriage in 2004, New Hampshire state Rep. Richard Kennedy seemed to be trying too hard to express his heterosexuality. "There are times when I see some comely young lady I would love to have as a house pet," he said. "But my wife won't let me, damn it. And I bought her a gun! That shows you how smart I am."

6 A 2009 Associated Press story out of Ohio began memorably: "James Mason had known his wife since she was a little boy." The story went on to explain that when the boy grew up, he had a sex-change operation. The boy-turned-girl, in her 30s, wed Mason, who was in his 70s. Their marital relations were perfectly legal, except when she forced him to exercise for more than two hours in a pool despite a heart condition. She was caught on videotape blocking his path 43 times as he tried to get out of the water. The old man collapsed and died, and his wife pleaded guilty to reckless homicide.

7 Why was it OK for Fred and Wilma Flintstone to sleep in the same bed in "The Flintstones" but not Rob and Laura Petrie on "The Dick Van Dyke Show"? Did cartoon characters have sex in the early '60s but real people did not? Some say "The Brady Bunch" or "The Munsters" was the first TV show to depict married couples sharing a bed, but in fact the first such program was "Mary Kay and Johnny," which began on the DuMont Television Network in 1947.

8 In the mid-1800s, Rumanika, the king of Karagwe in what is now Tanzania, had a special way of keeping his wives at home. The king fed them a steady diet of milk through straws, and if they resisted, a man with a whip forced them to keep sipping. As a result, the wives became so obese that they could not stand up on their own and instead wallowed on the floors of their huts.

9 Less than a century ago, boys could legally marry at age 14 and girls could wed at age 12 in Virginia, Louisiana and Kentucky.

10 LaRae Lundeen Fjellman was threatened with the loss of her massage therapist license for violating a Minnesota law banning people in her profession from having sex with former clients for two years. The man she had sex with was her husband, whom she married more than a year after he stopped being her client and started being her date. The state health department relented in the case in 2007 after three years of wrangling, and agreed to pay $5,800 of Fjellman's more than $13,000 in legal fees and expenses. Which meant that the state fined Fjellman at least $7,200 for having sex with her husband.

SOURCES: *"The White Nile" by Alan Moorehead; "Divorce With Decency" by Bradley A. Coates; "Commentaries on the Laws of England" by William Blackstone and William Carey Jones; "Family Law in the Twentieth Century" by Stephen Michael Cretney; "The Marriage Revolt" by William E. Carson; Newsweek; The New Yorker; The Globe and Mail; China Daily; anecdotage. com; snopes.com; Tribune news services.*

10 THINGS YOU MIGHT NOT KNOW ABOUT
TIPPING

1 The nation's best tippers dine in New Orleans, leaving an average gratuity of 19.7 percent, according to Zagat's 2012 America's Top Restaurants Survey. Americans overall tip at a 19.2 percent rate, up from 18 percent in 2000. Chicago's rate is the same as the nation's (19.2), and it's more generous than New York's (19.1) and Los Angeles' (18.7).

2 Some people believe tipping is aristocratic, undemocratic and un-American — that it promotes the idea of a servant class. In 1910, U.S. labor leader Samuel Gompers complained that tipping in Europe "borders on blackmail," and that many American travelers there suffered "mosquito bites" — demands for tips — almost hourly. Yet a century later, Americans are among the globe's premier tippers, sometimes criticized abroad for throwing supply-and-demand out of whack by being too generous.

3 A travel tip: Don't leave a gratuity in Japan. It would be considered an insult.

4 More than 100 Chicago waiters were arrested in 1918 amid accusations that restaurant workers were plotting to slip "Mickey Finn" drugs into the food and drink of bad tippers.

5 John D. Rockefeller gave away an estimated 20,000 to 30,000 coins in his lifetime. The tipping tycoon doled out dimes to adults and nickels to children, using the coins as icebreakers for conversations and as rewards for fellow golfers, amusing storytellers and others he met. When something was spilled on the floor, Rockefeller would cast dimes atop the stains to reward the person who cleaned up the mess. But he would sometimes play tricks, giving people horse chestnuts instead of coins, explaining that the chestnuts would ease their rheumatism. A dime in Rockefeller's day was the equivalent of $1.36 today.

6 "Autograt" is slang for an automatic gratuity — the built-in tip that restaurants may charge in certain cases, such as for large tables.

7 "Canadian" is a restaurant slang term for a presumably bad tipper, i.e. "Jodie just sat six Canadians in your section, dude." The term is not necessarily a slur against actual Canadians; some believe it is a racist code word aimed at blacks or other minorities.

8 Marwan al-Shehhi was not only a terrorist but a lousy tipper. After the September 11 attacks, an exotic dancer named Samantha remembered the hijacker being cheap as he patronized the Olympic Garden Topless Cabaret in Las Vegas. "I'm glad he's dead with the rest of them, and I don't like feeling something like that," Samantha told the San Francisco Chronicle. "But he wasn't just a bad tipper — he killed people."

9 Among the nicknames for a tip is baksheesh, from a Persian word for gift.

10 In June 2000, a British tourist in Chicago visiting the Leg Room appreciated his waitress so much he left a $10,000 tip for a $9 drink. The bar's manager didn't believe it — it was 3 a.m., after all — and photocopied the man's passport and had him sign a statement confirming his generous intentions. The credit card transaction was initially approved, but the British bank later rejected the charge. In the cold, sober light of day, the man decided he wouldn't pay the tip. "I don't recall the details," he told a British newspaper. "I had had a few drinks." But some stories do end well: The bar's owners made good on the tip.

SOURCES: *"Titan: The Life of John D. Rockefeller" by Ron Chernow; "Tipping: An American Social History of Gratuities" by Kerry Segrave; "Turning the Tables: Restaurants and the Rise of the American Middle Class, 1880-1920" by Andrew P. Haley; "Gratuity: A Contextual Understanding of Tipping Norms from the Perspective of Tipped Employees" by Richard Seltzer and Holona LeAnne Ochs; Bureau of Labor Statistics; drunkard.com; hospitality-industry.com; msnbc.msn.com; San Francisco Chronicle; Tribune archives.*

10 THINGS YOU MIGHT NOT KNOW ABOUT
CLASS WARFARE

1   Americans like to think they're in the middle — not rich or poor. An ABC poll found 45 percent identified themselves as middle-class, with 36 percent working-class and 11 percent upper-middle-class. Only 3 percent said they were better off than upper-middle-class, and 2 percent said they were worse off than working class (despite a poverty rate of 15 percent and a jobless rate over 9 percent at the time of the survey).

2   Marie Antoinette is said to have dismissed the plight of the poor by declaring, "Let them eat cake." But there's no evidence the queen ever said it, and plenty of evidence that Jean-Jacques Rousseau did. His autobiographical book, "Confessions," included the phrase about 1767, before Marie Antoinette even got to France. The quote in the original French refers to brioche, which is not really a cake and is better described as an enriched bread roll.

3   Speaking of food, communists sometimes have not put their appetites where their ideology is. China's Mao Zedong refused to eat as modestly as his fellow countrymen and once had a special fish transported alive 600 miles in a plastic bag with oxygenated water so that it could be prepared for him.

4   The Civil War was called a "rich man's war and a poor man's fight" because a conscripted man could pay $300 to hire a substitute to fight in his place. President Abraham Lincoln hired a substitute for $500, not because he had to but to show his support for the draft.

5   Many class warriors have found peace in Chicago-area cemeteries. Forest Home Cemetery in Forest Park features the Haymarket Martyrs' Monument, marking where executed labor activists were buried. It is also the final resting place of anarchist Emma Goldman and American Communist leader Gus Hall (birth name Arvo Kusta Halberg). And on the robber-baron side of the equation, there's George Pullman. When he was buried at Graceland Cemetery on the North Side, his coffin was sunk in a concrete block and covered with railroad ties to ward off possible grave defilers.

6   Karl Marx used the term "bourgeoisie" to describe the property-owning class, as opposed to the working-class "proletariat." In the 1920s, journalist and skeptic H.L. Mencken invented a new class called the "booboisie" to describe middle-class boobs, or idiots. The term was part of a list of "boob" words that included booberati and boobarian.

7 Hurricane Katrina exposed class distinctions — and inspired outrageous remarks. Radio commentator Randi Rhodes denounced federal efforts: "Conservatives ought to be really happy about New Orleans. This is what they always wanted, always wanted: eradication of the poor people, and less government." President George W. Bush's mother, Barbara, visited evacuees in Houston's Astrodome and cheerily declared, "So many of the people in the arena here, you know, were underprivileged anyway, so this is working very well for them."

8 One of the most memorable class wars in history was the slave revolt led by Spartacus against the Roman Empire, circa 72 BC. The climactic scene in the 1960 film "Spartacus" depicts warriors shouting in solidarity, "I am Spartacus!" The filmmakers recorded audio for that scene and others by getting 76,000 football spectators to shout phrases before a 1959 Michigan State-Notre Dame football game in East Lansing. Then the Spartans defeated the Irish (and the Romans defeated the slaves).

9 The exclusive enclave of Tuxedo Park, an hour north of Manhattan, was the creation in the 1880s of tobacco family scion Pierre Lorillard to provide a place for his "old-money" buddies and their families to get away from the riff-raff. To build it quickly, Lorillard imported European laborers and housed them on the grounds in a shanty town with muddy streets he called Broadway and Fifth Avenue. He named the mess hall Delmonico's, after the famous restaurant. The development was designed by Emily Post's father, who presumably had better manners.

10 Most Americans disagree with the notion that the U.S. is divided into haves and have-nots, but the idea is gaining support. In a 2005 survey, 38 percent thought the U.S. was divided in that way; now 45 percent think so. Curiously, the share of people who think they are on the have side held steady at 48 percent during that time.

SOURCES: *"Culture Wars" by Roger Chapman; "Hurricane Katrina" by Jamie Pietras; "Cassell's Dictionary of Slang" by Jonathon Green; "Encyclopedia of the American Civil War" by David Stephen Heidler, Jeanne T. Heidler, David J. Coles; "Best Little Ironies, Oddities, and Mysteries of the Civil War" by C. Brian Kelly; "Emily Post: Daughter of the Gilded Age, Mistress of American Manners" by Laura Claridge; Pew Research Center; New York Times; Washington Post; ABC News; pollingreport.com; Lansing CityPulse; imdb.com; graveyards.com; gracelandcemetery.org.*

ROYAL WEDDINGS

1   While actress Grace Kelly's wedding to Prince Rainier of Monaco in 1956 captivated millions of people around the world, the prince's idea of "courtship" left the Kelly family a little cold. First, Grace had to submit to a fertility test. Then, her father was told he would need to pay a dowry of $2 million before his daughter could become a princess. Outraged, he refused. Grace, also troubled by the demand but wanting to marry, finally persuaded her father to relent. Reportedly, Grace paid half the dowry herself.

2   Before there were Charles and Di, there were Akihito and Michiko, the current emperor and empress of Japan. In 1959, the crown prince's courtship and marriage to Michiko, a commoner, was a fairy-tale romance. And the much-anticipated nationally televised nuptials and procession proved a boon for the TV industry. In 1958, there were 1 million TV sets in Japan. A few months after the wedding, there were 3 million.

3   The phrase "close your eyes and think of England" is a bit of wedding-night advice that new bride Queen Victoria supposedly received or gave to her daughter. But the origin of the expression is in dispute, and the Victoria theory appears dubious. The Phrase Finder website notes that Victoria seemed to have a healthy sexual relationship with her husband and gave birth to four sons and five daughters. Which means she "thought of England" at least nine times.

4   Well into the 18th century in Europe, it wasn't uncommon on the wedding night for select guests to escort the lucky royal couple to their private chambers for the bedding ceremony, where they would watch the nightgowned couple get into bed together. Simply lying together under sheets was considered consummation.

5   Not all arranged marriages proved loveless. King Charles I of England met his bride, Henrietta Maria of France, on the day in 1625 when she arrived in Dover for the ceremony. Apparently the 15-year-old, 10 years his junior, was much younger than he expected. But after a rocky start, the pair fell deeply in love. They were openly affectionate with each other and couldn't bear to be parted. In fact, the king's councilors complained of how much time the couple spent together.

6   Japan's Prince Hirohito became engaged to Princess Nagako in 1918, but a government official questioned the match because color blindness ran in Nagako's family. Her father threatened to fatally stab his daughter and himself if the imperial family reneged. The wedding proceeded.

7   When India's Nawab of Junagadh held a royal wedding in 1922, he really put on the dog. The princely ruler hosted a lavish ceremony with thousands of guests to celebrate the wedding of his pet dog Roshanara to a golden retriever named Bobby. The bride was carried on a silver palanquin (a covered sedan chair), while the groom wore a gold necklace and silk cummerbund.

8   After Spain's King Alfonso XIII and Princess Ena of Battenberg were married in Madrid in 1906, a man tossed a bouquet at their bridal carriage. Inside the bouquet was a bomb. The royals were unhurt, but more than a dozen onlookers died.

9   When the king of Swaziland married his ninth wife in 2001, his subjects were not impressed. Mswati III, the world's last absolute monarch, had urged a chastity pledge for girls younger than 18 to help reduce the horrifying spread of HIV in his African kingdom. But his new bride was just 17. A group of girls who had taken the pledge protested in front of his residence. He eventually paid the fine: one cow.

10   King Henry VIII was a notorious husband, and he wasn't much better as a fiancé. Henry was reportedly out hunting on the day his second wife, Anne Boleyn, was beheaded. He rushed to Jane Seymour to share the good news. They were married the next day. And while the wedding was a relatively private ceremony, there were preparations to be made, invitations to be sent, cakes to be baked. All must have occurred even as Boleyn was still alive in the Tower of London.

SOURCES: *"A Dictionary of Catch Phrases"* by Eric Partridge; *"Once Upon a Time: Behind the Fairy Tale of Princess Grace and Prince Rainier"* by J. Randy Taraborrelli; *"Japan Pop!"* by Timothy J. Craig; *"Memoirs of the Queens of Henry VIII"* by Agnes Strickland; *"The Personal Rule of Charles I"* by Kevin Sharpe; *"The Yamato Dynasty"* by Sterling Seagrave and Peggy Seagrave; *"Sex with the Queen"* by Eleanor Herman; *"Queen and Consort: Elizabeth and Philip: 60 Years of Marriage"* by Lynne Bell, Arthur Bousfield and Garry Toffoli; *"Royal Babylon: The Alarming History of European Royalty"* by Karl Shaw; *"Royal Pains: A Rogues' Gallery of Brats, Brutes, and Bad Seeds"* by Leslie Carroll, *"Beyond Bizarre: Frightening Facts and Blood-Curdling True Tales"* by Varla Ventura; *"The History of Terrorism: From Antiquity to Al Qaeda"* by Gérard Chaliand and Arnaud Blin; New York Times; Times of London; The Phrase Finder (phrases.org.uk); CIA Factbook; englishhistory.net; Tribune archives.*

RACISM

1 "Honky," a slur against white people, probably originated in Chicago. Experts trace it to "bohunk," used to describe Bohemians, Hungarians and other Eastern European immigrants. Black workers in Chicago's South Side meatpacking plants are believed to have referred to their white co-workers as "hunkies," which later became "honkies" to refer to all whites.

2 A 1906 newspaper article in the Atlanta Constitution described how a white girl suffered a fatal heart attack after dreaming that a "big negro" with a knife was trying to kill her. The Constitution seemed to blame the fictional black man, headlining the story: "Negro, Seen in Dream, Causes Death of Girl." Such newspaper transgressions are easy to find. In 1921, The New York Times reported that South Africa's black population, which outnumbered whites 5-to-1, was pushing for political power. Some would view that as democracy in action. The Times saw it differently with this headline: "Negroes a Problem in South Africa."

3 The Tribune has its own embarrassing archives regarding race. About 40,000 people viewed the body of lynching victim Emmett Till when it was returned from Mississippi to Chicago in 1955, but the Tribune's article suggested that the key civil rights event might be a Marxist hoax. The article's third and fourth paragraphs described communists distributing "inflammatory literature" outside the church. The fifth and sixth paragraphs quoted a Mississippi sheriff who questioned whether the body was even Till's and said that "the whole thing looks like a deal made up by the National Association for the Advancement of Colored People."

4 There's nothing like a Disney movie to make some people whistle a happy tune and other people simply scream. The 1946 feature film "Song of the South" remains out of circulation because of the perceived offense it would give to African-Americans. The 1933 cartoon short "Three Little Pigs" featured the big, bad wolf dressed as a Jewish peddler. After complaints, the cartoon was revised so that the wolf posed as a Fuller Brush salesman. More recently, Arabs objected to a lyric in the 1992 film "Aladdin." It originally described Arabia as a place "where they cut off your ear if they don't like your face /

It's barbaric, but hey, it's home." That was changed to "Where it's flat and immense, and the heat is intense / It's barbaric, but hey, it's home." A Disney spokesman emphasized that the new lyric meant that Arabian weather patterns, not people, were "barbaric."

5 It's now a slur, but it once was the official name of a federal program. "Operation Wetback" was conducted in 1954 to drive illegal immigrants from the American Southwest. Federal officials claimed that 1.3 million people were deported or compelled to flee. The offensive name for the operation came from Gen. Joseph "Jumpin' Joe" Swing, a former West Point classmate of then-President Dwight Eisenhower who headed the Immigration and Naturalization Service.

6 A few weeks after the Japanese attack on Pearl Harbor in 1941, Life magazine published an article headlined "How to tell Japs from the Chinese." The Chinese, who were U.S. allies, found themselves mistaken for Japanese on American streets and treated rudely by angry Americans. Then Life came to the rescue, with annotated photos. The Chinese had "parchment yellow complexion." The Japanese had "earthy yellow complexion." The Chinese were "tall and slender." The Japanese were "short and squat." In their facial expressions, the Chinese "wear the rational calm of tolerant realists," while Japanese show the "humorless intensity of ruthless mystics." A person from China "never has rosy cheeks." A Japanese person has "sometimes rosy cheeks." The apparent message: If you feel compelled to angrily confront an Asian stranger, harass the one with the rosy cheeks.

7 Ethnic prejudice can look a lot like racism. In 1855, Chicago's lily-white rulers clashed with new German and Irish immigrants. The battleground: booze. Mayor Levi Boone tried to shut down Irish and German beer halls while leaving open the taverns that served the whiskey preferred by his kind of people. An immigrant mob protested the crackdown, and the Lager Beer Riot ensued, leading to one death and 60 arrests.

8 Two of Chicago's best-known roads — Sheridan and Roosevelt — are named after national icons who disparaged American Indians. The phrase "The only good Indian is a dead Indian" is often attributed to Gen. Philip Sheridan. He denied saying it, but there's no question he viewed Indians as inferior savages and that he imposed hard-line policies leading to the deaths of many innocent Indians. Future President Theodore Roosevelt addressed the "only good Indian" expression in an 1886 speech: "I don't go so far as to think that the only good Indians are dead Indians, but I believe nine out of every 10 are, and I shouldn't like to inquire too closely into the case of the 10th."

9 Marcus Garvey, founder of the Universal Negro Improvement Association and standard-bearer of the "Back to Africa" movement, met with the Ku Klux Klan in the early 1920s. Garvey said the two groups' attitudes were "similar," explaining: "Whilst the Ku Klux Klan desires to make America absolutely a white man's country, the Universal Negro Improvement Association wants to make Africa absolutely a black man's country." Four decades later, Malcolm X also met with the Klan. According to accounts by Malcolm X and an FBI informant, the black Muslim and the Klan shared their distaste for integration. But unlike Garvey, Malcolm X later expressed regret for consorting with Klansmen.

10 No matter how bad race relations are today, they are better than they used to be. In 1983, only 43 percent of Americans approved of marriage between blacks and whites. In recent surveys, 79 percent did. When blacks and whites were asked in 1997 whether they had "a fairly close personal friend" of the other race, 74 percent said yes. In 2008, 81 percent did. Will we be anywhere near 100 percent by 2042, when America is projected to become a "majority minority" nation?

SOURCES: *"An Original Man: The Life and Times of Elijah Muhammad" by Claude Andrew Clegg; "The End of Racism" by Dinesh D'Souza; "Whitewash: Racialized Politics and the Media" by John Gabriel; "The Facts on File Encyclopedia of Word and Phrase Origins," edited by Robert Hendrickson; "In Our Own Words: Extraordinary Speeches of the American Century," edited by Robert G. Torricelli and Andrew Carroll; "Phil Sheridan and His Army" by Paul Andrew Hutton; "Proverbs: A Handbook" by Wolfgang Mieder; "Walt Disney: The Triumph of the American Imagination" by Neal Gabler; "English with an Accent: Language, Ideology and Discrimination in the United States" by Rosina Lippi-Green; USA Today; Toronto Star; snopes.com; Tribune editor Jim Haglund; Tribune news services.*

10 THINGS YOU MIGHT NOT KNOW ABOUT

SCIENCE/TECHNOLOGY

THE COLOR GREEN

1   The green card, a permanent residency card for immigrants, hasn't been green for decades. It's mostly white and looks like a driver's license.

2   The left-field wall at Boston's Fenway Park is known as the Green Monster, but it wasn't always green. Until 1947, it was covered with advertisements. Another baseball icon, the scoreboard at Chicago's Wrigley Field, is green now but was a reddish-brown until the mid-'40s.

3   One of Dr. Seuss' classics is called "Green Eggs and Ham," but an early draft had the dish reversed as green ham and eggs. Author Ted Geisel soon came to his senses — or nonsenses. By switching the order, he created a nifty phrase that rhymed with the name of his character Sam-I-am.

4   When military helicopter pilots use night-vision goggles, they travel through a world that glows green. Little wonder that they sometimes say they are flying through "green air."

5   On New Year's Day 1965, Soupy Sales had extra time at the end of his children's TV show. So he asked his young fans to go find their parents' wallets, take out those "little green pieces of paper" and mail them to him. The TV comedian didn't get much money out of it — he hadn't announced his mailing address — but he did receive a lot of grief from parents and a suspension from his boss.

6   Fear of the color green is known as chlorophobia.

7   Only 3 percent of North Americans say green is their favorite car color. And in U.S. auto racing, the color is sometimes considered bad luck, perhaps dating to a 1911 crash of a green Knox racer in Syracuse, N.Y., that killed 11 spectators. Joe Weatherly, NASCAR's champ in 1962 and '63, was famously afraid of the color green. But the feeling isn't universal. "English racing green" is a popular color for cars sponsored by British automakers. And the very green Mountain Dew is a NASCAR sponsor.

8 According to a magazine-industry myth, green covers are lousy sellers. Glamour Editor Cindi Leive told Slate in 2006 about an "almost physical fight" she had when she was at Self magazine over a cover featuring model Stephanie Seymour in a dark green sweater. The art director "was screaming in a thick and impassioned Finnish accent and telling me that dark green was the color of death."

9 The Green Hornet, a super-serious superhero, got a comedic reinterpretation when Seth Rogen, star of "Knocked Up," donned the mask in 2011.

10 Research in December revealed that men's faces are more red than women's, while women's faces are more green than men's. The study was done at Brown University, which trumpeted the news on its website by announcing, "Men Are Red, Women Are Green, Brown Researcher Finds."

SOURCES: *"Dr. Seuss: American Icon" by Philip Nel, "The Color of Life" By Arthur G. Abbott, Stars and Stripes, snopes.com, doubletongued.org, cars.com, frontstretch.com, www.internationalhero.co.uk, slate.com, Tampa Tribune and brown.edu.*

CONTRACEPTIVES

1   The federal Comstock Act of 1873 labeled contraceptives obscene and effectively banned them. While poorly enforced, similar state laws survived until as late as 1965 before the U.S. Supreme Court threw them out in Griswold v. Connecticut.

2   A reader asked advice columnist Dear Abby: "Are birth control pills deductible?" Abby's answer: "Only if they don't work."

3   Margaret Sanger, the activist whose American Birth Control League was a predecessor of the Planned Parenthood Federation of America, was quite particular about how she and her movement were described. She popularized the straightforward term "birth control" and detested the more adman-friendly phrase "planned parenthood." According to Jean H. Baker's biography, Sanger's niece reflected her aunt's view by joking that "family planning" was so imprecise that it might refer to a family's plans for summer vacation.

4   The first tubal ligation in the United States was performed in Ohio in 1880, predating the first vasectomy by 19 years.

5   Long, long before there was the pill, first sold as a contraceptive in the U.S. in 1960, there was silphion. The root of the fennel-like plant, possibly the first oral contraceptive, was the go-to birth control method for ancient Greeks. Experts believe the plant was so popular that it was harvested to extinction.

6   Condoms' effectiveness and availability to the public took a huge leap forward in 1855 when they were first mass-produced using Charles Goodyear's new "vulcanized rubber." But those first rubbers were a far cry from what is available today: They had a seam and were as thick as a bicycle tire tube. The better latex rubber condoms arrived in the 1920s.

7   In the Middle Ages, women who wanted to avoid pregnancy were advised to spit three times into the mouth of a frog.

8   The Petrie Papyrus, an Egyptian document dating to 1850 B.C., is the oldest known guide to contraceptives. It recommended vaginal suppositories with such substances as gum, honey and crocodile dung.

9   One of the most popular birth control methods for American women in the middle of the 20th century was Lysol. It was heavily marketed as a product for feminine hygiene in U.S. newspaper advertisements, including the Tribune, but used as a contraceptive also.

10   The U.S. was alone among its World War I allies in not giving soldiers a valued piece of defensive equipment: the condom. Yet historians say the war was a turning point for condom use in this country because so many GIs adopted their use overseas and continued the practice back at home.

SOURCES: *"Margaret Sanger: A Life of Passion" by Jean H. Baker; "Devices and Desires: A History of Contraceptives in America" by Andrea Tone; "Vasectomy" by George C. Denniston; "Birth Control" by Aharon W. Zorea, "Sex. A User's Guide" by Stephen Arnott; "Contraception: A History" by Robert Jutte; "Importance of Condom Use" by A. Benjamin; "Desk Reference to Nature's Medicine" by Steven Foster, Rebecca L. Johnson; "Napoleon's Buttons: 17 Molecules That Changed History" by Penny Le Couteur and Jay Burreson; "A History of the Birth Control Movement in America" by Peter C. Engelman; "The Best of Dear Abby" by Abigail Van Buren.*

ELEPHANTS

1 African and Asian elephants are different species. The African savanna elephant is taller and heavier, has bigger ears and a concave back. The Asian's trunk ends with just one lip, versus two on African elephants. The Asian has one fewer pair of ribs but more toenails. And Asian elephants are hairier, which makes sense, as they are more closely related to the extinct woolly mammoth than to their contemporaries in Africa.

2 Duchess, Lincoln Park Zoo's first elephant, once escaped. In October 1892, she ran through a pond before leaving the zoo grounds at about Clark and what is now Dickens. During her rampage she demolished a brewery door and wreaked havoc inside a bar. A horse also died in the fray. Chased by zoo keepers, residents and police, Duchess fled down Cleveland Avenue, "plunging through the board sidewalks at every step," the Tribune reported. Zookeepers finally slowed her down by getting ropes around her legs and tying her to trees.

3 A rare intersection of elephants and opera is Giuseppe Verdi's "Aida," which has often been staged with pachyderms. Before soprano Maria Callas lost weight, a critic quipped that "it was difficult to discern Callas' ankles from those of the elephant in the scene." Another mammoth insult was delivered by composer Gioachino Rossini to hefty contralto Marietta Alboni. He called her "the elephant that swallowed a nightingale."

4 While the word jumbo possibly didn't originate with the massive African elephant in the Barnum and Bailey Circus, he certainly popularized it. Jumbo was billed as the largest elephant in the world and was a huge draw in the U.S. He was killed in 1885 by a train in St. Thomas, Ontario. (Railway City Brewing Co. there makes a beer called Dead Elephant Ale.) Jumbo's stuffed body, which toured with the circus for four more years, was given to Tufts University, and became the school's mascot.

5 For both Asian and African elephants, pregnancy lasts about 22 months. Because of gestation and lactation time, a female elephant may have only six offspring her entire life.

6 Sexually mature male elephants go through periodic states known as musth, in which they produce high levels of testosterone, are dangerously aggressive and secrete a foul-smelling liquid from a gland behind their eyes.

7 One of the most bizarre incidents in U.S. history — and a horrific example of animal cruelty — occurred in Erwin, Tenn., in 1916. A trainer with a traveling circus was killed by a five-ton elephant named Mary, and circus officials feared that surrounding towns would ban their show. So they took Mary to a rail yard and hanged her by the neck from a crane in front of 2,500 spectators, many of them children. The first attempt failed when the elephant's weight snapped a chain, causing her to fall and break her hip. A second try with a heavier chain succeeded. She was buried in a grave dug with a steam shovel.

8 Lincoln Park Zoo acquired Judy from Brookfield Zoo in 1943. But the 35-year-old elephant refused to ride in a flatbed truck, so she walked the 18 miles to her new home. Escorted by zoo staff and motorcycle cops, Judy set off at 7 p.m. and traversed the western suburbs and the West Side, resting for two hours in Garfield Park before reaching Lincoln Park at 2:15 a.m.

9 Walt Disney bought the rights to "Dumbo, the Flying Elephant" for $1,000 from Helen Aberson and Harold Pearl, a husband-and-wife team. Their original was published as a rare roll-a-book, a picture book on a scroll. The movie was released in 1941.

10 Ald. "Bathhouse John" Coughlin, one of Chicago's most corrupt and colorful politicians, bought a Lincoln Park Zoo elephant named Princess Alice for a reported $3,000 around 1905 and sent the elephant to his private zoo near Colorado Springs, Colo. The Chicago zoo was willing to give up the animal because its trunk was damaged when it got stuck in a door jamb.

SOURCES: *"Elephants" by Joyce Poole; "Asian Elephant" by Matt Turner; "Our Movie Houses" by Norman O. Keim, David Marc; "Walt's People" by Didier Ghez; "Maria Callas: An Intimate Biography" by Anne Edwards; "Strong on Music: Reverberations, 1850-1856" by Vera Brodsky Lawrence; "The Illustrated Encyclopedia of Elephants" by S.K. Eltringham and Jeheskel Shoshani; "The Moral Lives of Animals" by Dale Peterson; "Critical Regionalism" by Douglas Reichert Powell; "Lords of the Levee" by Lloyd Wendt and Herman Kogan; "The Ark in the Park" by Mark Rosenthal, Carol Tauber and Edward Uhlir; "Elephants: A Cultural and Natural History" by Karl Groning and Martin Saller; "In the Beat of a Heart" by John Whitfield; Tufts University; Tribune archives; blueridgecountry.com.*

EPIDEMICS

1   The 1918 pandemic was commonly known as the Spanish flu, but it did not start in Spain. (Many believe it began in Kansas.) The Spanish took the rap because their king, Alfonso XIII, got sick, and because their nation was neutral in World War I and allowed an uncensored press to report on the flu.

2   The word "quarantine" comes from the Italian word "quarantina," meaning a period of 40 days. During the Black Death, the city of Venice required ships suspected of carrying disease to sit at anchor for 40 days before they could land.

3   The 1918 flu reached far corners of the globe. In the Fiji islands, it killed 14 percent of the population in 16 days. In the remote eastern Canadian town of Okak, more than 200 of the 266 residents died. The virus struck Okak so quickly that citizens could not provide for their many dogs; the hungry animals invaded their homes, attacking both the living and the dead. One survivor, the Rev. Andrew Asboe, armed himself with a rifle and reportedly killed more than 100 dogs.

4   Mary Mallon was an Irish immigrant in New York City in the early 1900s. She was by all accounts a talented cook. But Mallon also was an asymptomatic carrier of typhoid. After she infected more than 20 people, with one dying, she was isolated in a hospital for nearly three years. Officials didn't know what to do with her, so she was given a second chance. Mallon, who likely never believed health officials who said she was infected, went back to cooking. Two more people died. This time, Typhoid Mary, as she became known, was given what amounted to a life sentence. She lived out her days — 23 years — isolated in a one-room cottage on an island in the East River.

5   When the Black Death ravaged Europe in the 14th century, learned men believed it was caused by an Italian earthquake or an alignment of the planets Saturn, Jupiter and Mars. No one knew the disease was spread by rats and fleas. A leading French doctor warned that people could become infected simply by looking at someone who was sick.

6   During World War I, the U.S. government considered venereal disease to be a formidable enemy threatening troop readiness. Taking the offensive, authorities in the U.S. incarcerated about 30,000 suspected prostitutes and shut down red-light districts. That included New Orleans' famed Storyville, described by one official as "24 blocks given over to human degradation and lust." New Orleans Mayor Martin Behrman complained about the crackdown, saying, "You can make prostitution illegal in Louisiana, but you can't make it unpopular."

7 Nobody calls "Monty Python and the Holy Grail" a documentary, but the British comedy's "Bring out your dead" scene rings true. During the European plague, when the bodies were piling up, funeral services and processions were prohibited. Instead, corpse-removers gathered up the dead in carts to get rid of them quickly. If a house was quarantined, a relative had to throw the body into the cart from a second-floor window.

8 English sweating sickness, which caused profuse sweating and sometimes led to a rapid death, remains a mystery more than five centuries later. After raging for more than 60 years, the last major outbreak of the disease in England was recorded in 1551. Then the "English sweat" simply vanished, with its cause never established.

9 In the early years of the AIDS epidemic, Canadian flight attendant Gaetan Dugas was identified as "Patient Zero," who brought the virus to North American cities in the 1970s and early '80s. But some believe Dugas' role was exaggerated, and there is evidence that the virus was on this continent well before his travels. Tissue from a teenager who died in St. Louis in 1969 was preserved for study and was later found to contain the AIDS virus.

10 One of the last smallpox outbreaks in Europe struck Yugoslavia in 1972. Josip Tito's totalitarian regime declared martial law. He imposed a strict national quarantine that saw the army seal off entire villages. He ordered the entire population of 20 million vaccinated. More than 10,000 people who had come into contact with infected people were shut up in hospitals and hotels for weeks. In the end, 35 of the 174 infected died.

SOURCES: *"A Distant Mirror," by Barbara W. Tuchman; "Daily Life During the Black Death," by Joseph Patrick Byrne; "The Great Influenza," by John M. Barry; "The Greatest Killer: Smallpox in History," by Donald R. Hopkins; "Encyclopedia of Plague and Pestilence," edited by George Childs Kohn; "And the Band Played On," by Randy Shilts; "Love for Sale," by Elizabeth Alice Clement; "Creating the Big Easy," by Anthony J. Stanonis; "No Magic Bullet," by Allan M. Brandt; "Typhoid Mary: Captive to the Public's Health," by Judith Walzer Leavitt; Collins English Dictionary; New York Times; pbs.org; npr.org; snopes.com.*

GASOLINE

1   The U.S. gasoline price was the 45th cheapest among 155 countries in a 2008 survey. Americans paid less than half what people paid in the United Kingdom. But for really cheap gas, there was Venezuela, where it was the equivalent of 12 cents a gallon.

2   Two states ban self-serve gasoline: Oregon and New Jersey. But while full-service gas usually is more expensive, Jersey residents get a break because the state's gas taxes are the third-lowest in the U.S. (after Wyoming and Alaska).

3   When lead was added to gasoline in the 1920s, the goal was to eliminate engine knock, but the result fouled the environment for more than half a century. Even the additive's developer, Thomas Midgley, got lead poisoning, yet he and others minimized the danger. More than a dozen production workers died, and one plant was labeled the "House of Butterflies" because the lead caused workers to have insect hallucinations. Production eventually was made safer, but cars spewed lead until the U.S. phased it out in the 1980s.

4   Move over, Robie House. There's a gas station in Cloquet, Minn., designed by Frank Lloyd Wright. It was supposed to be part of a utopian community called Broadacre City, but the filling station was the only part ever built. The station, outside Duluth, is still operating.

5   The "Molotov cocktail," a bottle filled with a fuel such as gasoline that is set afire and thrown during street fighting, got its name after the Soviet invasion of Finland in 1939. As the Soviets dropped cluster bombs, Soviet Foreign Minister Vyacheslav Molotov described the air operation as a food airlift for starving Finns. That led the Finns to sarcastically refer to the bombs as "Molotov bread baskets." When the Finns fought back against Soviet tanks, they called their gasoline bombs "Molotov cocktails."

6 Singer Bobby Fuller made a hit out of "I Fought the Law" and appeared in a movie with a quintessentially 1960s title, "The Ghost in the Invisible Bikini." In 1966, gasoline killed him. Fuller's body was found in his car, bruised, battered and doused with fuel. At first police said he swallowed gasoline to commit suicide. Later, authorities labeled it an "accidental death due to inhalation of gasoline." But many believe Fuller was murdered.

7 Four years ago, Hillary Clinton got in trouble for a gas-station joke. As she introduced a quote from Mohandas Gandhi during a speech, she quipped, "He ran a gas station down in St. Louis." Indian-Americans were none too pleased with the stereotype, and Clinton apologized for her "lame attempt at humor."

8 Celebrities who are former gas station workers include actors Michael Douglas and Steve Buscemi and singers Bono, Eddie Vedder and John Mayer. "My mission at the Mobil station was to become the best squeegee in the land — it's part of the full service," Mayer said. "I have long arms, and I thought, I'm going to show them art in motion: one full swipe, corner to corner. I never let a single drop of liquid remain. I could also make the pump stop exactly on $15. It's a rhythm thing."

9 "Gasoline Alley," a comic strip born in the Tribune in the late 1910s, is still around, though it is no longer published in the newspaper of its birth. Unlike most strips, its characters aged over the years. A baby named Skeezix, left on a doorstep in 1921, is 87 now.

10 Frank Sinatra referred to his favorite drink, Jack Daniel's whiskey, as "gasoline." And sometimes it works the other way. In some parts of Canada, a gas station is called a "gas bar." In countries that once were part of the British Empire, some people refer to gasoline as "motor spirit." So maybe what the world needs is a 12-step program.

SOURCES: *Tribune news services; InStyle; Rolling Stone; cnn.com; Toronto Star; "Fill 'er Up: An Architectural History of America's Gas Stations" by Daniel I. Vieyra; "The Secret History of Lead," by Jamie Lincoln Kitman in The Nation magazine.*

HAIR

1   A $24,000 haircut — perhaps the most expensive ever — was given to the Sultan of Brunei in August 2009. The main cost was the airfare of London barber Ken Modestou to Southeast Asia. Modestou's usual fee, when the customer comes to him, is about $45.

2   What's a "bar-code hairstyle"? That's when a balding man strings his few remaining hairs across the top of his head, in a pattern resembling a bar code.

3   Beehives are beautiful, according to Playboy magazine, which featured cartoon character Marge Simpson on its November 2009 cover. The beehive hairdo of another celebrity, the late British singer Amy Winehouse, came into play at her trial on charges of punching a fan in the face. Winehouse said she was only 5-foot-3 — too short to lay a serious blow on her 5-foot-7 accuser — and argued that her beehive made her seem taller. She was acquitted. Speaking of beehives, that's the name of an Alaska business where former Gov. Sarah Palin got her hair done: the Beehive Beauty Shop in Wasilla. But Palin's signature style is the updo, so chosen because it made her seem taller and because "Sarah wanted to look more professional and ready to work and not come across as high-maintenance and fussy," according to Beehive owner Jessica Steele.

4   Former North Korean despot Kim Jong Il was known for his bouffant, but he hated long hair on other men. He ordered followers in 2005 to keep their hair shorter than 5 centimeters (2 inches). The dictum came in a television campaign, titled "Let's Trim Our Hair According to the Socialist Lifestyle," that depicted long hair as a stinky indulgence that left the brain starved for oxygen.

5   Throughout his life, Incan emperor Pachakuti arranged for all of his body hair to be collected as it was cut or fell out. After Pachakuti died, his hair and fingernails were assembled into a statue in his memory.

6 For Lucille Ball's first movie, "Roman Scandals" in 1933, she was ordered to shave off her eyebrows. But after filming, the eyebrows didn't grow back properly, and for the rest of her life Ball had to use an eyebrow pencil.

7 When a St. Louis washerwoman named Sarah Breedlove feared she was going bald around 1900, she developed a hair conditioning product and became a marketing force named Madam C.J. Walker. Though often described as America's first black millionaire and sometimes as America's first female millionaire, she was neither. When she died in 1919, she was worth about $600,000 before taxes and charitable commitments. Though that fell short of a million at the time, it would be $7.5 million today, adjusted for inflation.

8 Joe Pepitone, the hip first baseman for the Yankees, Cubs, Astros and Braves in the '60s and '70s, was believed to be the first major leaguer to bring a hair dryer into a locker room.

9 African-American children are less likely than other American children to get head lice. That's because lice in the United States grasp the round-shaped hair of whites more easily than the oval-shaped hair of blacks.

10 A 9th-century warrior hero of Spain's Catalonia region was Guifré el Pelós, aka Wilfred the Hairy, so named because he had hair on a part of the body where it shouldn't have been, according to legend. What part? No one knows, but some think it was the soles of his feet. The Spanish attitude is summed up in an old saying: "Where there is hair, there is happiness."

SOURCES: *"Encyclopedia of Hair: A Cultural History" by Victoria Sherrow; "Hair: Sex, Society, Symbolism" by Wendy Cooper; "Barcelona" by Robert Hughes; "On Her Own Ground: The Life and Times of Madam C.J. Walker" by A'Lelia Bundles; "Cubs Journal: Year by Year and Day by Day with the Chicago Cubs Since 1876" by John Snyder; "The Incas" by Terence N. D'Altroy; wordspy.com, The New York Times; Irish Times; The Guardian; "Ball of Fire: The Tumultuous Life and Comic Art of Lucille Ball" by Stefan Kanfer.*

HEIGHT

1 Descriptions of Barack Obama often include his height, but plenty of presidents were taller, including two of the previous three. Histories are inconsistent on presidential heights, but it appears that Abraham Lincoln was tallest at 6 foot 4, with Lyndon Johnson between 6-3 and 6-4. Also listed as taller than Obama were Thomas Jefferson, Franklin Roosevelt, George H.W. Bush, Bill Clinton, George Washington and Chester Arthur. Obama and Ronald Reagan could see eye to eye — at 6-1. The shortest? James Madison at 5-4.

2 According to studies, tall people have higher incomes, higher IQs and longer life spans than short people.

3 Among the famous people afraid of heights: Steven Spielberg, Wayne Gretzky, Sarah Palin, Billie Jean King, Ray Bradbury, Adolf Hitler, Bridget Fonda, Frank Sinatra and Whoopi Goldberg. Even Spiderman — Tobey Maguire — has admitted to acrophobia.

4 A healthy fear of high places may be innate. In 1960, Cornell University psychologists Eleanor Gibson and Richard Walk conducted a "visual cliff" experiment. In the study, babies of various species (humans, rats, chickens, cats, goats and sheep) refused to venture onto a glass panel that covered what looked like a sharp drop-off. The 6- to 14-month-old human babies recognized the apparent danger of the drop-off and even refused to cross it, despite being coaxed by their mothers. Only three of the 36 infants ventured onto the glass, though some backed onto it without realizing it. None of the chicks, kittens, kids and lambs — some less than a day old — made the same mistake and mistakenly walked off the "cliff."

5 Because of spine compression, people lose height during the day, becoming 1 to 2 percent shorter than when they woke up. The same trend occurs long-term: In adulthood, the average person loses a half-inch every 20 years.

6 An American B-25 bomber collided with the 79th floor of the Empire State Building on a foggy Manhattan morning at the end of World War II. Three crew members died, along with 11 people in the building. A worker in the building survived a bizarre double accident: Badly burned by the fireball, she was taken to an elevator to be lowered to safety. But the impact had damaged the elevator cable, and it snapped, sending the woman and her helper hurtling toward the ground. An automatic braking system saved them.

7 How tall can grass grow? Up to 120 feet, if it's bamboo.

8 Mount Everest is not the highest point on the Earth. A dormant volcano in Ecuador beats out the 29,035-foot Himalayan peak. Mount Chimborazo, at just over 20,500 feet, gets a step-stool boost from Earth's equatorial bulge, which pushes the mountain an extra few miles into space and farther from the center of the planet. For the record, Mount Everest is the highest point above sea level.

9 According to a 1998 study, North America's Plains Indians were the tallest people in the world during the mid-19th century.

10 Language purists may get annoyed that the smallest coffee on the Starbucks menu is labeled "tall." But it wasn't always that way. The 12-ounce "tall" used to be a medium, in between the 8-ounce "short" and the 16-ounce "grande." Later, a 20-ounce "venti" was added and the "short" was taken off the menu (though some stores still sell it).

SOURCES: *"Facts about the Presidents" by Joseph Kane; "Tallest in the World: Native Americans of the Great Plains in the Nineteenth Century" by Richard H. Steckel and Joseph M. Prince; "Grande Expectations: A Year in the Life of Starbucks' Stock" by Karen Blumenthal; "The Tall Book" by Arianne Cohen; "Empire: A Tale of Obsession, Betrayal, and the Battle for an American Icon" By Mitchell Pacelle; "The Rat Pack" by Lawrence J. Quirk and William Schoell; "Great Mythconceptions: The Science Behind the Myths" by Karl Kruszelnicki and Adam Yazxhi; "The 'Visual Cliff'" by Eleanor J. Gibson and Richard D. Welk; npr.org; World Book Encyclopedia; New York Daily News; Associated Press; San Francisco Chronicle; Orange County Register; New Yorker; Anchorage Daily News; Vancouver Sun; Newark Star Ledger; Toronto Star; Houston Chronicle.*

HURRICANES

1 Hurricane, typhoon or cyclone? It isn't as simple as you might think, according to the Atlantic Oceanographic and Meteorological Laboratory. All are regional names for tropical cyclones. In the Atlantic, Caribbean and the eastern Pacific, call them hurricanes. But call them typhoons in the northwest Pacific, and cyclones in the southwest Pacific and the Indian Ocean.

2 After a hurricane battered Miami in 1926, a funeral was held for Thomas Gill, a worker on a dredge on Biscayne Bay. A minister was reading the 23rd Psalm when a man walked in and disrupted the service. It was Gill, who survived by swimming to shore from the vessel, where another body was misidentified as his.

3 A few days after Hurricane Katrina devastated New Orleans, TV's "The Price Is Right" broadcast a show offering a trip to New Orleans as a prize. The show was a rerun that was aired by mistake. The program apologized.

4 The naming of hurricanes has sometimes been controversial. In the '50s, lists were adopted with only female names, a practice that some people viewed as sexist. In 1979, male names were added. Further diversity has occurred with inclusion of Spanish and French names. But in 2003, Rep. Sheila Jackson Lee, D-Texas, complained about the lack of African-American names on the list.

5 An enduring story about Hurricane Camille in 1969 is that residents of the Richelieu Manor apartment building in Pass Christian, Miss., threw a "hurricane party," and that only one person survived. But that tale, told by survivor Mary Ann Gerlach, is in serious doubt. Other survivors have been identified, and one insisted that he and another person stayed not to party but to help a fellow resident. Contacted in 2011 by the Tribune, Gerlach stood by her story: "I don't care if anyone believes it or not. There was no reason for me to lie. I didn't get a penny out of it." Incidentally, when Gerlach was charged with killing her 11th husband (yes, 11th), years after Camille, her lawyer used an insanity defense, citing Gerlach's hurricane ordeal. That story didn't fly, and she did time in prison.

6 In December 1944, a U.S. Navy fleet under Adm. William "Bull" Halsey mistakenly steered straight into a typhoon in the Philippine Sea. Three destroyers sank and dozens of other ships were damaged. Nearly 900 people were killed. The aircraft carrier Monterey was badly damaged by fire. Among those who battled that blaze was Lt. Gerald Ford.

7 Generals and admirals had much to worry about during the bloody four years of the Civil War. What they didn't have to deal with was a hurricane. The longest hurricane-free period the continental United States has experienced in the last 160 years began in November 1861 and ended October 1865, roughly bracketing the War Between the States.

8 Beginning in the late 1950s, the U.S. Weather Service teamed up with the Navy on a research project to fight hurricanes. The plan was to bombard hurricanes with silver iodide in the hope it would collapse the storms' eyewall. Project Stormfury, as it was called, started meekly enough. Hurricane Daisy in 1958 shrugged off the attack. In 1961, Esther seemed to stagger — a segment of the eyewall did break down — but within two hours she returned to her original intensity. Other attempts showed some promise, but in the end were inconclusive. Stormfury died in 1983.

0 A hurricane's energy is the equivalent of a 10-megaton nuclear bomb exploding — every 20 minutes.

10 Chicago Bears fans' reputation for warmth and sensitivity took a hit after Hurricane Katrina. At the NFC championship game in January 2007, Soldier Field fans greeted the New Orleans Saints with signs such as "Bears Finishing What Katrina Started."

SOURCES: *"Florida's Hurricane History" by Jay Barnes;"Encyclopedia of Hurricanes, Typhoons, and Cyclones" by David Longshore; "Gerald R. Ford" by Douglas Brinkley; Congressional Record; "Hurricane Camille: Monster Storm of the Gulf Coast" by Philip D. Hearn; "Category 5: The Story of Camille" by Ernest Zebrowski and Judith A. Howard; "Roar of the Heavens" by Stefan Bechtel; Atlantic Oceanographic and Meteorological Laboratory; Biloxi Herald Sun; snopes.com; camille. passchristian.net.*

THE NOBEL PRIZE

1   When Alfred Nobel's brother Ludwig died in 1888, French newspapers reported erroneously that Alfred had died (One headline read: "The merchant of death is dead."). Some historians believe the newspapers' mistake gave Alfred a sneak peek at his legacy and inspired his desire to be remembered for something other than explosives. Hence the Nobel Prize was born.

2   The year 1912 was momentous for French scientist Alexis Carrel. He won the Nobel for medicine, and he began an experiment in which he took tissue from the heart of a chicken embryo and kept it alive for decades to test how long warm-blooded cells could be sustained in the laboratory. The news media oversimplified the project, annually marking the birthday of the "chicken heart." The Nobel laureate died in 1944, and the chicken tissue was euthanized two years later, having lived for 34 years.

3   The 1926 Nobel Prize in medicine went to Danish researcher Johannes Fibiger for discovering a cause for cancer. Problem was, Fibiger wrongly concluded that roundworms had caused the tumors in his lab rats. Within a decade of Fibiger's triumph, other research cast serious doubt on his findings, and the embarrassment led Nobel officials to shy away from honoring cancer research for years to come. Fibiger did not live long enough to suffer the same chagrin. He died in 1928 — of cancer.

4   Mohandas Gandhi never won the Nobel Peace Prize. James Joyce never won the literature prize. Both died before Nobel officials recognized their genius. Until 1974, a person could win the prize posthumously only if he or she died between the Feb. 1 deadline for nominations and the award announcement in October. That's how UN Secretary General Dag Hammarskjold won the Peace Prize in 1961, a month after dying in a plane crash. But in 1974, the rules became stricter. Only those who died between the announcement in October and the ceremony in December could be posthumous recipients.

5   University of Chicago graduate Edwin Hubble never won the Nobel Prize for physics despite transforming our view of the universe and providing the first evidence to support the Big Bang theory. Swedish engineer Gustaf Dalen, on the other hand, won the 1912 physics prize for improving gas flow to lighthouse beacons.

6 Portuguese neurologist Egas Moniz received the Nobel Prize for medicine in 1949 for pioneering the lobotomy. When Moniz developed this treatment to cut nerve connections in the frontal lobes of the brain, there was no other effective treatment for schizophrenia. But lobotomy soon was considered dehumanizing and subject to abuse, and drug therapies became far more effective. Today, some forms of "psychosurgery" are performed, but they are quite rare.

7 The most controversial honor in Nobel history? Perhaps the Peace Prize of 1973. Two members of the selection committee resigned to protest the choice of U.S. Secretary of State Henry Kissinger and North Vietnamese negotiator Le Duc Tho for crafting a Vietnam War peace deal. Tho rejected the prize, saying his nation was not yet at peace. Kissinger accepted, but in later years has been much criticized for his role in the secret war in Cambodia and the overthrow of a democratically elected government in Chile. Humorist-songwriter Tom Lehrer once said that "political satire became obsolete when Henry Kissinger was awarded the Nobel Prize."

8 An eccentric California optometrist named Robert Graham announced in 1980 that he was forming the Repository for Germinal Choice, which was quickly nicknamed the Nobel Prize Sperm Bank. Graham said he had commitments from three Nobelists, but the publicity chased away two of them, leaving only physicist William Shockley, who advocated paying people whose IQs were less than 100 to be sterilized. No children were born from laureate sperm, and the center closed in 1999.

9 Toni Morrison, the author who was the first African-American woman to win a Nobel Prize, has expressed regrets that her books aren't credited to Chloe Anthony Wofford. That was her name before she started going by "Toni" at Howard University and adopted the name Morrison from her husband, whom she later divorced.

10 When University of Chicago professor Robert Lucas won the Nobel in economics, he gave half of his $1 million prize money to his ex-wife. A clause in their divorce settlement in the late '80s required him to split the cash if he won before the end of October 1995. Lucas' prize came three weeks before he would have been free of the obligation.

SOURCES: *"The Nobel Prize: A History of Genius, Controversy and Prestige" by Burton Feldman; nobelprize.org; pbs.org; improbable.com; Tribune news services.*

NUMBERS

1 "Taking the No. 11 bus" is slang for walking, with the 1's representing your own two legs.

2 When restaurant workers cancel an order, they "86" it. For example, a waiter might tell the cook, "Eighty-six the French fries." There are competing theories for the origin of the term. Article 86 of the New York state liquor code spelled out when a customer should be refused alcohol. A soup kitchen during the Depression made only enough soup for 85 people. Delmonico's restaurant in New York City had rib-eye steak listed as No. 86 on the menu, and often ran out.

3 Formulaic screenwriting rules require that a protagonist face an episode of soul-searching despair before rising to conquer the world. Some call this a "low point" or a "dark night of the soul," but no-nonsense Hollywood producers refer to it simply as "Page 75."

4 "Leet" is a whimsical Internet language in which numbers and other typographical characters impersonate letters to create alternate spellings of words. The title of the TV show "Numb3rs" is an example. In Leet, 3's take the place of E's, 5's impersonate S's, 6's represent G's or B's, 1's pose as L's, and 7's are T's. The term Leet, slang for "elite," can be rendered as 1337. Leet is a constantly mutating bastardization of the language, including such affectations as using Z instead of S to form plurals and spelling "banned" as "B&." There are even Leet converters online. Type in "Shakespeare" and it comes out as S---4k35p34r3.

5 British musicians call a 128th note a quasihemidemisemiquaver.

6   One of Chicago's worst disasters was the fire at Our Lady of the Angels school on Dec. 1, 1958. Turning the death count into painful poetry, Chicago Sun-Times reporter Hugh Hough wrote: "Eighty-seven children. And three of the nuns who were their teachers. That, as near as any informed person could tell, was the terrible arithmetic of the fire that swept Our Lady of Angels School just 18 minutes before the day's final school bell." (The toll eventually reached 95.)

7   Cincinnati Bengals wide receiver Chad Johnson legally changed his name in 2008 to Chad Ocho Cinco, to reflect the Spanish translation of each number on his uniform. When No. 85 first started calling himself Ocho Cinco, his coach referred to the attention-craving athlete as "Ocho Psycho."

8   "1661" is slang for an older woman who dresses in young women's clothes. The sexist male term comes from the observation that some women look 16 years old from the back but 61 years old from the front.

9   Baseball fans love numerical slang. A "Lawrence Welk" is an old-fashioned term for a 1-2-3 double play (pitcher to catcher to first), in honor of the bandleader who started songs with "And a one, and a two, and a three." Then there's the phrase "on the interstate," which refers to a ballplayer hitting between .100 and .199. Such hitters' averages resemble interstate numbers. For example, .157=I-57.

10   The number 714 is an odd touchstone in American culture. It's the badge number of cop Joe Friday in the TV show "Dragnet." It's Babe Ruth's career home run total. It's the number of the "Friends" episode when Jennifer Aniston's character turns 30. It's a slang term for Quaaludes, because the number was marked on the tablets. And it's the area code for Disneyland.

SOURCES: *"The Penguin Companion to Classical Music" by Paul Griffiths; Toronto Globe and Mail; urbandictionary.com; espn.go.com; bbc.co.uk; Tribune news services.*

ROBOTS

1 The word robot, coined by Czech playwright Karel Capek in his 1921 play "R.U.R. (Rossum's Universal Robots)," is based on the Czech word "robota," meaning forced labor or serf. The fictional robots in Capek's play were created chemically, not mechanically.

2 Here's a nightmare scenario: Robots learn to build new robots, replicating without human aid and eventually achieving world domination. In theory, at least, that could happen through nanotechnology, the science of manipulating materials on an extremely small scale. Nanotechnology expert Eric Drexler once envisioned tiny machines replicating out of control, overwhelming the Earth in a wave of "gray goo."

3 "Proprioception" is sometimes called the sixth sense. It means knowing where each part of your body is without having to look for it. This is natural for people, but very difficult for robots.

4 As household robots such as the Roomba vacuum cleaner gain popularity, clashes with pets are becoming more common. Los Angeles graphic designer Rob Sheridan has posted a YouTube video called "Puppy Vs. Robot! Epic Battle for Territorial Domination!" The video, featuring confrontations between Sheridan's pet Lola and a toy called Roboquad, has been viewed more than 5.8 million times.

5 Cyborgs — part man and part machine — are coming. In fact, some would say they're already here. Is a person with a heart pacemaker a cyborg? How about a person who attaches a cell phone to his ear? Scientists are working on a robot suit or exoskeleton that people could wear to increase their physical strength. The happy application: Disabled people might be able to walk. The darker side: Soldiers could fight longer and better.

6 Scientists are studying swarming behavior among robots — the collective actions of robots that have individual intelligence. Robot enthusiasts enjoy staging soccer matches between teams of machines, such as the Sony robo-dog Aibo. Daniel H. Wilson offers scarier swarming scenarios in his tongue-in-cheek but science-based book, "How to Survive a Robot Uprising." An army of robots that communicated with each other would be effective at hunting down people because if one robot spotted a person, all of them would instantly know where the person was. Wilson also postulates how all the appliances in a "smart home" could conspire to kill the owner.

7 The "Uncanny Valley" is a theory by Japanese roboticist Masahiro Mori. He suggests that while people become more empathetic with robots as they become more humanlike, there is a drop-off — a valley — when the robot is not perfectly human but is alarmingly close. At that point, the robot comes across as creepy, like the living dead. Filmmakers and critics have cited the Uncanny Valley as the reason some animation fails: It is neither close enough to reality nor far enough away to be comfortable to the viewer.

8 While androids — humanlike robots — dominate popular perceptions, many roboticists believe that the robots of the future will be limited-function machines that look nothing like people. One example is a snakelike robot being developed to find people trapped in the rubble of an earthquake.

9 The U.S. military may be struggling to sign up soldiers, but it's recruiting plenty of robots. Predator drones have become a key part of the arsenal, and robots are being used to defuse roadside bombs. The U.S. military's Defense Advanced Research Projects Agency sponsors a competition to develop an unmanned vehicle that can operate in urban environments. Congress has set a goal that one-third of the military's "operational ground combat vehicles" be unmanned by 2015.

10 Many Americans view robots as threatening, but the Japanese have fully adopted them, consistent with their Buddhist and Shinto principles. "If you make something, your heart will go into the thing you are making," Mori told the Tribune in 2006. "So a robot is an external self. If a robot is an external self, a robot is your child."

SOURCES: *Tribune archives and news services; The Wall Street Journal; University of Texas at Austin's Robotics Research Group; the Economist; Forbes; darpa.mil; "How to Survive a Robot Uprising" by Daniel H. Wilson.*

SKIN COLOR

1   Melanin, the pigment that gives color to skin (and eyes) is produced in cells called melanocytes. Every person has about the same number of these cells, regardless of race, but those with darker skin have larger cells that produce more pigment. Melanin not only colors the skin but also protects it from the sun's harmful ultraviolet rays.

2   Crayola once had a color called "flesh," which was the color of Caucasian flesh. After complaints from civil rights activists, "flesh" became "peach" in 1962. A similar controversy involved "Indian red." Crayola said the color was based on a pigment found near India, but some thought it was a slur against native Americans, so the company solicited consumer suggestions for a new name. Among the ideas: "baseball-mitt brown" and "crab claw red." But "chestnut" was chosen in 1999.

3   A jaundiced baby has yellowish skin. A traveler suffering from seasickness takes on a greenish hue. And a silver miner suffering from argyria turns blue or bluish-gray.

4   The Incredible Hulk was born gray. It wasn't until issue No. 2 that Bruce Banner's alter ego turned green, and that was because the printer couldn't hold a consistent gray. The Hulk's skin shifted from light gray to almost black through the comic book.

5   It's difficult to understand how a painting of a woman in an evening dress could have scandalized 1884 Paris. But "Madame X," John Singer Sargent's portrait of Virginie Gautreau, caused a stir, and part of the reason was her skin color. In contrast to the black dress, her lavender-powdered skin was jarringly pale, except for her ears, which were adorned by rosy makeup. The result was an image of womanhood that was both corpselike and sexually dangerous, causing discomfort to upper-crust Parisians.

6   "The Simpsons" have jarringly yellow skin because, as animator Gabor Csupo told writer John Ortved, the characters were "primitively designed, so we thought we could counterbalance that design with shocking colors. That's why we came up with the yellow skin and the blue hair for Marge." John Alberti, in his intellectual treatise "Leaving Springfield," describes the Simpsons as "people of color" and notes that Bart has called himself "yellow trash."

7 African-American author Zora Neale Hurston offered this color scale for blacks: "high yaller, yaller, high brown, vaseline brown, seal brown, low brown, dark brown." The use of the word "yellow" (or "yaller") for light-skinned African-Americans is reflected in the song "Yellow Rose of Texas," referring to a mixed-race servant girl who, according to legend, distracted Mexican Gen. Santa Ana with her charms, contributing to his defeat at the battle of San Jacinto in 1836.

8 Former Soviet President Mikhail Gorbachev and supermodel Cindy Crawford have something in common: prominent birthmarks. Crawford's mole and Gorbachev's port-wine stain are just two forms of the skin discolor-ation that affects about 1 in 3 infants. Birthmarks come in two types: pigment (light-brown cafe au lait spots, dark-brown moles and gray or blue Mongolian spots) or vascular (port-wine stains, stork bites and hemangioma). Scientists don't know what causes birthmarks.

9 The first European references to Asians as "yellow" have been traced to the late 1600s and probably had nothing to do with skin color. They appear linked to the fact that the Chinese embraced yellow as a symbol of grandeur. By 1904, the color had a far scarier tinge when American adventure writer Jack London wrote an essay called "The Yellow Peril." But even London didn't think all Asians were yellow. He warned that the Western world would be threatened if "millions of yellow men" from China came under the control of "the little brown man" from Japan.

10 Actor George Hamilton said he had an "epiphany" as a young man: "Suntanning was going to be to me what the phone booth, funny blue suit and cape were to Superman. Without a tan, I was just another paleface in the crowd. With one, I could do some pretty amazing things."

SOURCES: *"Skin: The Bare Facts" by Lori Bergamotto; "Beautiful Skin of Color" by Jeanine Downie and Fran Cook-Bolden, with Barbara Nevins Taylor; "The Simpsons: An Uncensored, Unauthorized History" by John Ortved; "Was Superman a Spy?: And Other Comic Book Legends Revealed" by Brian Cronin; "Leaving Springfield: The Simpsons and the Possibility of Oppositional Culture" by John Alberti; "The Complete Stories" by Zora Neale Hurston; "Encyclopedia of Family Health" by David B. Jacoby, R.M. Youngson; "Strapless: John Singer Sargent and the Fall of Madame X" by Deborah Davis; "Don't Mind If I Do" by George Hamilton and William Stadiem; "Yellow: Race in America Beyond Black and White" by Frank H. Wu; "Savage Perils: Racial Frontiers and Nuclear Apocalypse in American Culture" by Patrick B. Sharp; "The Discourse of Race in Modern China" by Frank Dikotter; Texas Monthly; New York magazine; crayola.com; artble.com.; webmd.com; mayoclinic.com; encyclopedia.com.*

SNOW

1 In the nearly 130 years that snowfall records have been kept in Chicago, more than 4,600 inches of snow have fallen on the city. That would pile up to about the 30th floor of the Willis Tower — slightly more than a quarter of the way up.

2 A Vermont farmer named Wilson Alwyn Bentley began a decades-long hobby in the 1880s of taking thousands of photographs of snowflakes on black velvet. "Snowflake" Bentley believed that no two snowflakes are alike. Today, scientists say that no two complex snowflakes are alike but that more simple combinations of snow crystals may be alike. Bentley died in 1933 of pneumonia — contracted after he walked home in a blizzard.

3 The 1967 blizzard was one of Chicago's most bizarre weather events. On Jan. 24, the high temperature was 65, and there was a tornado watch. Two days later, a storm dropped 23.1 inches of snow in 29 hours. Chicagoans could feel picked on: Milwaukee got 2 inches, and Champaign got only rain. But the Windy City is not easily intimidated. Seven hours after the storm began, with snow falling at a rate of about an inch an hour, 193 people showed up at WGN-TV's studios for the "Bozo Show."

4 Chicago's 1979 snow crisis left the city crippled and opened the way for mayoral challenger Jane Byrne to go after Mayor Michael Bilandic's recovery efforts. Campaign manager Don Rose, a political consultant who occasionally writes for Perspective, later recalled shooting a TV ad with Byrne. "Snow was coming down, fortunately," he said. Otherwise, he confided, he would have had to fetch some cornflakes he had stashed in his car and throw them at Byrne, to mimic snow.

5 During World War I, when Italians and Austrians fought each other in the mountainous Southern Tyrol region, one of their chief weapons was snow. They purposely set off avalanches, leaving an estimated 60,000 soldiers on both sides dead, including thousands on a single day.

6 When the Montreal Canadiens won the 1924 hockey title, some of them put the Stanley Cup trophy in the trunk of their car and drove off to the victory party. But the car got a flat, and they took the trophy out and perched it on a snowbank so they could get to the spare tire. After changing the tire, they went to the party, only to realize they had forgotten the trophy. They found it where they had left it: on the snowbank.

7 The term "panked snow" is popular in Michigan's Upper Peninsula and other northern fringes of the country. It refers to snow that has settled or has been pressed down so that people can walk on it.

8 Snow comes in many colors beyond the familiar white and the unappetizing yellow. Glacier snow can appear blue. Algae growing on fallen snow can create hues of green or red, such as what hikers call "watermelon snow." When orange snow fell in Siberia last February, pollution was suspected, but officials said the likely cause was a heavy sandstorm in neighboring Kazakhstan.

9 Snow can occur even when the temperature is 50, according to climatologist Nolan Doesken of Colorado State University. Such a snow happens during a shower or thunderstorm, when the sun has warmed the ground but the air is still quite cold. In the Midwest, about the highest temperature for snow is around 40 degrees, Doesken said.

10 Some people say Philadelphia has the nation's worst sports fans. Exhibit A: At a 1968 Eagles game at Franklin Field, fans threw snowballs at Santa Claus.

SOURCES: *"Snow" by Ruth Kirk; Dictionary of American Regional English; The New Partridge Dictionary of Slang and Unconventional English; "Fighting Jane," by Bill Granger and Lori Granger; legendsofhockey.com; Science News; USA Today; Tom Skilling's Tribune weather page; Tribune archives and news services.*

SPACE

1 Where does Earth's atmosphere end and outer space begin? NASA defines an astronaut as someone who has flown 50 miles above sea level. But some international groups prefer to define space as the area beyond the Karman Line, which is about 62 miles above sea level.

2 Living in space can cause subtle changes in the human body. For example, some astronauts find that their tastes in food change. "One of my favorite foods on the ground is shrimp, and up here I can't stand it," said International Space Station astronaut Peggy Whitson.

3 Speaking of food and space, South Korean researchers spent more than $1 million on kimchee that astronaut Yi So-yeon took to the International Space Station in 2008. Scientists had to develop a special version of the pickled cabbage dish to address fears that it would offend crew members from other countries with its smell or that it would start "bubbling out of control" in space conditions.

4 Neil Armstrong misspoke when he uttered the first words on his moonwalk in 1969. He was supposed to announce, "That's one small step for a man, one giant leap for mankind." But he left out the "a," producing a sentence that didn't really make sense. (Without the "a," "man" would mean the same thing as "mankind.") But, of course, everyone knew what he meant.

5 Sitting in the Centaurus constellation about 20 light years from Earth is star BPM 37093, also named Lucy. The white dwarf is one huge diamond, scientists say, that weighs in at 10 billion trillion trillion carats and is about the size of our moon.

6 In 1993, a meteoroid destroyed the European Space Agency's communication satellite Olympus. Don't think Hollywood explosion. Scientists suspect it was damaged by a few pebbles, and in trying to regain control, so much fuel was lost the satellite was rendered useless. While space shuttles, space stations and satellites have received minor damage from flying space rocks, the Olympus is the only satellite to be rendered useless.

7 Before "The Big Bang Theory" was a TV show, it was an explanation for the development of the universe, and much of the credit (for the theory, not the TV show) goes to a former Chicagoan. Edwin Hubble set the Illinois high jump record while at Wheaton High School, won a Rhodes scholarship, and earned a doctorate at the University of Chicago. But the ultimate honor — the Nobel Prize — eluded him because some Nobel officials didn't think astronomy fit into the physics category.

8 The word "jovial" comes from Jove, another name for the god (and the planet) Jupiter. The god was considered jolly, so those who are similarly good-natured are jovial. But in space terms, a "jovian planet" is not at all jolly — it's a planet that, like Jupiter, is composed primarily of gases rather than solid matter.

9 When you point out the Big Dipper to your child, be careful not to call it a constellation. It's an asterism, or a collection of stars within a constellation or in multiple constellations that form another shape. Another famous asterism is Orion's Belt. There are 88 official constellations, including Orion, Gemini, the zodiac signs and Ursa Major, which includes the Big Dipper.

10 The ashes of more than 100 humans have been launched into space, including those of "Star Trek" creator Gene Roddenberry and hippie icon Timothy Leary. But the first human ashes to leave the solar system are expected to be those of Clyde Tombaugh. The remains of the astronomer who discovered Pluto are aboard the New Horizons spacecraft, scheduled to fly past Pluto in 2015 and take photographs, then depart our solar system.

SOURCES: *"Handbook of Space Engineering, Archaeology, and Heritage" by Beth Laura O'Leary; "The Complete Idiot's Guide to Weird Word Origins" by Paul McFedries; "Meteors in the Earth's Atmosphere" by Edmond Murad, Iwan Prys Williams; "The Nobel Prize" by Burton Feldman; "Don't Know Much About the Universe" by Kenneth C. Davis; "Star Clusters and How to Observe Them" by Mark Allison; "The Handy Astronomy Answer Book" by Charles Liu; spaceflight now.com; The New York Times; snopes.com; chicagomaroon.com; "People of the Century" by CBS News; BBC News; Toronto Globe and Mail; planetfacts.org; science.nasa.gov; dictionary.reference.com; universetoday.com.*

TV TECHNOLOGY

1 Philo Farnsworth was a 14-year-old Idaho farm boy when he came up with a brainstorm that eventually led to the first practical electronic television. Working with a horse-drawn harrow to harvest potatoes one row after another, it occurred to him that an electronic image could be scanned and reproduced line by line — one row after another.

2 Why is there no Channel 1 on American TV? Because in the 1940s, TV and radio shared some frequencies, raising the prospect of interference. Channel 1 was used only by low-watt TV stations, so the industry was willing to surrender the frequency to radio. TV could have reordered its remaining channels to start with 1, but it chose not to.

3 The late 1940s and early '50s were a freewheeling time in Chicago TV. When NBC-owned WNBQ used a special effect to split one image into dozens, network execs in New York asked about this new "image multiplier." The Chicagoans refused to explain. The New York bosses insisted. Finally, the Chicagoans shipped them the cutting-edge technology: a common glass building block that they had held in front of the lens.

4 The yokels got cable TV first. We think of cable as a means to deliver 200-plus channels, but its first customers had no choices at all — people in remote areas whose TV reception was terrible. "Community antennas" were built on high ground in Arkansas, Oregon and Pennsylvania in 1948. Then cables carried the signals to individual homes.

5 The wireless TV remote control was born in the Chicago area in 1955. Zenith engineer Eugene Polley created the Flash-Matic, which sent a light signal to the television. Trouble was, sunlight could cause confusion. A year later, Zenith's Robert Adler devised a remote called the Space Command that used ultrasound and was state of the art for decades. Eventually, infra-red signaling took over. When Adler died in 2007, some admirers called for a sitting ovation.

6 Japanese manufacturer Ikegami Tsushinki invented a hand-held TV camera that it called a "handy-looky," mimicking the slang term "walkie-talkie." The product caught on. The nickname did not.

7 Because history is written by the victors, few people have heard of the DuMont Television Network, which went out of business in 1955. Founder Allen DuMont pioneered development of cathode ray tubes and launched his own TV manufacturing company and broadcast network. He lacked the clout of rival companies that had been involved in radio for decades, though many believe his studio equipment and home sets were technologically superior. And he didn't lack for marketing pluck. A 1946 print ad quoted actress Betty Hutton as saying: "I'll be practically in your lap — on DuMont television!"

8 In a technological feat that some saw as pointless, CNN unveiled "hologram" reporting on Election Night 2008. Correspondent Jessica Yellin was sent to Chicago's Grant Park, and her three-dimensional image was beamed back to the studio, as if she had never left. CNN exec Jon Klein explained: "The hologram allowed us to pull people figuratively out of a very noisy environment in Grant Park and actually have a conversation with them. One day all TV news will be done that way." Or not. Holography experts noted that CNN wasn't really using holograms, since the 3-D images weren't projected in space, but only on screen. Technically, that meant they were tomograms, not holograms.

9 Early TV cameras sometimes were thrown off by certain colors. After Soviet broadcaster Olga Vysotskaya gave a gymnastics demonstration while wearing a certain hue in 1938, she got letters from viewers asking her why she had appeared in the nude.

10 If Hitachi has its way, the remote control will be inside your head. The company is researching a "brain-machine interface" in which the TV would sense that you wanted to change channels, and would do so instantly. All the more reason to make friends with your technology, before your spouse does.

SOURCES: *"The Quotable Tycoon" by David Olive; "Eureka! Scientific Breakthroughs That Changed the World" by Leslie Alan Horvitz; "The Box: An Oral History of Television, 1920-1961" by Jeff Kisseloff; "Television Innovations" by Dicky Howett; "Please Stand By: A Prehistory of Television" by Michael Ritchie; "Canned Laughter" by Peter Hay, National Cable & Telecommunications Association; cbsnews.com; The Observer; ikegami.com; Penton Insight; TVNewser; snopes.com.*

TWINS

1   Many of us started out as twins, whether we know it or not. An estimated one in eight natural pregnancies begins that way. In the quite common "vanishing twin syndrome," one of the twins is reabsorbed by the mother during the first trimester while the other remains viable.

2   One in 80 deliveries in the United States results in twins, but the rate is much higher among the Yoruba ethnic group in Nigeria: One in 11 people is a twin. In ancient times, the Yoruba viewed twins with suspicion, and sometimes sacrificed them. But now twins are considered lucky. In contrast to the Western view, the firstborn twin is considered the younger of the two. The Yoruba believe that the "senior" twin sent the younger one out first to scout the world.

3   Peggy Lynn of Danville, Pa., delivered fraternal twins Eric and Hanna 84 days apart — one in November 1995, one in February 1996.

4   Fraternal twins can be the result of two acts of sexual intercourse that occur days apart. For that reason, it is possible for fraternal twins to have different fathers, as demonstrated in an 1810 case in the U.S. in which one child was white and the other was what people then called mulatto, mixed black and white.

5   Of particular interest to psychologists are lifelong "twinless twins," people whose twin died at or near birth. According to psychologist Peter Whitmer, such surviving twins go to great lengths to assert their uniqueness, yet often feel as if they're living for two people. Perhaps the most famous was Elvis Presley, whose identical twin brother, Jesse, was stillborn. Others include painter Diego Rivera, pianist Liberace and writers Thornton Wilder and Philip K. Dick.

6   Actresses Scarlett Johansson and Parker Posey are twins. No, not with each other. Each of them has a twin brother.

7 Frederick and Susan Machell were a happily married couple in Australia in the 1980s. They both knew they had been adopted and thought it was an amusing coincidence that they had been born in the same hospital on the same day. But after 20 years of marriage, they investigated further because their child had a genetically related illness. Yes, they were twins. But they stayed married anyhow.

8 Identical twins can vary markedly in certain skills. Jose Canseco had 7,057 at-bats in the major leagues and hit 462 home runs. His identical twin brother, Ozzie, had 65 at-bats with no homers. You might guess that Jose's edge was steroid use, but Ozzie was exposed in the steroid scandal too.

9 Painter Ivan Albright's meticulously detailed work is displayed at the Art Institute of Chicago and featured in the 1945 film "The Picture of Dorian Gray." But Ivan was only half of his own story. He had a twin named Malvin. The two attended the School of the Art Institute, flipping a coin to determine which of them would study painting and which would learn sculpture. Though the coin flip put Ivan in the painting classes, Malvin eventually embraced that medium as well, but less successfully. Malvin signed his paintings "Zsissly," so that when the twins' work was displayed together, the catalog would have Albrights at the beginning and the end.

10 Other famous twins: Diplomat Kofi Annan (sister), journalist Seymour Hersh (fraternal brother), model Gisele Bundchen (fraternal sister), actor Montgomery Clift (sister), actor Vin Diesel (fraternal brother), actor Ashton Kutcher (fraternal brother), singer-songwriter Alanis Morissette (brother), writer Sarah Vowell (fraternal sister) and actor Billy Dee Williams (sister).

SOURCES: *"Entwined Lives," by Nancy L. Segal; "The Inner Elvis," by Peter O. Whitmer; "Yoruba Customs and Beliefs Pertaining to Twins," in Twin Research (April 2002); salon.com; baseball-reference.com; Tribune archives and news services.*

AIR TRAVEL

1   A cat flew across the Atlantic Ocean eight years before Charles Lindbergh. The cat, named Wopsie or Whoopsie, was a stowaway aboard the dirigible R34 when it traveled from Scotland to New York in 1919. The cat wasn't the only creature who beat Lindy to a trans-Atlantic flight. More than 80 people also did. But Lindbergh was the first to fly solo.

2   Qantas, the Australian airline, is a former acronym for Queensland and Northern Territories Air Service. That name is strange, but others may be stranger. Airline pilot Patrick Smith, who writes a column for salon.com, suggested that two of the worst airline names ever were Russia's Kras Air ("always just an H away from infamy," wrote Smith) and Taiwan's U-Land Airlines ("That's right. U-buy, U-fly and U-Land it yourself.").

3   In 1987, American Airlines removed one olive from each first-class salad for a savings of about $40,000 a year. In a more recent cost-cutting move, American announced in 2004 that it would get rid of pillows on its MD-80 planes for an annual windfall of about $300,000. The next year, Northwest Airlines ditched free pretzels in coach class on its domestic flights, saving $2 million a year.

4   Joseph of Cupertino, a 17th century Italian priest, is a Roman Catholic patron saint of pilots and air passengers. Known as the "flying friar" because of his reported ability to levitate, Joseph annoyed his fellow churchmen, who banned him from attending choir or visiting the refectory for 35 years.

5   National Airlines launched an ad campaign in the early 1970s featuring attractive young flight attendants — then known as stewardesses — and slogans such as "I'm Margie. Fly me." A group called Stewardesses for Women's Rights picketed the airline's offices and complained to the Federal Trade Commission about the ads. National was forced to tone down the campaign by including other airline workers. But somehow the idea of "flying" someone like, say, Ralph the baggage handler seemed a bit less alluring.

6   The producers of the 1980 comedy film "Airplane!" considered talk show host David Letterman and singer Barry Manilow for the lead role of washed-up pilot Ted Striker before settling on actor Robert Hays. The co-pilot played by basketball great Kareem Abdul-Jabbar was originally written for baseball star Pete Rose. According to the Internet Movie Database, Rose was offered $30,000 but lost the part after asking for $35,000, which he wanted to spend on an Oriental rug.

7   Ten soldiers boarded a plane at California's Fort Hunter Liggett in the early 1960s, expecting a routine training mission. Instead, once they were airborne, the crew announced that an engine had stalled, the landing gear was inoperable and the plane would attempt to ditch in the ocean. Then the crew issued an odd demand: The soldiers would have to fill out insurance forms. After they dutifully did so, the plane landed, safely and routinely. The episode was an Army experiment to measure soldiers' performance under stress. Not surprisingly, a control group on the ground filled out the same insurance forms more accurately.

8   Passengers preparing to take off in 2008 on an Aeroflot jet from Moscow to New York revolted when the pilot appeared to slur his words over the loudspeaker. Officials of the Russian airline tried to calm them. According to the Moscow Times, an airline official said, "It's not such a big deal if the pilot is drunk. Really, all he has to do is press a button and the plane flies itself." But the passengers stood their ground, and the crew was replaced. The incident was another black eye for Aeroflot, remembered for a 1994 flight in which a pilot let his 15-year-old son take the controls. The boy accidentally disabled the autopilot, sending 75 people to their deaths.

9   When Amelia Earhart helped organize the New York, Philadelphia and Washington Airways in the early years of commercial aviation, the in-flight lunch consisted of hard-boiled eggs and saltine crackers, chosen because they seemed unlikely to contribute to airsickness.

10   A passenger boarded a Chicago-bound plane in Washington, D.C., in 2003 and handed a note to a flight attendant, asking her to take it to the pilot. The note read, "Fast. Neat. Average." The pilot had no idea what it meant and alerted authorities, who detained the passenger for questioning. The note was part of a well-known code at the Air Force Academy, based on cadets' answers on a dining-hall survey. If all had gone well, the passenger's note would have been returned with a note reading "Friendly. Good. Good," and the passenger would have been invited to visit the cockpit. But the pilot was not an Air Force grad, and the passenger missed his flight. As an Air Force spokesman noted, "Obviously, the world has changed since 2001."

SOURCES: *"Travia: The Ultimate Book of Travel Trivia" by Nadine Godwin; "Amelia: A Life of the Aviation Legend" by Donald M. Goldstein and Katherine V. Dillon; "How to Make a Tornado," a New Scientist book edited by Mick O'Hare; "Working the Skies" by Drew Whitelegg; London Telegraph; Sacramento Bee; Denver Post; "Ask the Pilot" by Patrick Smith on salon.com; imdb.com, straightdope.com; newadvent.org; snopes.com; consumerist.com.*

10 THINGS YOU MIGHT NOT KNOW ABOUT

FOOD/LEISURE

BEER

1 Why did the Pilgrims land at Plymouth Rock instead of pushing on to Virginia? Well, for one thing, they were nearly out of beer. A Mayflower passenger's diary reads: "We could not now take time for further search or consideration; our victuals being much spent, especially our beere."

2 In the 1600s and 1700s, midwives in Europe and Colonial America gave delivering mothers "groaning ale," which was fermented for seven or eight months and tapped when contractions began. After the birth, the child might even be bathed in the ale, since it was likely to be more sanitary than the water then available.

3 As president, James Madison proposed creation of a national brewery and appointment of a "secretary of beer." But Congress wouldn't go along. If such a Cabinet position existed today, who might fit it? Actor George Wendt of "Cheers," perhaps? Or Windell Middlebrooks, who portrays the Miller High Life truck driver who confiscates beer from overpriced establishments?

4 Beer can kill, but it usually doesn't do it nine at a time. The exception occurred in London in 1814 when the rupture of a brewery tank sent a giant wave of 3,500 barrels of beer cascading upon nearby residents. Two houses were demolished, and nine people died.

5 The North Side's Diversey Parkway and Lill Avenue were named after two early Chicago brewers, Michael Diversey and William Lill.

6 The Great Chicago Fire of 1871 devastated the local beer industry, allowing Milwaukee brewers to swoop in and seize market share. After grabbing a strong foothold in Chicago, Schlitz and other Milwaukee companies took advantage of Chicago's railroad hub to purvey their products across the country.

7 "The Guinness Book of World Records" was begun in 1955 at the suggestion of Guinness Brewery's top executive to settle gentlemanly disputes, such as those that would arise over mugs of beer.

8 Joe Charboneau, a Belvidere, Ill., native who played outfield for the Cleveland Indians in the early '80s, used to open beer bottles with his eye socket and drink beer through a straw in his nose.

9 You've heard of "beer goggles" — the idea that someone who has had a few quaffs finds members of the opposite sex more attractive. A study at Glasgow University in 2002 confirmed the effect. Tipsy students were 25 percent more likely to rate a person as sexually attractive than students who were sober.

10 During Prohibition, only "near beer" (less than 0.5 percent alcohol) could be sold. Such beer was sometimes illegally turned into high-octane "needle beer" when alcohol was injected into the barrel. The opposite of near beer might be called severe beer, such as Samuel Adams' Utopias. At 25 percent alcohol, its kick is five times as strong as Budweiser's. Reportedly, it tastes like cognac. It is so alcoholic that it violates the laws of 14 states, not including Illinois.

SOURCES: *"The Big Book O' Beer" by Duane Swierczynski; "From Beer to Eternity" by Will Anderson; "Beer: A History of Brewing in Chicago" by Bob Skilnik; snopes.com; samueladams. com; realbeer.com.*

CANDY

1   The Arabs are often credited with inventing caramel. But an early use of the hot, sticky substance was not so sweet: Women in harems applied it as a hair remover.

2   Most Americans knew nothing about chocolate in 1893, when the World's Columbian Exposition in Chicago featured a display of chocolate-making equipment from Germany. Among the fairgoers was Milton Hershey, who bought every piece of equipment on display and went into the chocolate business.

3   Early American chocolate-makers often touted their products' nutritional value. During the Depression, candy bars had such names as Chicken Dinner, Idaho Spud and Big Eats. The Hershey's chocolate wrapper once carried the slogan "More sustaining than meat."

4   The Chicago area has been at the center of the U.S. candy industry, producing such treats as Tootsie Rolls, Atomic Fireballs, Lemonheads, Baby Ruths, Butterfingers, Milk Duds, Milky Ways, 3 Musketeers, Snickers, Oh Henry! bars, Frango Mints, Cracker Jacks, Turtles, Doves, Jelly Bellies and Pixies. Candy historian Tim Richardson credits Chicago candymakers with popularizing the tradition of giving sweets to Halloween trick-or-treaters, calling it "a simple marketing ploy that emanated from the city's confectioners."

5   The Baby Ruth candy bar debuted in 1921, and even today the origin of the name remains in dispute. The Chicago-based Curtiss Candy Co. insisted that it named the bar after President Grover Cleveland's daughter Ruth. But some historians find it odd that a company would name a new candy after a girl who had died 17 years earlier. They also find it mighty suspicious that the candy's name was similar to that of baseball star Babe Ruth, who never collected royalties and was prevented from selling his own Babe Ruth Home Run Bar because of a Curtiss lawsuit.

6 When the Mars candy company marketed Snickers in Britain, it changed the name to Marathon to avoid any jokes about Snickers rhyming with knickers. (Many years later, Mars renamed Marathon as Snickers.)

7 Producers of the film "E.T." wanted to use M&Ms as the candy that lured the extraterrestrial from hiding. But when Mars said no, Hershey jumped at the chance to showcase Reese's Pieces instead. Sales soared.

8 Cotton candy is known as "candy floss" in Britain and "fairy floss" in Australia.

9 The rock band Van Halen had a contract clause requiring a bowl of M&Ms backstage at its concerts — but all of the brown M&Ms had to be removed. The clause is sometimes cited as an example of ridiculous rock-star demands, but it made practical sense, singer David Lee Roth has written. If a concert venue got the M&Ms wrong, it was a red flag that promoters hadn't read the contract closely and were likely to mess up on other, more important details.

10 The National Confectioners Association says 90 percent of parents admit sneaking Halloween goodies out of their kids' treat-or-treat bags.

SOURCES: *"The Emperors of Chocolate" by Joel Glenn Brenner; "Candy: The Sweet History" by Beth Kimmerle; "Sweets: A History of Candy" by Tim Richardson; candyusa.org; snopes.com.*

DRUNKENNESS

1   St. Cummian of Fota, a 7th Century Irish priest, distributed rules for the drinking clergy such as: "If a monk drinks till he vomits, he must do 30 days' penance; if a priest or deacon, 40 days. But if this happens from weakness of stomach, or from long abstinence, and he was not in the habit of excessive drinking or eating, or if he did it in excess of joy on Christmas or on Easter Days, or the commemoration of some saint, and if then he did not take more than has been regulated by our predecessors, he is not to be punished..."

2   Among the slang terms for being drunk: Ossified, boiled as an owl, squiffy, sozzled, torn off the frame, pie-eyed, seeing two moons, Boris Yeltsinned, locked out of your mind, three sheets to the wind and holding up the lamp-post. "Plotzed" is another term, based on the Yiddish word "platsn," meaning to crack, split or burst. Also, "gaysted" is slang for being so wasted that you flirt with men even though you are a heterosexual man.

3   In the 1820s, Michigan Territory Gov. Lewis Cass complained that the Midwest's Indians "give themselves up to the most brutal intoxication whenever this mad water can be procured." But sometimes it was procured from the U.S. government. Cass ordered 932 gallons of whiskey for the Ottawa, Chippewa and Potawatomi when they held treaty talks in Chicago in 1821.

4   W.C. Fields wasn't always a drunk. Quite the opposite. As a young man in vaudeville, his act demanded sobriety and precision: He was a juggler. Only later when he became a comedian did Fields also become a souse. "Always carry a flagon of whiskey in case of snakebite," he said. "And furthermore, always carry a small snake."

5   William Faulkner was stereotyped as a drunken novelist. But he rarely drank while writing and could abstain for long periods of time. He built his bad reputation through binges, such as the time at the Algonquin Hotel in New York when he drunkenly fell onto a radiator, badly burning himself. Faulkner's drinking was rivaled or surpassed by fellow Southern writers, such as Tennessee Williams and Carson McCullers. One summer in Nantucket, Williams and McCullers wrote in the same room while passing a whiskey bottle back and forth.

6 Drunkenness is a common excuse when people do stupid things. Rarer is it for a person to perform brilliantly and say he was "half drunk," as New York Yankees pitcher David Well did after throwing a perfect game in 1998. More accurate would be to say that Wells was hung over and sleep deprived, having partied until 5 a.m. and slept 3½ hours before reporting for a day game.

7 Imagine the shame of being considered a drunk when you haven't consumed any alcohol. That's the burden of some people who suffered inner-ear damage from the antibiotic gentamicin. Their poor sense of balance makes some people think they're boozers. They prefer the term "wobblers" and have formed a support group called Wobblers Anonymous.

8 Three co-workers went out drinking one night in 1990. Two of them shared seven pitchers of beer, and a third had 15 rum-with-colas. A few hours later, they reported for work — as the pilots of a Northwest Airlines Boeing 727. Their 91 passengers arrived safely on the flight from Fargo, N.D., to Minneapolis. The pilots were fired and served at least a year in prison.

9 Drunken driving is a scourge that has cost many innocent lives. But some civil libertarians believe preventive measures have overreached. Exhibit A: Keith Emerich, who was never accused of drunken driving but told his doctor he drank six or more beers a day at home after work. Pennsylvania law required the doctor to report anything that might impair a patient's driving ability, and in 2004 the state revoked Emerich's driver's license.

10 Dean Martin fostered a boozy reputation, sporting a vanity license plate of DRUNKY and declaring, "You're not drunk if you can lie on the floor without holding on." The singer commonly appeared onstage holding a whiskey glass, but it was often filled with apple juice.

SOURCES: *"Alcohol: The World's Favorite Drug" by Griffith Edwards; "Perfect I'm Not" by David Wells with Chris Kreski; "White Man's Wicked Water" by William E. Unrau; "Dean and Me" by Jerry Lewis and James Kaplan; "The Lonely Hunter" by Virginia Spencer Carr; Urban Dictionary; Moderndrunkardmagazine.com; doubletongued.org; Reason magazine; Newsweek; the Patriot-News of Pennsylvania; Tribune news services.*

EGGS

1   When the Bulls' Michael Jordan and Scottie Pippen were in their prime, Jordan liked to say that they were "ham-and-egging." Which meant that one of them would start strong and the other would finish strong. And opponents were toast.

2   At breakfast, President Woodrow Wilson drank two raw eggs in juice.

3   To demonstrate his versatility, the Japanese master artist Hokusai sometimes painted using the stick end of the brush, or with his fingers, or with chicken eggs.

4   Paul McCartney came up with the melody for "Yesterday" long before he had the words. While searching for just the right lyrics, he and John Lennon referred to the song as "Scrambled Eggs," which had the same meter as the eventual title. "We called it 'Scrambled Eggs' and it became a joke between us," Lennon said. "...Then one morning Paul woke up and the song and the title were both there, completed. I was sorry in a way, we'd had so many laughs about it."

5   A common numbers racket in the 1930s and '40s was called "butter and eggs." Gamblers would bet on the closing commodity prices for butter and eggs. Before that, a "butter-and-egg man" was slang for a visitor with a lot of money, a yokel ready to be separated from his funds.

6   In golfing slang, a ball half-buried in a sand bunker is called a "fried egg." In diner slang, if you want to order scrambled eggs on toast, you say, "Adam and Eve on a raft, and wreck 'em."

7   Nobody seems sure about the Benedict who was honored by eggs Benedict. According to one story, LeGrand Benedict, a customer at the famed New York restaurant Delmonico's, asked the chef to invent a new egg dish. But a rival story says the dish was inspired by Harry Benedict, a customer at the Waldorf Astoria in New York who wanted a meal to help him overcome a hangover.

8 The Easter bunny must have been wearing jackboots in Tumwater, Wash., in February 2006. Residents found neo-Nazi leaflets taped to plastic Easter eggs and scattered on their front lawns. The ethnic slurs were appalling, but residents found the Easter motif to be particularly offensive. "They shouldn't be doing the eggs," said Shirleyann Westman. "That's not right at all."

9 Joseph Coyle, who ran a small newspaper in the 1910s in British Columbia, quit the news business after inventing a different paper product: the egg carton.

10 Birds generally lay eggs that are 1 to 10 percent of their body weight. But the kiwi produces a single egg that is about a fifth of its weight. The San Diego Zoo's website compares it to a 120-pound human female giving birth to a 24-pound baby.

SOURCES: *"Hokusai: Life and Work" by Richard Lane; "The Berghoff Family Cookbook" by Carlyn Berghoff and Nancy Ross Ryan; "Eggs, Nests and Baby Dinosaurs" by Kenneth Carpenter; "Woodrow Wilson" by Arthur Walworth; "The Beatles Anthology" by the Beatles; "Cassell's Dictionary of Slang" by Jonathon Green; Seattle Times; Hiway 16 Magazine; king5.com; double-tongued.org; mygolfrounds.com; sandiegozoo.org; Tribune news services.*

10 THINGS YOU MIGHT NOT KNOW ABOUT
CHICAGO FOOD

1 Centuries ago, one place along Lake Michigan developed a stinky reputation. Smelly plants (variously described in history books as wild onions, leeks and garlic) grew so abundantly there that Indians referred to the place by the same word they used for the plants themselves and for skunks. That word sounded something like "Chicago."

2 During the Civil War, one of the most popular restaurants in Chicago was operated by two runaway slaves. Ambrose & Jackson, on Clark Street, fed such prominent people as Sen. Stephen A. Douglas, inventor-industrialist Cyrus McCormick and Chicago's first mayor, William Ogden.

3 Many people associate Wrigley Field with the Wrigley chewing gum company, but its origins had more to do with the fast-food industry. For its first few years, the ballpark was called Weeghman Park, in honor of co-owner Charles Weeghman, who operated a chain of quick-lunch places. The stadium at Clark and Addison was a pioneer in ballpark food, operating the first permanent concession stand.

4 As former Bears star Walter Payton was dying of a rare liver disease in 1999, he embarked on a gourmet mission with friend and former teammate Matt Suhey. They bought a Zagat's restaurant guide and resolved to eat at Chicago's 10 best restaurants before Payton died. "We picked out a few, but never got to finish the project," Suhey said.

5 When an anarchist attempted to kill many of Chicago's most powerful men in 1916, his weapon was chicken soup. At a welcoming banquet for new Roman Catholic archbishop George Mundelein that was attended by Illinois' governor, a former Chicago mayor and many titans of industry, a cook named Jean Crones spiked the soup with arsenic. While Mundelein said he felt no ill effects, many guests vomited amid the splendor of the University Club. But no one died. Crones' escape led to a series of reported sightings, including a tip that he was disguised as a nun in Pittsburgh. He was never captured.

6 The elaborate process of serving saganaki at Greek restaurants — setting the cheese on fire at the table, extinguishing the flames with lemon juice, and chanting "opaa!" — appears to be a Chicago invention. The Parthenon restaurant in Greektown claims credit.

7 Boxer Joe Louis' trainer, Chappie Blackburn, tried to toughen him up by taking him to Chicago's stockyards to drink blood from the slaughterhouse.

8 Deep-dish pizza was invented during the '40s in a lumber baron's former mansion at 29 E. Ohio St. — now the site of Pizzeria Uno. But the inventor is unclear, with credit going variously to restaurant co-owners Richard Novaretti (a.k.a. Ric Riccardo) and Ike Sewell and their employee, Rudy Malnati Sr. The invention of deep-dish pizza might not have happened if not for a twist of fate. At first, Sewell wanted to open a Mexican restaurant. But a test meal went wrong, sickening Riccardo. He suggested they try Italian instead.

9 Perhaps the most universal description of a Chicago-style hot dog is that it includes no ketchup. In November 1995, Tribune columnist Mike Royko denounced Sen. Carol Moseley Braun for including ketchup in a recipe that she (or her staff) contributed to a hot dog cookbook. He also didn't like the fact that she omitted celery salt.

10 Chicago-based potato chip entrepreneur Leonard Japp Sr. ran into a public relations problem: the Japanese attack on Pearl Harbor. His solution: Japp's became Jays Potato Chips.

SOURCES: *"Fabulous Chicago" by Emmett Dedmon; "The Man Who Got Away: The Bugs Moran Story" by Rose Keefe; "History of Cook County, Illinois," edited by Weston A. Goodspeed and Daniel D. Healy; "Never Die Easy: The Autobiography of Walter Payton" by Walter Payton with Don Yaeger; "The Olive and the Caper: Adventures in Greek Cooking" by Susanna Hoffman; "Secret Chicago: The Unique Guidebook to Chicago's Hidden Sites, Sounds & Tastes" by Sam Weller; "Crunch!: A History of the Great American Potato Chip" by Dirk Burhans; "For the Love of Mike: More of the Best of Mike Royko" by Mike Royko; "Encyclopedia of Chicago"; diningchicago. com; Tribune reporter James Janega; Tribune archives.*

ICE CREAM

1 Haagen-Dazs is not an exotic Scandinavian recipe. It's a brand name created by a Polish immigrant and his wife in the Bronx. Reuben Mattus' family sold ice cream for decades, but the product didn't really take off until the early 1960s, when Mattus and his wife, Rose came up with the Haagen-Dazs name out of thin air and put a map of Denmark on the carton. They used an umlaut (two dots) over the first letter "a" in Haagen even though there's no such usage in Danish.

2 The Evinrude outboard motor was invented because of ice cream. A young man named Ole Evinrude was picnicking with his fiance on a Wisconsin lake island in 1906 when she expressed interest in a dish of ice cream. Evinrude rowed to shore to satisfy her desire, and en route realized that if he had a motor, the errand would be a lot easier — and the ice cream would be less likely to melt. So inspired, he designed an outboard motor that made him famous.

3 When comedian Jackie Gleason dined out, he sometimes ordered roast beef with a scoop of ice cream on it.

4 In the ice cream industry, "overrun" is a term for the amount of air that's inserted into ice cream as it's produced. Without some aeration, ice cream would be a solid mass, difficult to scoop and serve. So overrun is a good thing, within limits: Cheaper ice cream has more overrun. Long before Margaret Thatcher became Britain's prime minister, she was a chemist investigating the air in ice cream. As the Times of London put it, she studied "methods for preserving the foamy quality of ice cream by injecting it with air."

5 Ice cream vendors in the Mexican town of Dolores Hidalgo have featured such flavors as beer, cheese, cactus petal, avocado, tequila, corn, black and red mole, pigskin and shrimp.

6 The Library of Congress houses many of Thomas Jefferson's writings, including a draft of the Declaration of Independence and his recipe for vanilla ice cream. Jefferson, an obsessive foodie, kept his ice house carefully stocked and corresponded with acquaintances in Paris to secure vanilla beans.

7 Who was the nation's first great ice cream entrepreneur? We nominate Augustus Jackson, an African-American. In the late 1820s — when nearly 2 million other black Americans were still in bondage — Jackson was a free man who left his job as a chef at the White House and moved to Philadelphia to establish a successful catering business that supplied ice cream to restaurants.

8 It's surprising that the Republicans didn't raise the ice cream issue against Barack Obama in 2008. Most Americans like ice cream; Obama apparently doesn't. In an "Access Hollywood" interview during the campaign, Obama's daughter Malia said: "Ice cream is my favorite food. I could eat ice cream forever." Then Obama's younger daughter, Sasha, said: "Everybody should like ice cream. Except Daddy. My dad doesn't like sweets." Perhaps Obama's distaste stems from his part-time job at Baskin-Robbins as a teenager in Hawaii. But one of the most romantic scenes in the Obama biography also involves ice cream. On his first date with Michelle Robinson, Obama took her to a Baskin-Robbins. He later described the scene: "I asked if I could kiss her. It tasted of chocolate."

9 When actor Clint Eastwood ran for mayor of Carmel, Calif., in 1986, a major issue was ice cream. Town leaders had banned the sale of ice cream cones, incensing Eastwood and his supporters. They won, and overturned the ordinance.

10 People for the Ethical Treatment of Animals wrote a letter to Ben & Jerry's in 2008 urging the company to start making its ice cream with the milk of nursing mothers rather than the milk of cows. A PETA spokeswoman acknowledged that the idea was "somewhat absurd" but said it was intended to publicize the alleged cruelty of the dairy industry. There was no comment from People for the Ethical Treatment of Nursing Mothers.

SOURCES: *International Dairy Foods Association; Tribune reporter Hugh Dellios; "The Great Clowns of American Television" by Karin Adir; "Slavery in the United States" by Jenny B. Wahl of Carleton College on eh.net; "Ice: Great Moments in the History of Hard, Cold Water" by Karal Ann Marling; "Famous Wisconsin Inventors & Entrepreneurs" by Marv Balousek; "The Scoop" by Lori Longbotham; "Chocolate, Strawberry and Vanilla" by Anne Cooper Funderburg; "The Audacity of Hope" by Barack Obama; evinrude.com; San Francisco Chronicle; Tribune news services.*

MARIJUANA

1 In 19th Century Nepal, the marijuana harvest was performed by men who ran naked through fields of flowering plants and then had the sticky resin scraped off their bodies and formed into bricks of hashish.

2 Marijuana is known for its mellowing effect, but it has fueled many warriors in history. The word "assassin" is believed to come from the hashish used a millennium ago by Middle Eastern killers (called "hashshashin" or "hashish eaters"), though some historians doubt they were under the influence while on their missions. Mexican bandit Pancho Villa's henchmen were pot smokers. And some believe Zulu fighters in southern Africa were high on dagga — a.k.a. marijuana — when they attacked the Boers at Blood River in 1838. The Zulus lost 3,000 fighters, while only four Boers were wounded. Talk about a buzzkill.

3 Louisa May Alcott, author of "Little Women," wrote a short story called "Perilous Play" about marijuana. In it, a character declares, "If someone does not propose a new and interesting amusement, I shall die of ennui!" Another character produces a box of hashish-laced bonbons, and hedonism ensues.

4 Around 1900, the U.S. government briefly grew marijuana along a stretch of the Potomac River to study the plant's medicinal value. A more potent plant has since risen on that site: the Pentagon.

5 A white Chicago jazz musician named Milton "Mezz" Mezzrow moved to Harlem in 1929, declared himself a "voluntary Negro," and began selling marijuana. Known as "The Man Who Hipped the World" and "The Link Between the Races," Mezzrow sold fat joints called mezzrolls. Soon a new piece of Harlem slang emerged: Something genuine was described as "mezz."

6 Marijuana interferes with short-term memory so that users forget what they just said or did. Not only that, marijuana interferes with short-term memory so that users forget what they just said or did.

7   Billy Carter, the late brother of former President Jimmy Carter, believed the illegality of marijuana was part of its attraction. "Marijuana is like Coors beer," he said. "If you could buy the damn stuff at a Georgia filling station, you'd decide you wouldn't want it."

8   Before Congress voted to ban marijuana in 1937, the birdseed industry got the bill amended to exempt marijuana seeds (known as hemp seeds) as long as they were sterilized and could not be used to grow plants. An industry spokesman denied that the seeds made birds high, but an ardent marijuana foe, Dr. Victor Robinson, had previously written that the seeds had caused birds to "dream of a happy birdland where there are no gilded cages, and where the men are gunless and the women hatless."

9   One of the least typical supporters of the decriminalization of marijuana was conservative icon William F. Buckley, who died in 2008. Buckley once sailed his yacht into international waters so that he could smoke pot without breaking U.S. laws.

10   Former President Bill Clinton said famously that he smoked marijuana but "didn't inhale." Former President George W. Bush never admitted taking the drug, but his drug use was strongly suggested in recorded conversations between him and a friend — the interestingly named Doug Wead. Two of the top 2008 presidential contenders, Hillary Clinton and John McCain, denied that they had ever smoked pot. Barack Obama, on the other hand, said, "When I was a kid, I inhaled frequently. That was the point."

SOURCES: *"Marihuana, The First Twelve Thousand Years," by Ernest L. Abel; "Marijuana: Opposing Viewpoints," edited by Jamuna Carroll; Encyclopedia Britannica; High Times; Tribune news services.*

MEAT

1 The Roman emperor Elagabalus ordered 600 ostriches killed so his cooks could make ostrich-brain pies.

2 A 1655 book by English physician Thomas Muffett advocated torturing animals before slaughter to make them more tender as food. The book said animals should be killed slowly and painfully, with "fear dissolving the hardest parts."

3 Jesse James refused to rob a bank in McKinney, Texas, because his favorite chili parlor was in the same building.

4 On a 1965 space flight, astronaut John Young smuggled a corned beef sandwich on board for crew mate Virgil "Gus" Grissom.

5 In 1971, when Tokyo got its first McDonald's, the company's Japanese partner, Den Fujita, made this politically incorrect statement: "The reason Japanese people are so short and have yellow skins is that they have eaten nothing but fish and rice for 2,000 years. If we eat McDonald's hamburgers and potatoes for 1,000 years, we will become taller, our skin will become white, and our hair will become blond."

6 Chicago artist Dwight Kalb made a statue of Madonna from 180 pounds of ham.

7 Turkeys have been bred to have such large breasts that they can't have sex and must be artificially inseminated.

8 Jazz trumpeter Dizzy Gillespie gave up meat around age 60, explaining: "My intestines wrote me a letter."

9 There's no chicken in chicken fried steak, so why is it called that? Probably because the beefsteak is coated in flour or batter, much as is done with fried chicken. Like many Southerners, Elvis Presley loved chicken fried steak, which he called "ugly steak."

10 In Francois Mitterrand's dying days in 1995, the retired French leader ate an illegal dish: the ortolan, an endangered bird that is turned into dinner in a most cruel way. The small birds are captured alive, their eyes are poked out, they are force-fed millet, then they are drowned in Armagnac liqueur. Roasted and put into the diner's mouth whole, they are eaten bones and all. Mitterrand devoured ortolan in the traditional French way, with a linen napkin over his head. Some say the napkin helps capture the aroma of the roasted bird; others say the person who eats an ortolan is merely hiding from God.

SOURCES: *"The Food Chronology" by James Trager; "The Great Food Almanac" by Irena Chalmers; "The Encyclopedia of American Food and Drink" by John F. Mariani; "Jazz Cooks" by Bob Young and Al Stankus; People magazine; foodtimeline.com; London Daily Telegraph; Tribune news services.*

SALT

1 Salt has seasoned English in many ways. Because Romans put salt or brine on their vegetables, the word "salad" developed. Because Roman soldiers were given money to buy salt, "salary" was coined.

2 "Glitter" is 1950s prison slang for salt.

3 In promoting the Louisiana Purchase, President Thomas Jefferson cited reports of a "salt mountain" in the territory. "This mountain is said to be 180 miles long and 45 in width, composed of solid rock salt, without any trees or even shrubs on it." The New York Evening Post mockingly asked whether there was "an immense lake of molasses, too." The salt mountain was never found; some think the reports referred to Oklahoma's Great Salt Plains.

4 The adult human body contains about 250 grams of salt — about half a pound.

5 According to a superstition, spilling salt can cause bad luck — an idea that may have originated with Leonardo da Vinci's painting "The Last Supper," which shows Judas Iscariot knocking over a salt container.

6 Dozens of advice books tell the story of a job applicant who went to lunch with his prospective boss, only to lose the job because he salted his food before tasting it — thus demonstrating a closed mind. But one of the most famous Americans, Elvis Presley, routinely showered his food with salt before taking a single bite.

7 Chicago is America's salty center, thanks to the Morton Salt Co. The company was owned by Joy Morton, a man who got his first name from the maiden name of his mother, Caroline Joy. Morton's father was agriculture secretary under President Grover Cleveland and is credited with starting Arbor Day. Reminders of the family's philanthropy include the Morton Arboretum in Lisle and the Morton Wing of the Art Institute of Chicago.

8 Though salt is necessary for human life, overconsumption contributes to heart disease and other problems. However, modern table salt addresses a separate health concern: iodine deficiency, which can cause low IQ and goiter, an enlargement of the thyroid gland. A century ago, goiter was so prevalent around the Great Lakes that the area was considered part of a "goiter belt." Doctors pushed for adoption of a Swiss tactic of adding iodine to table and cooking salt, and Morton Salt began selling its iodized salt in 1924.

9 Michael Jordan's mother, Deloris, and sister, Roslyn, wrote a children's book in 2000 called "Salt in His Shoes," about how young Michael was upset about being smaller than his basketball-playing friends and was comforted when his mom told him he would grow taller if he put salt in his shoes and prayed.

10 There is an enormous salt mine under the city of Detroit, about 1,200 feet below ground. According to Detroit Salt Co., the century-old mine spreads out more than 1,500 acres and has more than 100 miles of underground roads.

SOURCES: *"Salt: A World History" by Mark Kurlansky; "Salted: A Manifesto on the World's Most Essential Mineral" by Mark Bitterman; "Cassell's Dictionary of Slang" by Jonathon Green; "Dictionary of Word Origins" by Jordan Almond; "Thomas Jefferson and the New Nation" by Merrill D. Peterson; "The Road to Monticello" by Kevin J. Hayes; "The Story Behind Salt" by Heidi Moore; International Council for the Control of Iodine Deficiency Disorders; mortonarb.org; mortonsalt.com; detroitsalt.com; wadeburleson.org; Detroit News.*

TOMATOES

1 The tomato originated in South and Central America, and the earliest variety was probably a yellow cherry tomato. The Aztecs, who called them "tomatl," grew an amazing variety, including the bigger, red fruit we know today.

2 Originally, there was no tomato in ketchup. Early versions relied on such ingredients as fish, vinegar, shallots and wine. The origin of the word "ketchup" is debatable, but one popular theory traces it to the word "ke-tsiap" from China's Amoy dialect, meaning "the brine of pickled fish."

3 When Nelson Mandela was a political prisoner in South Africa, he grew tomatoes and other produce, carefully studying proper soils and fertilizers. Knowing that his letters were censored, he sometimes wrote in metaphor, including two letters to his wife, Winnie, about how he had nurtured a tomato plant only to see it wither and die. He later said the story reflected his worries about their marriage.

4 Seeds of the Galapagos tomato — unique to the islands lying 600 miles west of Ecuador — need to be softened for a few weeks in the digestive system of a giant tortoise to germinate. This also helps disperse the plant because even a giant tortoise gets around in a few weeks.

5 Latomatina.org, the official website of the famous tomato throwing festival in Bunol, Spain, offers a number of tips. They include: Bring a change of clothing (because you can't get on the bus out of town soaked in tomatoes), wear goggles (acidic tomato juice really stings) and squash the tomato before you throw it (the goal isn't to hurt anyone).

6 Ever heard of a tomato called Radiator Charlie's Mortgage Lifter? A West Virginia auto mechanic named M.C. Byles, aka Radiator Charlie, crossbred large tomatoes in the 1930s and came up with a whopper that he sold for $1 a plant, making enough money that it was appropriately called the Mortgage Lifter.

7 When Romanian dictator Nicolae Ceausescu visited New York City in 1978, protesters threw tomatoes and eggs at his motorcade. Ceausescu protested to Mayor Ed Koch, who downplayed the incident, asking, "A couple of tomatoes and a few eggs?" Responded Ceausescu: "They could have been hand grenades." The dictator joined a long history of tomato targets. Others include Margaret Thatcher, Sarah Palin, Frank Sinatra and Cubs slugger Hack Wilson. And the Paris debut of Igor Stravinsky's "Rite of Spring" was tainted by tomato tossers.

8 Europeans once thought the tomato was poisonous — and not without reason. The plant is related to deadly nightshade, and tomato leaves are toxic in quantity. German legend held that nightshade could be used to summon werewolves, so the earliest German name for tomato translated to "wolf peach." It took centuries for the tomato to repair its reputation.

9 Tomatoes are far and away the most popular grow-it-yourself food. According to the National Gardening Association, 86 percent of the nation's backyard plots included tomatoes in 2009. The cucumber was a distant second at 47 percent.

10 If the fruit or vegetable debate confuses you, you're not alone. The U.S. Supreme Court muddied the issue way back in 1893 when it ruled — for tax purposes and contrary to scientific fact — that the tomato was a vegetable. The court's reasoning: People eat them at dinner and not for dessert. The federal government famously weighed in again in 1981 when the Reagan administration, in an attempt to save money, briefly suggested that tomato ketchup should satisfy the vegetable requirement for school lunches. Finally, Arkansas declared in 1987 that the tomato was both the state fruit and the state vegetable.

SOURCES: *"In Praise of Tomatoes" by Ronni Lundy with John Stehling; "Pure Ketchup" by Andrew F. Smith; Federal News Service; "Long Walk to Freedom" by Nelson Mandela; "Part of My Soul Went With Him" by Winnie Mandela; "Red Horizons: The True Story of Nicolae and Elena Ceausescus' Crimes, Lifestyle, and Corruption" by Ion Mihai Pacepa; "The Great Tomato Book" by Gary Ibsen with Joan Nielsen; U.S. Supreme Court's "Nix v. Hedden"; "The Galapagos" by Robert I. Bowman; "Ecology and Evolution: Islands of Change" by Richard Benz; "Galapagos: A Natural History" by John C. Kricher; "Eat Your Food! Gastronomical Glory From Garden to Gut" by Aaron Brachfeld and Mary Choate; National Gardening Association; Journal of Laboratory and Clinical Medicine; Latomatina.org; Tribune archives.*

TOYS

1 Play-Doh was invented as a wallpaper cleaner.

2 When Milton Bradley bought the concept for a game called Pretzel, it changed the name to Twister. The game soared in popularity in 1966 after Johnny Carson played it with actress Eva Gabor on his television show.

3 The Chicago area has been a healthy playground for toymakers. The Radio Flyer red metal wagon was born in Chicago, and the headquarters remains here, though the metal wagons are now made in China. Tinkertoys were designed in Evanston by Charles Pajeau. Donald Duncan, a businessman from Oak Park, popularized the yo-yo, bringing joy to millions, but perhaps not making up for his nefarious promotion of another product, the dreaded parking meter.

4 The 1964 television special "Rudolph the Red-Nosed Reindeer" featured the Island of Misfit Toys, where unwanted playthings were exiled. The original program omitted the misfits in its happy ending — an oversight that brought viewer complaints. For the rebroadcast the next year, footage was added to show Santa delivering the misfits on Christmas Eve.

5 Gumby toys were ubiquitous in the 1960s as the television show gained popularity. The claymation character's name came from Michigan farm slang: Creator Art Clokey's father referred to a muddy clay road as a "gumbo."

6 You know her as Barbie. But her full name is Barbara Millicent Roberts. By various estimates, 10 percent to 25 percent of adults who collect Barbies are men — not that there's anything wrong with that.

7 When Hooters waitress Jodee Berry won a 2001 beer-sales contest at her Florida restaurant, she thought the prize was a Toyota. Instead, the restaurant gave her a "toy Yoda" — a "Star Wars" doll — in what her manager called an April Fool's joke. Berry laughed all the way to her lawyer's office. The case was settled, with Berry getting enough money to buy a car, the lawyer said.

8 llinois-based RC2 Corp., maker of Thomas the Tank Engine, recalled more than 1 million of its wooden trains in 2007 because of lead paint from China. Then RC2 sent free boxcars to aggrieved customers as a goodwill gesture. Trouble was, some of those boxcars had lead paint too.

9 You know it's a bad, bizarre year for toys when a children's product is mentioned in the same sentence as "date-rape drug." In November 2007, 4 million craft kits called Aqua Dots were recalled because their beads were coated with a chemical that metabolizes into the drug GHB when swallowed. A Chinese company had substituted a cheaper — and toxic — chemical for the proper one. The Australian version of Aqua Dots, called Bindeez, had the same problem, and from now on will be coated in Bitrex, an extremely bitter "taste aversive" agent that discourages kids from putting it in their mouths.

10 In 2005, the Mujahedeen Brigades posted a grainy picture on a website, claiming it showed a U.S. soldier named John Adam who had been captured in Iraq and soon would be beheaded. But the U.S. military said no such soldier was missing. The hoax was exposed when a California toymaker reported that the soldier looked an awful lot like Cody, its foot-tall doll.

SOURCES: *"Warman's 101 Greatest Baby Boomer Toys" by Mark Rich; Fortune magazine; Tribune archives and news services.*

TURKEY

1 Hunting a wild turkey is exceedingly difficult. The bird may appear dumb and slow, but looks can be deceiving. In fact, Tom Turkey has fantastic hearing, amazing eyesight, can flat-out run (15 mph and three-foot strides) and can fly even faster. And he is paranoid — because everyone is out to get him — so he'll flee at the slightest provocation.

2 Eccentric billionaire Howard Hughes liked Swanson's frozen TV dinners, especially the turkey entree. But Hughes was a picky eater. He didn't approve of Swanson's mixing of white and dark meat. And he wished the dinner came with a dessert of peach cobbler rather than apple cobbler. Through an aide, Hughes asked Swanson's to switch to peach cobbler in its turkey dinners. When Swanson's refused, Hughes tried to buy the company but was unsuccessful.

3 In the spring, a wild male turkey's head can turn a brilliant red, white or blue, often changing in just seconds. That fact was not one of Benjamin Franklin's arguments for why the turkey would be a better national symbol than the bald eagle.

4 Joe Engel, an executive with the minor league Chattanooga Lookouts baseball team, was famous for stunts, such as having his players ride into the ballpark on elephants. The topper came in 1931 when he traded his shortstop to Charlotte for a Thanksgiving turkey. The trade turned out badly, he said, because the turkey meat was tough.

5 Before the Turkey Trot became the go-to name for a 5K race in November, it was a controversial ragtime-style dance in the early 1900s. It was considered quite vulgar, and it was often banned, which, of course, just made it insanely popular.

6 Italian composer Gioacchino Rossini claimed that he wept only three times in his life: when his opera "Tancredi" was booed on opening night, when he heard Nicolo Paganini play the violin and when his truffle-stuffed turkey fell out of a boat during a picnic.

7 Playwright Arthur Miller and his wife, photographer Inge Morath, were counterfeit carnivores during Thanksgiving. "Since we're vegetarians," Morath told The New York Times in 1981, "I usually make a pretend turkey out of vegetables — a piece montee. I put a loaf of bread underneath, and over the top I arrange carrots, leeks, beans, apples, all kinds of cold cooked and raw vegetables, Chinese vegetables bought at Korean markets, like a painting. With pieces of avocado I make beautiful wings. It looks more like a live turkey than a dead one."

8 If an adult male turkey is a tom, what's a young male turkey? A jake.

9 During family Christmas celebrations, Gen. George Patton turned the carving of the turkey into a circus act. He waved the knife like a saber, explained that the warrior Saladin wielded a sword so sharp it could cut a floating feather in half, then he shouted a rebel yell and plunged a carving fork into the turkey's breast. His daughter Ruth Ellen recalled: "Then he would carefully withdraw the fork, put his ear to the turkey's breast, nod in a sad, wise way, and say, 'She's gone alright,' and then start carving."

10 If you feel like taking a nap after your Thanksgiving feast, don't blame the turkey. The whole tryptophan-in-the-turkey-makes-you-sleepy idea is a myth. In fact, turkey doesn't contain any more tryptophan than many other meats. The real culprit is the sheer quantity of food you just inhaled.

SOURCES: *"Hunting Tough Turkeys" by Brian Lovett; "Hunting the First State: A Guide to Delaware Hunting" by Steven Kendus; "Howard Hughes: The Hidden Years" by James Phelan; "The Private Correspondence of Benjamin Franklin, Vol. 1"; National Wildlife Turkey Federation; "The Gourmet Cookbook," edited by Ruth Reichl; "The Wicked Waltz and Other Scandalous Dances" by Mark Knowles; "General Patton: A Soldier's Life" by Stanley Hirshson; heritagetur- keyfoundation.org; snopes.com; baseball-reference.com; engelfoundation.com; New York Times; Tribune archives.*

10 THINGS YOU MIGHT NOT KNOW ABOUT

PLACES

FRANCE

1   The French don't call someone an April fool. They use the term poisson d'avril — an April fish.

2   Who says the French are rude? When Marie Antoinette was taken to the guillotine, she stepped on the foot of her executioner, and her last words were: "Monsieur, I beg your pardon. I did not do it on purpose."

3   On the night of May 23, 1920, French President Paul Deschanel was traveling by train and retired to his car early. A few hours later, a man wearing pajamas showed up along railroad tracks south of Paris, claiming he had fallen off a train. It was Deschanel. Aides explained that Deschanel had opened a window to get a breath of fresh air and fallen out, unnoticed.

4   French author Georges Perec wrote a novel, "La Disparition," without using the letter "e." The English translation is titled "A Void," and most readers indeed have avoided it. Perec, who died in 1982, engaged in other literary gymnastics, such as taking famous poems and replacing each word with the seventh word after it in the dictionary.

5   Some of history's greatest military figures have been French, including Napoleon Bonaparte and Joan of Arc. And if the French hadn't helped the American revolutionaries defeat the British, we might be eating bangers and mash today. Yet some Americans insult the French as "cheese-eating surrender monkeys." When France balked at helping the U.S. invade Iraq in 2003, conservative commentator Jed Babbin said, "Going to war without France is like going deer hunting without an accordion. You just leave a lot of useless, noisy baggage behind." Even today, if you type "French military victories" into Google, one of the first hits is a joke site that mimics Google and asks, "Did you mean 'French military defeats.'"

6 A prominent French-basher in 2003 was Rep. Bob Ney (R-Ohio), who ordered the House cafeterias to refer to french fries as freedom fries. Four years later, Ney lost his own freedom when he was imprisoned in a bribery scandal. Ney's payoffs had included free trips to places such as New Orleans, home of the French, er, Freedom Quarter.

7 France has a special relationship with African-Americans. During World War I, black American soldiers, including Chicago's "Fighting 8th" regiment, served under French command because the racist U.S. military would not allow them into battle. African-American emigres such as writer James Baldwin and entertainer Josephine Baker were welcome there.

8 Parisian night watchman Noel Carriou was convicted of killing two wives because they were bad cooks. One wife, he complained, undercooked the roast. The other overcooked it. For his second conviction, in 1978, he got only eight years. In passing such a light sentence, the sympathetic judge noted that good cooking is an important part of marriage.

9 In May 2007, Republican presidential candidate Mitt Romney declared that among the French, "I'm told that marriage is now frequently contracted in seven-year terms where either party may move on when their term is up." A Romney spokesman later conceded there was no such French tradition. Even so, marriage is indeed slipping there. In the last generation, the French marriage rate has plunged more than 30 percent, and is close to half of the U.S. rate.

10 French President Nicolas Sarkozy might be lucky to spend even seven years with Carla Bruni, considering what she told Le Figaro newspaper: "Monogamy bores me terribly."

SOURCES: *"Marie Antoinette" by John Hearsey; "5 People Who Died During Sex" by Karl Shaw; "The Best, Worst and Most Unusual" by Bruce Felton and Mark Fowler; "The Crazy Years: Paris in the Twenties" by William Wiser; Time magazine; London Telegraph; Tribune news services.*

IRAN

1 Iran is a major exporter of crude oil, but it has to import gasoline because of its limited refinery capability. This shortcoming would make Iran particularly vulnerable to any blockade.

2 The CIA helped overthrow Iran's democratically elected government and installed a dictator in 1953. The joint U.S.-British covert action known as Operation Ajax turned Prime Minister Mohammed Mossadegh into a political prisoner and led to decades of repression, torture and assassination under Shah Mohammad Reza Pahlavi.

3 Barely half of Iranians — 53 percent — speak the official language, Farsi, or a dialect of Farsi as their primary language. Iran has sizable and sometimes restive minorities, including Azeris and Kurds. (And while we're talking about ethnic groups, let's remember that Iran is not an Arab nation.)

4 Iran's fundamentalist Islamic leaders have a well-earned reputation as repressors of women's rights, imposing strictures on how women dress and even a ban on women attending soccer matches. But more than half the country's university students are women, and female literacy is relatively high: 70 percent, compared with 64 percent in Iraq, 59 percent in Egypt and 48 percent in India.

5 Although white-bearded clerics are familiar symbols of Iran, the nation's young people may be as powerful a force. The country's median age is 26.8, way below the U.S. median, which is 37.2 and climbing. Until 2007, Iranian 15-year-olds were allowed to vote. The age limit was raised to 18 after elections embarrassing to Mahmoud Ahmadinejad.

6 Iran, whose president has called for the destruction of Israel, has the second-highest Jewish population in the Middle East. (Israel, of course, is first.) Ahmadinejad has expressed support for Iran's 25,000 Jews by donating money to the Jewish hospital in Tehran. But his extreme statements about Israel and the Holocaust have made him a loathed figure in many quarters.

Long ago, another Iranian leader was a hero to the Jewish people: Cyrus the Great conquered Babylon (in present-day Iraq) in 539 B.C. and freed the Israelites from slavery.

7 The ancient Iranians (also known as Persians) were pioneers in mathematics and architecture. The world's first windmills were created in Iran, as was one of the world's oldest monotheistic religions, Zoroastrianism.

8 Possession of 30 grams or more of heroin is punishable by death in Iran. Still, the country has one of the highest heroin addiction rates in the world. In a population of 79 million, an estimated 1.2 million to 3.5 million Iranians use heroin or opium. (It is next door to the world's leading opium producer, Afghanistan.)

9 Satellite dishes are common in Iran despite an official ban and sporadic roundups. In recent years, Oprah Winfrey's show was especially popular. Dozens of unauthorized television and radio stations beam their signals into Iran, a few of them funded by the U.S. and many of them based in Los Angeles, where the large Iranian community is nicknamed "Tehrangeles."

10 In past visits, Tribune correspondents have found that Iranians generally like Americans. After chanting "Death to America" at Friday prayers, a group of Iranian women asked a Tribune correspondent where she was from. When told America, one woman said, "Oh, we didn't mean you. It's just something we say." Another woman gave our correspondent an apple.

SOURCES: *CIA Factbook; cnn.com; unmultimedia.org; thefix.com; Tribune archives and news services.*

OHIO

1 Eight U.S. presidents have hailed from Ohio, and half have died in office. The last of them was likely the worst of them: Warren Harding, who was chosen as the 1920 Republican nominee by party bosses in the original "smoke-filled room" at Chicago's Blackstone Hotel. While Harding spent his career philandering, his cronies were busy filling their pockets. More sordid details are expected in 2014 when the Library of Congress is allowed to unseal Harding's love letters to a secret paramour. Those who have seen the letters say Harding was an even worse poet than president.

2 Cleveland is a typo. The city's founder was Moses Cleaveland, and even today there's no consensus for why the letter A disappeared in the 1830s. Among the theories: A local newspaper editor dumped the 'A' because it didn't fit on the masthead; an early map contained a spelling error; or store signs posted by brothers named Cleveland made residents think that was the city's correct spelling.

3 Ohio once went to war with Michigan — and not just on the football field. The Toledo War of 1835 was a dispute over 500 square miles of land, including the town of Toledo. Militias from Ohio and Michigan confronted each other along the Maumee River, but reportedly the only injury was a single stab wound to the leg. The federal government settled the issue: Ohio got Toledo, and Michigan received the western Upper Peninsula.

4 Halle Berry, born in Cleveland, was named after the city's now-defunct Halle Brothers department store chain. The Oscar-winning actress is part of an impressive cast of African-Americans from Ohio. They include Nobel Prize-winning author Toni Morrison of Lorain; poets Paul Laurence Dunbar of Dayton and Rita Dove of Akron; Olympic hero Jesse Owens of Cleveland; and comedian Dave Chappelle, who lives on a farm outside Yellow Springs.

5 Chef Boyardee was no Betty Crocker or Aunt Jemima — he was a real person. Italian immigrant Hector Boiardi ran a restaurant in Cleveland whose spaghetti sauce was so popular that he began manufacturing it for home cooking.

6 Ohio wasn't officially admitted into the union until 1953. Back in 1803, Congress approved the state's constitution but neglected to adopt a resolution formally accepting it as the 17th state. A century and a half later, historians noticed the oversight, which was rectified by Congress and President Dwight Eisenhower.

7 Ohio is home to the Rock and Roll Hall of Fame, so you would think that the "official state rock song" would be world-class. Instead, it's "Hang On Sloopy," popularized by a Dayton group called the McCoys in 1965. The song is a favorite at Ohio State football games.

8 Among the greatest Ohioans were the Wright brothers, bicycle-makers from Dayton who made the first powered airplane flight. But while Orville and Wilbur are remembered as pioneers, they impeded the development of aviation by filing incessant lawsuits against business competitors. Some historians believe the lawsuit-happy Wrights are a major reason U.S. aviators in World War I had to fly foreign-made planes

9 The Longaberger Basket Co.'s headquarters in Newark, Ohio, is a seven-story building shaped like a basket.

10 The logo of the Chicago International Film Festival features the eyes of an Ohioan named Theda Bara, the original "vamp" of silent films. Her movie studio invented an exotic back story for her, noting that her name was an anagram for "Arab Death" and claiming that her father was a French artist and her mother was an Arab princess. In truth, she was Theodosia Goodman, a bookish, middle-class Jewish girl from Cincinnati.

SOURCES: *Tribune news services; Ohio Historical Society; Cleveland Plain Dealer; Detroit Free Press; snopes.com.*

TEXAS

1 The congressional resolution that brought Texas into the union in 1845 allowed it to be subdivided into five separate states. Such a partition has never been seriously considered, to the Democrats' relief. Otherwise, there might be 10 Republican senators from what is now Texas.

2 The Confederates won the last battle of the Civil War. It took place at Palmito Ranch, Texas, a month after the war effectively ended with Robert E. Lee's surrender at Appomattox Court House, Va. Three Union regiments attacked a rebel camp at Palmito Ranch and were driven back, with more than 100 soldiers killed.

3 The King Ranch in south Texas covers nearly 1,300 square miles — bigger than all of Cook County and DuPage County combined.

4 The founders of Reklaw, Texas, wanted to call the town Walker, but that name was taken, so they spelled it backward. Same for the settlers of Sacul, whose first choice was Lucas. Then there's the town of Uncertain, Texas. According to one story, town fathers hadn't picked a name when they sent their application to the state, so they wrote "uncertain" on the form, planning to choose the name later.

5 Texas has produced some eccentric members of Congress. When newly elected Rep. J.J. Pickle arrived in Washington, President Lyndon Johnson sent a limousine to the airport and invited him to stay at the White House. Pickle sent the limo back empty, explaining that he had arranged to stay with a friend and it would be rude to change his plans. Then there's Rep. Sheila Jackson Lee, whom critics call "Hurricane Sheila" because she once complained that hurricanes didn't have distinctly African-American names. And let's not forget Rep. Tom DeLay, who posed for one of the happiest police booking shots ever. Accused of conspiracy and money-laundering, DeLay apparently decided that if he looked miserable in his mug shot, it would give comfort to his enemies.

6 Since 1976, more people have been executed for crimes committed in Texas' Harris County (home of Houston) than in any state outside Texas. During that time, about 4 in 10 U.S. executions have been in Texas. A state website once included a list of condemned prisoners' last meals, but it was removed after complaints of bad taste. According to the book "Texas Curiosities," one prisoner requested dirt as his last meal because he wanted to use it in a voodoo ritual. "He did not get dirt; he got yogurt," said Texas correctional spokeswoman Michelle Lyons.

7 The Dr Pepper Museum is in Waco, which is appropriate because the soft drink was invented there and was originally known as a "Waco." There is no truth to the legend that the drink includes prune juice, but it is indeed true that there's no period after "Dr" in its name.

8 Texans love their nicknames, but not all of them are officially sanctioned. Gubernatorial candidate Richard "Kinky" Friedman was allowed to put his nickname on the ballot in 2006, but rival Carole Keeton "Grandma" Strayhorn had to drop her nickname. Poker legend Doyle Brunson became "Texas Dolly" after Jimmy "the Greek" Snyder tried to introduce him as "Texas Doyle." Either Snyder mispronounced the name or reporters heard it wrong. Either way, it was printed as "Texas Dolly," and the name stuck.

9 Two musical daughters of Texas who died too young, Janis Joplin and Selena, are well remembered. The slide rule that Joplin used in school is displayed at the Museum of the Gulf Coast in Port Arthur. A bronze statue in Corpus Christi honors Selena. Sculptor H.W. Tatum produced both a smiling Selena head and a solemn one. The family chose solemn. The smiling head resides at the Corpus Christi Museum of Science and History.

10 Texas has produced some of the nation's most famous TV journalists, including Walter Cronkite, Dan Rather, Linda Ellerbee, Bob Schieffer and Sam Donaldson. On the air, Rather once described Texas as "the big enchilada or, if not an enchilada, then a huge taco."

SOURCES: *"Finding Anything About Everything in Texas" by Edward Walters; "Texas Curiosities" by John Kelso; "The Civil War" by Shelby Foote; pokerpages.com; Tribune news services; "Texas Death Row," edited by Bill Crawford.*

WISCONSIN

1 Wisconsin is known as the Badger State because of lead miners in the 1800s who were nicknamed badgers because they lived underground in tunnels and mine shafts.

2 Even when Wisconsin had the deadliest fire in American history, it was overshadowed by Chicago. The Peshtigo disaster in the Green Bay area began Oct. 8, 1871 — the same day as the Great Chicago Fire, which dominated the nation's attention. Chicago's disaster killed about 250, while Peshtigo's death toll was at least 1,200, and perhaps twice that many.

3 The QWERTY keyboard layout was invented in Wisconsin. Christopher Latham Sholes, a Milwaukee printer and inventor, realized he could prevent his typewriter from jamming by separating the most popular keys.

4 Wisconsin ranks No. 1 among states in high school graduation rate (90.7 percent). But it also has been No. 1 in drunken driving, according to the state's Transportation Department. A 2008 federal study found that 26.4 percent of Wisconsin adults surveyed admitted driving drunk in the previous year. (Illinois' percentage was 16.5.)

5 Wisconsin rightfully boasts it is "America's Dairyland" on its license plates. In the late 1960s, it went one step further with a bright yellow version that people called "butter plates."

6 Because of an insult, Wisconsin is home to the fantastical House on the Rock in Spring Green. A Madison architect named Alex Jordan Sr. hoped to impress Frank Lloyd Wright with his building designs for a women's dormitory, according to Jordan's biographer, Marv Balousek. Wright was blunt: "I wouldn't hire you to design a cheese crate or a chicken coop." A furious Jordan vowed to build his own masterpiece to spite the famed architect. House on the Rock officials dispute this account and say the house was conceived and built by his son, Alex Jordan Jr. Today, more than 500,000 people flock annually to his House on the Rock. Spring Green's other big attraction, Wright's Taliesin house, draws less than a 10th of that.

7   Madison is known as a center of political correctness, but it took a wrong turn in 2000 when the University of Wisconsin-Madison admissions office promoted diversity by digitally adding a black student into a photo of white people at a football game. The virtual spectator, Diallo Shabazz, said he'd never attended a UW game.

8   Before Tommy Bartlett thrilled thousands with his water-skiing show in the Wisconsin Dells, he worked in Chicago radio. He was just 17 in 1931 when he started at WBBM-AM, where he went on to host two very popular daytime programs targeted at housewives, "Meet the Missus" and "The Missus Goes to Market."

9   In 1951, divorced dressmaker Margaret Jorgenson of Oshkosh left nearly $100,000 in her will to a man after spending only four hours with him. The two began chatting in a hotel elevator while both were visiting Chicago, and they decided to have lunch together. Afterward, they parted, maintaining a correspondence but never again meeting face to face. Jorgenson's will left her relatives nothing, and they sued, winning more than half of the money intended for Jorgenson's four-hour friend.

10   Wisconsin boasts some funny names. There are places like Imalone, Uhet, Embarrass, Footville and Spread Eagle. Then there are people, such as the pride of Wisconsin Rapids, retired race car driver Dick Trickle.

SOURCES: *National Center for Education Statistics; "Cassell's Dictionary of Slang" by Jonathon Green; "The New Partridge Dictionary of Slang and Unconventional English" by Eric Partridge; "The Complete Idiot's Guide to Cheeses of the World" by Steve Ehlers and Jeanette Hurt; "Famous Wisconsin Inventors & Entrepreneurs" by Marv Balousek; "Firestorm at Peshtigo" by Denise Gess and William Lutz; "Wisconsin Biographical Dictionary" by Caryn Hannan; dot.wisconsin.gov; Wisconsin State Journal; Milwaukee Journal Sentinel; wisconsinhistory.org; usgs.gov; imdb.com; snopes.com; channel3000.com.*

IOWA

1 The Ringling Brothers circus nearly expired in northeast Iowa in the 1880s. Bedraggled by bad weather and bad luck, the fledgling circus lurched through thick mud to Cascade at imminent risk of collapse. But Cascade's mayor, doubtless aware that the death of a circus wouldn't help Cascade's image, turned out huge crowds. The Ringlings were so appreciative of Cascade's generosity that they decreed free admission for Cascade residents — forever. Nearly 130 years later the circus, now owned by Virginia-based Feld Entertainment, stands proudly by the brothers' promise.

2 The University of Iowa Writers' Workshop boasts that it was the first creative writing degree program in the United States. Among its students: Stuart Dybek ("The Coast of Chicago"), John Irving ("The World According to Garp") and Flannery O'Connor ("Wise Blood"). The acerbic O'Connor once said: "Everywhere I go, I'm asked if I think universities stifle writers. I think they don't stifle enough of them."

3 The most famous thing about Riverside, Iowa, hasn't even happened yet. According to the "Star Trek" saga, the captain of the starship Enterprise was born in an unspecified Iowa town on March 22, 2228. Seeing that reference, Riverside postal worker Steve Miller persuaded town officials to call the town the "future birthplace of Capt. James T. Kirk," and "Star Trek" creator Gene Roddenberry reportedly went along with it. Today, the town's slogan is "Where the trek begins," and an annual Trekkie festival is held there.

4 One of the most dramatic U.S. air disasters occurred in Sioux City in 1989 when a Chicago-bound jetliner suffered catastrophic engine failure and crash-landed, killing 111. Heroic crew efforts saved 185 others. Iowa also was the scene of crashes fatal to boxer Rocky Marciano (1969, near Newton), members of the Iowa State women's cross-country team (1985, in Des Moines), and South Dakota Gov. George Mickelson (1993, near Dubuque). But none was as famous as the tragedy on Feb. 3, 1959, "The Day the Music Died." Buddy Holly, Ritchie Valens and the Big Bopper, J.P. Richardson, were lost in an air accident near Clear Lake.

5 Iowa wasn't 15 years old as the Civil War approached, and would never host a battle. Yet Iowa contributed a higher percentage of its men to war than did any other state, North or South: Of the 116,000 Iowa men subject to military duty, 75,000 fought for the Union, according to the Iowa Official Register, a state government factbook.

6 Iowa's caucuses haven't always been so important. It wasn't until South Dakota's George McGovern and his campaign manager, Gary Hart, realized how, under new party protocols, the state's 1972 vote could launch his long-shot presidential bid that they rose to prominence. The campaign recruited many Iowans and convinced national political reporters to cover the caucuses. McGovern stole the show and headlines from front-runner Edmund Muskie. He won the nomination but lost to Richard Nixon in November. In 1976, an obscure Georgian named Jimmy Carter repeated the feat by shocking the Democratic field, but he went on to win it all.

7 Which of these show business figures was not born in Cedar Rapids: Ashton Kutcher ("Two and a Half Men"), Elijah Wood ("Lord of the Rings"), Ron Livingston ("Office Space") or Fran Allison ("Kukla, Fran and Ollie")? The answer: Allison, who attended Coe College in Cedar Rapids but was born in La Porte City.

8 Drive from Dyersville to the "Field of Dreams" baseball diamond, and you'll traverse the same undulating farm-to-market roads that bring hundreds of vehicles to the site in the 1989 movie's final, twilight scene. How did filmmakers choreograph the movements of all those cars on crowded two-lane roads so they could shoot the scene from the sky? A radio station in Dubuque, 25 miles east, surrendered its airwaves for the evening: All the drivers tuned to WDBQ-AM for precision commands on when the enormous entourage should come forward toward the ballfield, or cautiously retreat in reverse gear.

9 A remarkable Iowan died in 2011: Norma "Duffy" Lyon, who fascinated Iowa State Fair visitors with her life-size butter sculptures of cows, Elvis Presley, Dwight Eisenhower and even Jesus Christ and his disciples at the Last Supper.

10   Iowans demand efficient government. Exhibit A is the Squirrel Cage Jail, which served Council Bluffs from 1885 until 1969 and is now a museum. The jail, a three-story Lazy Susan and the only one of its size ever built, allowed one jailer to control more than 60 inmates in pie-shaped cells that revolved at the turn of a hand crank. An 1881 patent noted that the design would provide "maximum security with minimum jailer attention." An inmate could exit his cell only when the jailer ratcheted it to the sole doorway on that level.

SOURCES: *"Conversations with Flannery O'Connor," edited by Rosemary M. Magee; "The Iowa Precinct Caucuses: The Making of a Media Event" by Hugh Winebrenner; "Ashton Kutcher" by Marc Shapiro; "Amazing Iowa" by Janice Beck Stock; Encyclopedia Britannica; Des Moines Register; Quad City Times; Newsweek; WDBQ-AM; Feld Entertainment; Historical Society of Pottawattamie County; iowahawkeyes.net; imdb.com; Tribune archives and news services.*

10 THINGS YOU MIGHT NOT KNOW ABOUT
MICHIGAN

1   Is a person from Michigan called a Michiganian or a Michigander? There's no official answer, but respected sources such as the Michigan Historical Center prefer Michiganian. University of Michigan professor Richard Bailey traced the word Michigander to an 1848 speech by then-Rep. Abraham Lincoln of Illinois. The future president combined the words "Michigan" and "gander" (a male goose and was slang for a dandy) to poke fun at Lewis Cass, a political foe from Michigan.

2   People from Michigan love using stage names. The state has produced Kid Rock, Iggy Pop, Della Reese, Alice Cooper, Del Shannon, Eminem and Stevie Wonder — previously known as, respectively, Robert James Ritchie, James Newell Osterberg Jr., Deloreese Patricia Early, Vincent Damon Furnier, Charles Weedon Westover, Marshall Bruce Mathers III and Stevland Hardaway Judkins.

3   There was a Lake Michigan before there was a Michigan. The body of water was once called "Lake of the Illinois" by Native Americans. But the French preferred an American Indian word for "great water" — Michigan. Only later did the land east of the lake take on the name Michigan as well.

4   Former Michigan Gov. Jennifer Granholm has a far better chance of becoming a U.S. Supreme Court justice than president or vice president. That's because she was born in Canada, which means she can't be president, according to the U.S. Constitution. But she could join the high court, as have six other foreign-born Americans.

5   A boy named Leslie Lynch King Jr. became the only Michigan resident to serve as president of the United States. Born in Omaha, Neb., King moved with his mother to Grand Rapids, Mich., after her divorce. She married a paint salesman, and her son took his stepfather's name: Gerald Ford.

6 A school massacre deadlier than Columbine or Virginia Tech occurred in the central Michigan town of Bath in 1927. School board treasurer Andrew Kehoe blamed property taxes for the struggles of his farm, and he plotted revenge. Over weeks, he planted explosives in a school, and then his fury erupted. First, he bludgeoned his wife to death and blew up his farm. Then he drove to the school to witness the deadly explosion he had set by timer. Part of the school blew up with children inside, but Kehoe wasn't done. As towns-people rushed to the scene, he arrived in a truck packed with explosives and loose metal, setting off a blast that killed himself and others. The final death toll: 45 people, including 38 children. In the aftermath, authorities discovered that some of Kehoe's dynamite in the school had failed to explode, suggesting that the worst school massacre in U.S. history could have been even worse.

7 The phrase "jump the shark" was born at the University of Michigan in Ann Arbor. It refers to the point in a TV series when its plot becomes so ri-diculous that fans know it is on the way out. The classic example — and the inspiration for the phrase — occurred when Fonzie of "Happy Days" went water-skiing and leapt over a shark. "Jump the Shark" was coined by Sean Connolly in a conversation with Jon Hein at the U. of M. in the mid-'80s. They formed a website, which was bought in recent years by tvguide.com and turned into a typical Hollywood celebrity gossip site. At that point, jump-theshark.com jumped the shark.

8 In the peace talks that ended the Revolutionary War, the new United States gave Britain two options for drawing the border between the U.S. and Canada in the area around Michigan. The Brits could follow the lines of some of the Great Lakes, or they could establish the border at the 45th Parallel. They chose the former, of course. If they had chosen the latter, Canada would have gained Michigan's Upper Peninsula and the section of the Lower Peninsula north of Traverse City. But Toronto would have become an American city.

9 Motown Records founder Berry Gordy Jr. helped make Detroit the epi-center of soul, but he sometimes had a tin ear. When Marvin Gaye recorded "I Heard It Through the Grapevine" in February 1967, Gordy seemed unim-pressed and refused to release it. Instead, he gave the song to Gladys Knight and the Pips, who made it a hit. Gaye's version appeared on an album in August 1968 but was not released as a single. Legendary disc jockey E. Rodney Jones of Chicago's WVON-AM played the album track, agitating for recog-nition of its brilliance. In late November 1968, nearly two years after it was recorded, Gaye's version was released as a single, and is now considered one of the greatest soul recordings ever.

10 It would be natural to assume that Michigan is called the Wolverine State because there are a lot of wolverines there. Wrong. The wolverine — a voracious eater also known as a "skunk bear" — generally dwells farther north. The 2004 discovery of a wolverine 90 miles north of Detroit was the first confirmed sighting in Michigan's wilds in two centuries. A popular the-ory of how Michigan got its nickname is that American Indians in the 1830s called the white settlers "wolverines" to insult them for their gluttony.

SOURCES: *"Michigan: A History of the Wolverine State" by Willis F. Dunbar and George S May; "Motown: Music, Money, Sex, and Power" by Gerald Posner, "Weird Michigan" by Linda S. Godfrey; "Turn the Beat Around: The Secret History of Disco" by Peter Shapiro; michigan.gov; Michigan Today News; Legal Times; npr.org; jumptheshark.com; Tribune news services.*

10 THINGS YOU MIGHT NOT KNOW ABOUT

POLITICS

DIRTY POLITICS

1   When unscrupulous British political operatives show up at nursing homes with premarked absentee voter ballots, it's called "granny farming."

2   Once upon a time, Roman Catholics were very, very scary. Running for U.S. president in 1928, Catholic Al Smith, a Democrat, was called a "rum-soaked Romanist." His opponents circulated construction photos of New York's Holland Tunnel, saying they showed the beginnings of a tunnel to the Vatican.

3   In the 1946 Democratic primary race for Georgia governor, Eugene Talmadge appealed to white racists by hiring a look-alike of his opponent to campaign in a limousine with two cigar-puffing blacks in the back seat. It worked, but Talmadge died before Inauguration Day.

4   According to political lore out of Florida, Democratic primary challenger George Smathers defeated Florida Sen. Claude Pepper in 1950 by declaring Pepper was a "shameless extrovert" whose sister "was once a thespian" and who "habitually practiced celibacy" before his marriage. But that speech probably was apocryphal. A Time magazine article at the time cited it as a "yarn," but some believed it despite Smathers' denials.

5   Hairdressers, beware. When Republican Mike Taylor challenged Democratic Sen. Max Baucus in Montana in 2002, a Democratic ad cited financial irregularities in Taylor's hair-care business decades earlier. The ad featured old footage of Taylor with his shirt half-open while he applied lotion to a man's temples as disco music played. The Village People didn't appear in the ad, but the suggestion was obvious. Taylor, a father of two who had been married 22 years, was defeated.

6   Former Bush aide Karl Rove admitted a "youthful prank" in Chicago in 1970. As a 19-year-old, he stole campaign stationery for Alan Dixon, a Democratic candidate for Illinois treasurer, and printed 1,000 fliers promising "free beer, free food, girls and a good time" at a Dixon rally. The leaflet was distributed to street people, creating unexpected diversity at the event.

7   Dirty tricksters love telephone "push polls," which pretend to be surveys but ask leading questions, such as the one in the South Carolina 2000 primary: "Would you be more or less likely to vote for John McCain if you knew he had fathered a black child out of wedlock?" (The child was his adopted Bangladeshi daughter.) Another phone prank is the "Super Bowl scheme," in which a caller pretends to be from an opponent's campaign and annoys voters by interrupting them during the football game.

8   Many historians believe Chicago Mayor Richard J. Daley's Democratic machine stuffed the ballot box to win Illinois for John F. Kennedy in the 1960 race for the White House. But it's often wrongly assumed that Illinois was crucial. In fact, JFK would have captured the presidency without Illinois. After the election, a joke went around Washington: Kennedy, Secretary of State Dean Rusk and Daley were in a lifeboat with enough food for one. Two of them would have to jump overboard. But whom? Daley suggested the three of them vote on it and he won, 8-2.

9   It's known as "oppo," or opposition research, in which investigators hunt for damaging information. William Casey was a master. Working for Richard Nixon in 1960, he investigated John F. Kennedy's medical condition but was never directly tied to a break-in at the office of Kennedy's doctor. Two decades later, Jimmy Carter's debate briefing book went missing, and a congressional probe later cited Casey as the chief suspect, despite his denials. When Ronald Reagan defeated Carter, Reagan decided Casey was well-qualified for a key job: CIA director.

10   Whispering campaigns often label candidates as drunkards. But in Wisconsin in 1956, the opposite was true. Republican gubernatorial candidate Vernon Thompson was from Richland Center, which banned alcohol sales. His opponents went to taverns in resort areas and struck up conversations about how Thompson was from a dry town and wanted to turn the whole state that way. Thompson won, barely.

SOURCES: *"How to Get Elected" by Jack Mitchell; "Dirty Politics" by Bruce L. Felknor; "American Pharaoh" by Adam Cohen and Elizabeth Taylor; "Going Dirty" by David Mark; Newsweek; Time; doubletongued.org; Washington Monthly; Tribune news services.*

ELECTION DAY

1 Jose Lira, a native Spaniard who had become an American citizen, flew 3,000 miles from Spain to Detroit to vote in the November 1960 election, only to be turned away on Election Day because Michigan required residence for the six months prior to voting.

2 The New York Times crossword puzzle for Election Day 1996 included the clue "Lead story in tomorrow's paper." Because of ingenious construction by puzzle builder Jeremiah Farrell, the answer could have been either CLINTON ELECTED or BOB DOLE ELECTED. The crossing clues were written so that either one would work. For example, the "down" clue for the first letter was "black Halloween animal," which could have been either "cat" or "bat."

3 On Nov. 5, 1968, when Illinois helped elect Richard Nixon president, one citizen had a heightened sense of alarm. The Chicago pedestrian alerted authorities that the under-construction John Hancock Center on North Michigan Avenue appeared to be on fire. In fact, the 100-story building was enveloped in clouds, not in smoke. Eventually, Chicagoans would get used to it.

4 If you receive a letter telling you that Election Day is Nov. 5 instead of Nov. 4, or that there's a "rain date" if the weather is bad, ignore it. That's a classic "vote suppression" scheme.

5 Forget about term limits — we need terminal limits. Three candidates were re-elected in 2006 despite the ultimate disqualification: death. Sam Duncan lost his life but retained his county Soil and Water Conservation Board seat in North Carolina. Texas state Rep. Glenda Dawson won a new term after her campaign cynically sent out literature failing to mention she was dead. Katherine Dunton was very much alive when she ran for the Adak, Alaska, school board, but she passed away on Election Day. Just because Dunton was dead didn't mean she was unlucky: The election ended in a tie, and she won the coin toss.

6 On Election Day 1994, the Willis family of Chicago was driving near Milwaukee when a mudflap-taillight assembly fell off a truck, puncturing the gas tank of their minivan and causing a fire that killed six of the family's children. On that same day, Illinois Secretary of State George Ryan was re-elected. The events seemed unrelated until years later, when it was revealed that the truck driver involved in the accident got his license through corruption in Ryan's office. In 2007, on the 13th anniversary of that terrible Election Day accident, Ryan served his first full day in prison on unrelated corruption charges.

7 George W. Gibbs Jr. was the first black explorer to reach the Antarctic ice shelf, but he held another distinction: He was born on Election Day 1916, when Woodrow Wilson won the presidency, and he died on Election Day 2000, when George W. Bush was elected.

8 One of the shortest Election Days in the U.S. takes place in Dixville Notch, N.H. Residents cast their ballots at midnight and then close the polls. But the town is not exactly representative of the nation as a whole: When Democrat Bill Clinton won the presidency in 1992, he finished fourth in Dixville Notch behind Republican George H.W. Bush, independent Ross Perot and Libertarian Andre Marrou.

9 As many as a dozen United Airlines employees said they saw a flying saucerlike object hovering over O'Hare International Airport on Election Day 2006. Also on that day, Democrats completed their takeover of Illinois' state government. Not that one event had anything to do with the other, necessarily.

10 On that same day when the United workers spotted a UFO above O'Hare, Republican Sarah Palin was elected governor of Alaska. We report, you decide.

SOURCES: *Editor & Publisher; legacy.com; mazes.com; fun-with-words.com; Tribune news services.*

THE G-8

1   Germany took some controversial security steps when it hosted the 2007 summit in the small Baltic resort town of Heiligendamm. One was "scent tracking," in which authorities collected samples of suspected radicals' sweat so that sniffer dogs could pick them out during protests.

2   The G-8 represents about 14 percent of the world's population and 44 percent of its economic output. Both those numbers are on the decline. China's economic expansion has prompted calls to redefine the G-8 to include the Beijing regime and other surging nations.

3   Russia is the summit's stepchild. The G-7 became the G-8 when Russia joined in 1997, but it has a smaller economy than at least three non-members. At the summit in Halifax, Nova Scotia, in 1995, Russian President Boris Yeltsin put on such an odd performance that there was dueling speculation over whether he was drunk or affected by a blood transfusion. In recent years, President Vladimir Putin has cracked down on civil rights, prompting calls for Russia to be suspended from the G-8.

4   Each country appoints a top official to negotiate the G-8's communique. The eight officials are called "sherpas," a reference to the Tibetan guides who lead climbers to mountain summits. Their assistants are known as "sous sherpas," from the French word "sous," meaning "under."

5   President Bill Clinton learned that the summit is conducted under a microscope when he made offhand comments at the Naples, Italy, gathering in 1994 that were interpreted to mean that the U.S. wouldn't defend the value of the dollar. The currency took a plunge.

6   The conference is sometimes held in remote locations. At the 2002 meeting in Kananaskis in the Canadian Rockies, authorities put radio collars on six grizzly bears in the area so that the animals could be tracked during the proceedings.

7 In 2005, French President Jacques Chirac ridiculed the Scottish dish of haggis and said of the British: "We can't trust people who have such bad food." The remarks were made just before the G-8 in Gleneagles, Scotland. Chirac was the only G-8 leader not greeted by Scottish First Minister Jack McConnell upon arrival, but the Scots politely kept haggis off the menu at the opening banquet.

8 The London suicide bombings on July 7, 2005, overshadowed President George W. Bush's bike accident at the G-8 summit the day before. The bicycling Bush rode toward police, said, "Thanks, you guys, for coming," and took a hand off the handlebars to wave. He lost control, slamming into a constable and skidding along the ground. Bush suffered abrasions; the constable was treated at a hospital. The cop received an apology from Bush, who was described in the Scottish police report as a "moving/falling object."

9 At the 2006 meeting in St. Petersburg, Russia, Bush was caught by a live microphone using a curse word to refer to Hezbollah. Then a Russian TV camera captured him sneaking up behind German Chancellor Angela Merkel and giving her a quick massage of her neck and shoulders. The 5-second video, popular on YouTube, showed the chancellor hunching her shoulders, throwing her arms up and grimacing, but she appeared to smile as Bush walked away. White House spokesman Tony Snow said the president believes in "putting people at ease, so that you can have a candid conversation."

10 Scottish crime writer Ian Rankin sets his 2006 novel "The Naming of the Dead" against the backdrop of the G-8 summit. His detective hero's case — a politician's mysterious plunge from Edinburgh Castle during a diplomatic dinner.

SOURCES: *The Globe and Mail; Scotland on Sunday; the Guardian; Tribune archives and news services.*

INAUGURATIONS

1   George Washington had to borrow money to go to his own inauguration.

2   Perhaps the greatest myth of U.S. inauguration history is that William Henry Harrison's long speech in chilly weather caused his death in 1841. True, Harrison didn't wear a hat or overcoat while speaking for an hour and 40 minutes. But the 68-year-old Harrison conducted extensive presidential business for weeks after his address. It's unclear when Harrison caught the cold that led to his pneumonia, but he didn't summon a doctor until 23 days after the inauguration. He died about a week later. The "fatal speech" idea seems predicated on the common but false notion that cold weather causes a cold.

3   The outgoing president often gets little attention, but rarely has it been as obvious as in 1857, when James Buchanan succeeded Franklin Pierce. The swearing-in ceremony had to be delayed for 20 minutes because officials forgot to pick up Pierce at his hotel and had to go fetch him.

4   Ulysses Grant was inaugurated for his second term on a day in 1873 when the noon temperature was 16 degrees. A temporary wooden structure was built for the inaugural ball, and the weather turned it into an icebox. The food froze while guests danced in their coats. The musicians' violin strings snapped because of the chill, and 100 canaries, brought in to provide pleasant sounds, froze to death in their cages.

5   Pierce and Herbert Hoover both "affirmed" rather than swore the oath of office because of religious convictions.

6   Because of gas rationing during World War II, there was no parade for Franklin Roosevelt's fourth inauguration in 1945.

7   Dwight Eisenhower's 1953 parade was covered by a 24-year-old reporter who worked for the Washington Times-Herald as the "Inquiring Camera Girl." Her name was Jacqueline Bouvier, soon to become Jackie Kennedy.

8   One of America's greatest poets, Robert Frost, had a miserable time when called upon to recite verse for John Kennedy's inauguration in 1961. The 86-year-old poet was blinded by the bright sunlight and unable to read the new poem he had written. Instead, the flustered Frost switched to an old poem he had memorized, dedicating it to "the president-elect, Mr. John Finley." (Finley was a classics scholar at Harvard.)

9   Lyndon Johnson was the only president to take the oath of office from a woman, Federal District Judge Sarah Hughes. He also was the only president to be sworn in on an airplane, taking office after Kennedy's assassination in 1963.

10   Before Richard Nixon's 1973 inaugural parade, officials applied a chemical bird repellent to tree branches along the route. The product, called Roost No More, was supposed to keep pigeons off the trees by making their feet itch. Instead, the birds ate the repellent and keeled over, leaving Pennsylvania Avenue decorated with sick and dead pigeons.

SOURCES: *Joint Committee on Inaugural Ceremonies; inaugural.senate.gov; nara.gov; History News Network; Washington Post; "Ask Not: The Inauguration of John F. Kennedy and the Speech That Changed America" by Thurston Clarke; "Democracy's Big Day: The Inauguration of Our President, 1789-2009" by Jim Bendat; "Old Tippecanoe: William Henry Harrison and His Time" by Freeman Cleaves; "President James Buchanan" by Philip Shriver Klein; "Presidential Inaugurations" by Paul F. Boller Jr.; Tribune news services.*

LIEUTENANT GOVERNORS

1 It's an office that people love to hate — or at least want to abolish. In 2009, South Carolina senators, the Louisiana governor and lawmakers in California and Wisconsin have talked about doing away with the office. "I cannot think of one solitary contribution our lieutenant governors have made to the operation of state government other than sitting around, waiting for the current officeholder to pass on or leave town," said state Sen. Alan Lasee, a Wisconsin Republican.

2 Despite calls to abolish the job of lieutenant governor elsewhere, New Jersey just added the position. Republican Kim Guadagno became the state's first second banana in January 2010.

3 Tennessee's lieutenant governor, Ron Ramsey, didn't shy from the "birther" controversy with his 2010 comments to Nashville Republicans. Asked about suspicions that President Barack Obama was not born in the U.S., he said: "I've got a tableful of advisers sitting over there and they'll probably start cringing right about now when I start talking about some of this stuff right here. ... I'm going to tell you something. I don't know whether President Obama is a citizen of the United States or not. I don't know what the whole deal is there."

4 Former Wisconsin Lt. Gov. John Strange was an enemy of beer. While German forces were ravaging Europe in World War I, Strange discovered danger closer to home. "We have German enemies in this country too," he said. "And the worst of our German enemies, the most treacherous, the most menacing, are Pabst, Schlitz, Blatz and Miller."

5 Only two U.S. presidents have been lieutenant governors. Ironically, one succeeded the other. Maybe Warren Harding saw the value of such experience when he selected Calvin Coolidge to be his running mate. It proved important, because Coolidge took over in 1923 when Harding died in office. Maybe not so ironically, both are considered second-rate presidents.

6 In 1825, Illinois Gov. Edward Coles told Lt. Gov. Adolphus Hubbard that he would be traveling out of state for about three months and that Hubbard would take over temporarily. When Coles returned about 10 weeks later, Hubbard claimed Coles had forfeited his job. But the Illinois Supreme Court thought differently. In another coup attempt by a lieutenant governor, Florida's William Gleason tried to replace Harrison Reed in the aftermath of the Civil War. Gleason proclaimed himself governor and started signing documents from his hotel. It backfired. Not only did a court rule he wasn't governor, but it also found he was ineligible to be lieutenant governor because he hadn't been a state resident long enough.

7 In the early 19th century, the British-held island of Malta was administered by a lieutenant governor with a particularly macho name: Manley Power.

8 From 1985 to 2010, 24 lieutenant governors moved into the governor's mansion without winning election to the job. The majority of those — 14 — moved up because the sitting governor accepted a higher post, such as president (Bill Clinton and George W. Bush). Five moved up after scandal-forced resignation or ouster (adios, Rod Blagojevich). Another five took over because of the death of the elected officeholder.

9 Pinckney Benton Stewart Pinchback, the son of a freed black slave and a white planter, became the first African-American governor in the U.S. in 1872. Known as P.B.S. Pinchback, he achieved that high office without election. When Louisiana's lieutenant governor died, Pinchback was appointed in his place. Then the governor was impeached, and Pinchback served as the state's leader for 35 days. It would be 118 years before another black American (Virginia's Douglas Wilder) gained a governorship.

10 John W. Brown, Ohio's lieutenant governor for 16 years, served as the state's governor for only a week and a half, but he made the most of it. When the governor quit early to take a U.S. Senate seat in 1957, his elected successor could not take office until 11 days later. Brown moved into the governor's office, replacing portraits of Democrats with those of Republicans. He called a joint session of the General Assembly and made a State of the State speech. He commuted the sentences of several murderers. He demanded the governor's salary for 11 days — and got it.

SOURCES: *"Duty, Honor, Victory: America's Athletes in World War II" by Gary L. Bloomfield; "200 Quick Looks at Florida History" by James C. Clark; "Ohio Politics" by Alexander P. Lamis and Mary Anne Sharkey; "Ambitious Brew: The Story of American Beer" By Maureen Ogle; "Governor Edward Coles" edited by Clarence Walworth Alvord; "The Bench and the Bar of Illinois: Historical and Reminiscent, Vol. 1," edited by John McAuley Palmer; Larry Sabato, director, University of Virginia's Center for Politics; nashvillescene.com; sos.louisiana.gov; britishempire.co.uk.*

PHILANDERING POLITICIANS

1   The man pictured on the $10 bill had to spend his own legal tender to cover up sex. In 1791, Treasury Secretary Alexander Hamilton was duped into a sexual affair with a married woman and then was blackmailed by her husband.

2   Judith Exner, girlfriend of both President John Kennedy and Chicago mobster Sam Giancana, served as a go-between as they plotted the "elimination" of Cuban President Fidel Castro. Exner said later that she would have been more frightened if she had known "elimination" meant Castro's assassination, not just his removal from office.

3   U.S. Rep. John Schmitz (R-Calif.) won more than 1 million votes in 1972 as the American Independent Party nominee for president. A decade later, the ultraconservative's political career was over with the revelation that he had a pregnant mistress and a son born out of wedlock. Today, he is far less famous than his daughter, Mary Kay Letourneau, the teacher who went to prison for having sex with an underage pupil and later married him.

4   In 1980, lobbyist Paula Parkinson went on a Florida golf trip with three congressmen. One of them, Thomas Evans (R-Del.), lost his re-election bid when the dalliance was revealed. Another, Dan Quayle (R-Ind.), did not, and later became vice president. Said Quayle's wife, Marilyn: "Anyone who knows Dan Quayle knows he'd rather play golf than have sex any day."

5   The unwanted advances of U.S. Sen. Robert Packwood (R-Ore.) prompted more than two dozen women to file complaints in the early 1990s. His undoing was his diary. One passage described a female bridge player who wore a jacket "showing, as best I could tell, bare breasts. God was she a good player. I was so fascinated in watching her bid and play that I could hardly concentrate on the breasts."

6 Elizabeth Ray, an office worker for Rep. Wayne Hays (D-Ohio) whose only duty was sex, famously said, "I can't type, I can't file, I can't even answer the phone." The 1976 scandal erupted only because of Hays' bad manners. When Hays got a divorce and married someone else, Ray was insulted that she was the only Hays staffer not invited to the wedding reception. She called The Washington Post.

7 Few political paramours are as dumb as Ray. Donna Rice, whose relationship with U.S. Sen. Gary Hart (D-Colo.) wrecked his presidential bid in 1988, was a magna cum laude graduate of the University of South Carolina. Monica Lewinsky, who trysted with President Bill Clinton, earned her master's degree in social psychology in 2006 from the London School of Economics and Political Science.

8 A chief Clinton foe was U.S. Rep. Henry Hyde (R-Ill.), who had a four-year extramarital affair in his 40s and later called his actions "youthful indiscretions." At least seven Republican House members who voted to impeach Clinton have been involved in sex scandals or adulterous affairs: Hyde, Robert Livingston (La.), Ken Calvert (Calif.), Newt Gingrich (Ga.), Steven Latourette (Ohio), Mark Foley (Fla.) and Helen Chenoweth (Idaho).

9 One of the seven, Livingston, was on the verge of becoming House speaker in 1998 but quit when his affair was revealed. His successor? Last week's "D.C. Madam" associate, Sen. David Vitter (R-La.). Vitter's wife, Wendy, was once asked if she could forgive her husband if he ever strayed, and she recalled Lorena Bobbitt, who cut off her sleeping husband's penis. "I'm a lot more like Lorena Bobbitt than Hillary [Clinton]. If he does something like that, I'm walking away with one thing, and it's not alimony, trust me."

10 Los Angeles Mayor Antonio Villaraigosa's original name was Villar. But when he married Corina Raigosa in 1987, they merged names. After the mayor admitted to an affair in 2007, his wife dumped both him and his name, going back to Raigosa. The mayor kept the full Villaraigosa.

SOURCES: *Tribune news services; "Scandal" by Suzanne Garment; "Alexander Hamilton, American" by Richard Brookhiser; "The Dark Side of Camelot" by Seymour M. Hersh.*

POLITICIANS' KIDS

1 Samantha Thompson, daughter of Illinois' longest-serving governor, James Thompson, runs her own New York-based fashion design company, Eloise Carr.

2 Was the Baby Ruth candy bar named after Grover Cleveland's daughter? Probably not, even though Chicago-based Curtiss Candy Co. insisted it was so. Curtiss' story made it easier to avoid paying royalties to Babe Ruth, who was a baseball star when the candy debuted in 1921. Ruth Cleveland, on the other hand, had died of diphtheria 17 years earlier and hardly would have been top of mind when considering the name of a candy bar.

3 Elizabeth Ann Blaesing, who grew up in Chicago and died in Oregon in 2005, believed she was the "love child" of President Warren Harding. Her mother, Nan Britton, wrote a tell-all book about Elizabeth being conceived on a Senate office couch, and Harding's reputation has lent credibility to her account. But in recent years, neither the Blaesing family nor the Harding family has been interested in DNA testing that might confirm a link.

4 President James Madison did not have any children, but he married Dolley, who had two by a previous marriage. John Payne Todd proved to be a bane to both. He was a womanizer, gambler and alcoholic who would disappear for weeks at a time. He would run up debts of tens of thousands of dollars, huge sums at the time, which James and Dolley would pay. Even in the final year of Dolley's life, as she struggled to make ends meet because of him, Todd wanted more. He successfully harassed her to change her will to make him the sole beneficiary. She realized her error the next day and worked to nullify the new will. She died shortly thereafter, but Todd continued the fight in court.

5 John Scott Harrison, the son of President William Henry Harrison and the father of President Benjamin Harrison, has a bizarre niche in American history. When he died in 1878, relatives attending his burial in Cleves, Ohio, noticed that the nearby grave of another relative had been robbed. The next day, family members went to a local medical college hoping to find that relative's body, but instead found the body of ... John Scott Harrison, robbed from his grave. The other relative's body was later found in Ann Arbor, Mich. Both bodies had been stolen for use in medical education.

6 Before it was the norm to shelter a president's younger children from media attention, there was Gerald Ford's daughter Susan. She hosted her high school's prom at the White House, served as hostess at official functions (while her mother, Betty, was recuperating from illness), sat for a People magazine cover story and photo spread, and even wrote a monthly column for Seventeen magazine.

7 In several Asian nations, daughters of politicians have reached prominence equaling or surpassing their fathers'. They include Nobel Peace Prize winner Aung San Suu Kyi of Myanmar, former Pakistani Prime Minister Benazir Bhutto and former Indian Prime Minister Indira Gandhi. But prominence has not meant safety. Suu Kyi, who was elected to her nation's lower house of parliament in 2012, was imprisoned in her own house for nearly 15 years, and Bhutto and Gandhi were both assassinated.

8 Margaret Truman Daniel, the author of best-selling mysteries, once had aspirations as an opera singer. And although being the daughter of the president may have advanced her career, it didn't protect her from criticism. After a December 1950 concert, a Washington Post reviewer wrote, "Miss Truman cannot sing very well" and "There are few moments during her recital when one can relax and feel confident that she will make her goal, which is the end of the song."

9 When Dwight Eisenhower and Richard Nixon campaigned as the GOP presidential ticket in 1956, it was the start of something great. Yes, the two were running for re-election, but during the second campaign, Ike's grandson and Nixon's daughter met. In 1968, Dwight D. Eisenhower II, known as David, and Julie Nixon married. The Rev. Norman Vincent Peale officiated, and the best man was future "Love Boat" actor and U.S. Rep. Fred Grandy.

10 Nancy D'Alesandro, the young daughter of Baltimore Mayor Tommy D'Alesandro, wanted to be a priest when she grew up. Eventually, her mother broke the news that this was impossible. "Well, then, I'll go into politics instead," she responded, according to a biography of the girl who became Nancy Pelosi, speaker of the House.

SOURCES: *"Woman of the House: The Rise of Nancy Pelosi"* by Vincent Bzdek; *"Benjamin Harrison: Centennial President"* by Anne Chieko Moore; *"America's Royalty: All the Presidents' Children"* by Sandra L. Quinn-Musgrove and Sanford Kanter; *"The First Ladies Fact Book"* by Bill Harris; *"Truman"* by David McCullough; Cleveland Plain Dealer; People magazine; Life magazine; snopes.com; barrypopik.com; eloisecarr.com,; Tribune archives and news services.

REPUBLICANS

1 The Iowa Republican Party platform has nearly 400 planks. One of them is: "We support the definition of manure as natural fertilizer."

2 Elizabeth Dole, transportation secretary under President Ronald Reagan, was the first woman to command an armed service, the Coast Guard. As secretary, she gets credit for the rear-window brake light in cars.

3 Republicans were pioneers on civil rights for blacks and women. Their role in abolishing slavery is well known. Less understood is that the GOP proclaimed support for some women's rights 40 years before the Democrats. Its 1876 platform declared that the party "recognizes with approval the substantial advances toward the establishment of equal rights for women." Its 1896 document called for "equal pay for equal work." The Democrats didn't address women's rights until they supported women's suffrage in 1916, just four years before the passage of the 19th Amendment.

4 Abraham Lincoln was among our most admired presidents, but he wasn't above playing politics even in wartime. Worried that he would lose the 1864 election, he arranged for soldiers who were unfit for immediate duty to leave the warfront and return to their home states to vote.

5 Newt Gingrich was born with the name Newton Leroy McPherson to a 16-year-old mother and 19-year-old father whose marriage broke up in three days.

6 Col. Robert McCormick, publisher of the Tribune, was such a stalwart Republican that when Rhode Island Democrats won a political battle in 1935, McCormick ordered that Rhode Island's star be cut out of the American flag that flew in the Tribune Tower lobby. But an employee pointed out that mutilating the flag was a crime punishable by a fine and jail time, and the colonel relented.

7 Republican National Chairman Michael Steele's half-sister married Mike Tyson after the boxer's rape conviction, and later divorced him. Tyson endorsed Steele's unsuccessful bid for the U.S. Senate in 2006.

8 Four cities call themselves "the birthplace of the Republican Party." Activists in Ripon, Wis.; Exeter, N.H.; and Crawfordsville, Iowa, held meetings in 1853-54 to discuss forming a new party. The first official meeting of the Republican Party took place in Jackson, Mich., in July 1854.

9 A Republican named Pinckney Benton Stewart Pinchback was the nation's first African-American governor, serving 35 days in 1872-73 after Louisiana's governor was impeached.

10 Margaret Chase Smith was just a freshman Republican senator from Maine when she denounced much-feared demagogue Joseph McCarthy on the Senate floor in 1950. One memorable line: "I don't want to see the Republican Party ride to political victory on the Four Horsemen of Calumny — Fear, Ignorance, Bigotry and Smear." Despite earning McCarthy's wrath, she served for two more terms.

SOURCES: *"American History Revised" by Seymour Morris Jr.; "Post Biographies of Famous Journalists" by John E. Drewry; "Bill Clinton: Mastering the Presidency" By Nigel Hamilton; "The Pact: Bill Clinton, Newt Gingrich, and the Rivalry That Defined a Generation" by Steven M. Gillon; "Ripples of Hope: Great American Civil Rights Speeches," edited by Josh Gottheimer; the American Presidency Project at presidency.ucsb.edu; Center for Public Integrity; newsweek.com; iowagop.org; notablebiographies.com; senate.gov; public.coe.edu; pbs.org; sos.louisiana.gov; blackpast.org; Washington Post; New York Times; Tribune archives and news services.*

TAXES

1 Did 7 million American children suddenly disappear in 1987? On paper, it seemed so. That's the year the IRS began requiring Social Security numbers for dependent children, and the number dropped dramatically.

2 Before there was Al Capone, there was a South Carolina bootlegger named Manny Sullivan. In the 1927 ruling United States vs. Sullivan, the U.S. Supreme Court declared that income derived from illegal means was taxable. Sullivan argued that reporting his ill-gotten gains would violate his 5th Amendment rights against self-incrimination. The court unanimously disagreed. That set the table for Capone's conviction in October 1931, and for today's requirement in some states that marijuana dealers buy tax stamps.

3 There might be no such thing as Busch Stadium if Fred Saigh hadn't cheated on his taxes. Saigh, owner of the St. Louis Cardinals baseball team in the early 1950s, was forced to sell the team after being sentenced to 15 months in prison for tax evasion. The Busch family bought the team and owned it for four decades.

4 What did actress Sophia Loren have in common with Chicago Mayor Harold Washington, Illinois Gov. Otto Kerner, rock 'n' roller Chuck Berry, hotel magnate Leona Helmsley, comedian Richard Pryor, lobbyist Jack Abramoff and evangelist Sun Myung Moon? They all did jail time on tax charges.

5 In 1697, England taxed homeowners based on the number of windows in their houses. Glass was expensive, so a tax on windows was a somewhat fair gauge of wealth. Nevertheless, some citizens viewed the tax as the ultimate daylight robbery. When today's tourists see bricked-up windows on old English buildings, it's often a testament to their owners' efforts to avoid the tax, which was repealed in 1851.

6 Nearly 99 million federal taxpayers used e-file in 2010, meaning almost 70 percent of all federal returns were paperless.

7   The man who helps formulate tax policy for the world's largest economy messed up his own taxes by filing through the TurboTax software program. But Treasury Secretary Timothy Geithner blamed himself, not TurboTax, for failing to report more than $34,000 in International Monetary Fund income, a stumble that complicated but did not derail his Senate confirmation.

8   The Stamp Act of 1765, the first direct tax on American colonists, is familiar to students of the Revolutionary War. But less understood is how pervasive the tax was. Nearly every commercial, legal and government document had to be written on special paper carrying an embossed stamp. That included marriage licenses, wills, college diplomas, calendars, almanacs and newspapers. That's not all: The act taxed playing cards and even dice.

9   Here's a little-known American hero: Donald Alexander, the Internal Revenue Service commissioner from 1973 to 1977 who found that President Richard Nixon was using a secret cadre of IRS investigators to attack people on his "enemies list." Alexander disbanded the unit, and later wrote: "The evening of the same day, President Nixon made his first effort to fire me." But Alexander outlasted his boss. He died in 2009, honored for withstanding political pressure and simply doing his job.

10   Another former IRS boss, Joseph Nunan Jr., is less fondly remembered. In 1952, Nunan was convicted of tax evasion for failing to report at least $86,000 in income, including his winnings when he bet that President Harry Truman would be elected in 1948. Nunan wagered $200 on Truman with 9-to-1 odds, earning $1,800 — and a five-year prison sentence.

SOURCES: *"1927: High Tide of the Twenties" by Gerald Leinwand; CIA Factbook; U.S. Supreme Court; Federal Bureau of Investigation; Encyclopedia Britannica; ushistory.org; irs.gov; snopes. com; Washington Post; Tribune news services.*

THIRD PARTIES

1 Nevada is the only state that includes "none of the above" as a ballot option. But if "none" finishes No. 1, the second-highest vote-getter wins.

2 A high point for third parties was 1912, when Teddy Roosevelt tried to win a third term in the White House because he was disgruntled with his successor, William Howard Taft. Roosevelt's Bull Moose Party beat Taft but lost to Woodrow Wilson. Roosevelt won 27 percent of the popular vote and got 88 electoral votes.

3 In 1967, the citizens of Picoaza, Ecuador, were treated to a series of advertisements with slogans such as "For Mayor: Honorable Pulvapies" and "Vote for any candidate, but if you want well-being and hygiene, vote for Pulvapies." The honorable Pulvapies was elected mayor by write-in votes, but could not take office. Why? Because Pulvapies was a foot powder.

4 For nearly seven years, former Alaska Gov. Sarah Palin's husband, Todd, was a registered member of the Alaskan Independence Party, which advocates that state residents be allowed to vote on seceding from the United States.

5 Socialist Party presidential candidate Eugene Debs finished third in 1920 with 913,664 votes — about 3.5 percent of those cast — even though he couldn't go on the campaign trail or even vote for himself. Debs had been thrown in prison because he protested against American involvement in World War I.

6 When President Richard Nixon visited communist China in 1972, right-wing California politician John G. Schmitz quipped: "I have no objection to President Nixon going to China. I just object to his coming back." Schmitz was the American Independent Party's 1972 presidential candidate, winning more than 1 million votes. Many more millions have heard of Schmitz's daughter, whom he nicknamed "Cake." She is Mary Kay Letourneau, the teacher who was imprisoned for having sex with an underage pupil and married him upon her release.

7   By definition, the third-party route is an uphill battle. But for the crusading Victoria Claflin Woodhull, it was particularly daunting. Running as the Equal Rights Party presidential candidate in 1872, her most likely supporters—women—couldn't even vote.

8   Jesse Ventura, a former professional wrestler who shocked the political establishment in 1998 when he won the Minnesota gubernatorial race, may have been the first political candidate to launch his own action figure. One of his campaign ads featured two boys playing with custom-made Ventura action figures dressed in a suit. It didn't take long before the dolls were available for sale.

9   A third-party presidential candidate has never won a general election in Illinois—not even Rockford native Rep. John B. Anderson, who ran as an independent in 1980 against President Jimmy Carter and Ronald Reagan. Anderson, who won just 7 percent of the vote in his home state, had become considerably more liberal since first being elected to the U.S. House in 1960. Early in his career, he repeatedly pushed a constitutional amendment that would have recognized "the law and authority of Jesus Christ."

10   When H. Ross Perot announced on "Larry King Live" in February 1992 that he would run for president if supporters got him on the ballot in all 50 states, the most surprised person may have been his wife, Margot.

SOURCES: *Presidency Project at University of California-Santa Barbara; National Heritage Museum; "Citizen Perot" by Gerald Posner; "The Bull Moose Years: Theodore Roosevelt and the Progressive Party" by John Allen Gable; "Encyclopedia of U.S. Campaigns, Elections, and Electoral Behavior, Vol. 1" by Kenneth F. Warren; "Democracy's Prisoner: Eugene V. Debs, the Great War, and the Right to Dissent" by Ernest Freeberg; "Run the Other Way: Fixing the Two-Party System, One Campaign at a Time" by Bill Hillsman; "Victoria Woodhull's Sexual Revolution" by Amanda Frisken; Seattle Post-Intelligencer; Los Angeles Times; Reuters; Rockford Register Star; Washington Post; snopes.com; u-s-history.com; uselectionatlas.org; akip.org.*

THE U.S. SUPREME COURT

1   Nicknames for justices include "Old Bacon Face" (Samuel P. Chase, who had a reddish complexion), "Scalito" (Samuel Alito, characterized as a mini-me of Antonin Scalia), "The Lone Ranger" (William Rehnquist, for his contrarian positions) and "Hugo-to-Hell" (Hugo Black, a strict sentencing judge). But if you see a reference to Thurgood Marshall as "Thoroughgood," that's not a nickname—that's the first name he was born with, before changing it in the second grade.

2   While delivering a speech to the Utah Bar Association in 1982, Justice Byron White was attacked by a man who shouted "Busing and pornography don't go!" and hit the judge. After the man was hauled away, White referred to his younger days as a University of Colorado running back, quipping, "I've been hit harder than that before in Utah."

3   In 1985, the Supreme Court had no Jews and one Catholic. Now there are three Jews and six Catholics.

4   Jimmy Carter was a tough-luck president, with crises at the gas pump and in the embassy at Tehran. So it's little wonder that Carter was shut out at the Supreme Court, becoming the only president in U.S. history to serve at least a full term without making a high court nomination.

5   When conservative Robert Bork was nominated to the court in 1987, all aspects of his life were examined, even his video rentals. A leaked list of his videos included nothing sexually explicit and many classics, such as Alfred Hitchcock's "North by Northwest" and Orson Welles' "Citizen Kane." Among the surprises: Federico Fellini's "8 1/2." Bork also rented "The Star Chamber," a film about a secret society imposing vigilante justice. Bork's nomination was rejected, but it left legacies such as the term "Borked," based on the nominee's rough treatment, as well as a federal law banning disclosure of video rentals.

6   Douglas Ginsburg withdrew his nomination to the court in 1987 amid revelations that he had smoked marijuana. Within a few years, that was no longer a fatal flaw. Our last three presidents have smoked pot, as has at least one current justice, Clarence Thomas. When Thomas was nominated only four years after the Ginsburg debacle, the White House confirmed that Thomas had smoked marijuana "several times" in college and "perhaps once" in law school. "We believe this matter is inconsequential," said White House spokeswoman Judy Smith, and she turned out to be right.

7 The chief justice of the United States earns $223,500, while associate justices get $213,900. When Justice John Paul Stevens stepped down in 2010, he started collecting that same salary for lifetime under a policy that applies to all federal judges who retire at age 65 or later with at least 15 years of service. The idea is that federal judges never fully retire and are available as needed.

8 President Richard Nixon, smarting from the rejection of nominee Clement Haynsworth, presented Harrold Carswell in 1970 as his second choice for justice. When critics called Carswell mediocre, Sen. Roman Hruska, R-Neb., issued a most unhelpful defense: "Even if he were mediocre, there are a lot of mediocre judges and people and lawyers. They are entitled to a little representation, aren't they, and a little chance?" Carswell, forever cast as a symbol of mediocrity, was rejected by the Senate. Six years later, he was fined $100 for making sexual advances to an undercover police officer in a shopping mall restroom in Tallahassee, Fla.

9 Justice Scalia, who is considered one of America's finest legal minds, was rejected by the college of his choice. "I was an Italian boy from Queens, not quite the Princeton type," Scalia said. He went to Georgetown instead.

10 Historians generally agree that the court's low point came in 1857 when it ruled that Dred Scott must remain a slave. But the second worst? Perhaps the case of Chicagoan Myra Bradwell, who passed the Illinois bar exam in 1869 but was denied a license because of her sex. Bradwell appealed to the U.S. Supreme Court but lost, with Justice Joseph Bradley writing: "The paramount destiny and mission of woman is to fulfill the noble and benign offices of wife and mother. That is the law of the Creator." About two decades later, Bradwell finally won her law license, retroactive to 1869.

SOURCES: *"American Original: The Life and Constitution of Supreme Court Justice Antonin Scalia" by Joan Biskupic; "The Supreme Court: the Personalities and Rivalries that Defined America" by Jeffrey Rosen; "Hugo Black and the Judicial Revolution" by Gerald T. Dunne; "Supreme Court for Dummies" by Lisa Paddock; "More Than Petticoats: Remarkable Illinois Women" by Lyndee Jobe Henderson; Christian Science Monitor; Milwaukee Journal; Washington City Paper; supremecourt.gov; slate.com; cnn.com.*

10 THINGS YOU MIGHT NOT KNOW ABOUT

HOLIDAYS & RELIGION

APRIL FOOLS' DAY

1   The origin of April Fools' Day may be lost to history. One theory centers on people confused by the transition to the Gregorian calendar, but even before that time, there were April Fools'-like hoaxes. In 1983, Boston University professor Joseph Boskin said the practice began when court jesters and fools told the Roman emperor Constantine that they could do a better job than he did, and Constantine made one of them king for a day. Many newspapers picked up Boskin's story—which was an April Fools' Day joke.

2   Ranked by the Museum of Hoaxes as the best April Fools' prank ever was a 1957 BBC report about Switzerland experiencing an early spaghetti harvest. The television show included video of peasants pulling spaghetti from trees and explained that a uniform length for the spaghetti had been achieved through expert cultivation. The BBC got hundreds of phone calls, with most callers asking serious questions, such as where could they buy spaghetti trees.

3   Oh, those Brits. Astronomer Patrick Moore told BBC Radio 2 on April 1, 1976, that the alignment of the planets Pluto and Jupiter would cause a temporary decrease in Earth's gravity at 9:47 a.m. If people jumped in the air at that time, Moore said, they would float for a short while. Indeed, many listeners called the station to say they had floated.

4   Most people know they need to read the Web with a healthy skepticism, but that doesn't mean hoaxes about the Internet don't catch the unwary. In 1994, PC Computing magazine wrote that Congress was considering a bill making it illegal to surf the Internet while drunk. The outcry was great enough that Sen. Edward Kennedy was forced to deny being the sponsor of the nonexistent legislation. In 1996, an e-mail, purportedly from the Massachusetts Institute of Technology, informed people that the Internet would be shut down for a day for spring cleaning. The day that users were told to disconnect computers? April 1.

5   In 1997, newspaper readers found chaos on the comics pages. Billy from "Family Circus" was joking with Dilbert. The "Family Circus" mom sported a Dilbert boss-like pointy hairdo. What was going on? The Great Comic Switcheroo. Urged on by "Baby Blues" creators Rick Kirkman and Jerry Scott, more than 40 cartoonists swapped strips for the day. Among the other switches: Blondie and Garfield, and Shoe and Beetle Bailey.

6   Chicago's WXRT-FM 93.1 has a history of April Fools' hoaxes going back to the 1970s. In 1980, the station promoted the Mayor Jane Byrne April Fool Fest on Navy Pier. On a warm spring day, hundreds of people showed up at what was then a rather derelict padlocked Navy Pier to hear live music, despite the fact that some of the promised artists were dead. In 1998, the station announced it had been purchased by Playboy, was changing the call letters to XXXRT and was touting itself as True Adult Radio. Outraged listeners bombarded not only the station with calls but also Playboy.

7   Chicago's downtown streets devolved into gantlets of tomfoolery in the 1880s and 1890s when armies of newsboys gathered to harass and taunt passers-by. In 1880, the Tribune reported that one ingenious youngster created a wooden apparatus that chalked the words "April Fool" when tapped lightly on a victim's back.

8   Australian businessman Dick Smith had long discussed his plans to tow an iceberg from Antarctica into Sydney Harbor so he could sell especially pure ice cubes to the public for 10 cents apiece. So, when a barge towed a huge white object into the harbor on April 1, 1978, Sydney residents got excited. But then it rained, which dissolved the faux berg—a giant mound of firefighting foam and shaving cream that had been piled on sheets of white plastic.

9   On April 1, 1998, Burger King took out a full-page ad in USA Today to announce a fast-food breakthrough: the Left-Handed Whopper. It featured the same ingredients as the regular Whopper, except the condiments were rotated 180 degrees. According to Burger King, thousands of customers requested the new burger, and others asked for a right-handed version.

10   Among the true things that have happened in April 1: The first speaker of the House was elected (1789); American forces landed on Okinawa (1945); the first U.S. weather satellite was launched (1960); and Steve Wozniak and Steve Jobs founded Apple (1976). Born on April 1, 1929, were Czech author Milan Kundera ("The Unbearable Lightness of Being") and University of Michigan football coach Bo Schembechler ("The Unbearable Heaviness of Losing to Ohio State").

SOURCES: *museumofhoaxes.com; snopes.com; infoplease.com; The Independent of London; St. Paul (Minn.) Pioneer Press; babyblues.com; WXRT-FM 93.1; Tribune news services.*

ATHEISTS

1   Poet Percy Bysshe Shelley was expelled from Oxford University for co-writing a pamphlet called "The Necessity of Atheism" in 1811. When Shelley drowned in a boating accident at age 29, a British newspaper observed that "now he knows whether there is a God or not."

2   To 20th Century philosopher Bertrand Russell, dogmatic belief in God was irrational. He said it would be like him demanding that people believe there was a china teapot orbiting the sun between Mars and Earth, too small to be detected by any telescope.

3   A contemporary version of Russell's teapot is the Flying Spaghetti Monster. In 2005, when the Kansas School Board considered allowing the theory of intelligent design to be taught alongside evolution, an Oregon State University physics graduate named Bobby Henderson wrote a letter to the board demanding equal time for the Church of the Flying Spaghetti Monster. Since then, the church has become an Internet sensation, embraced by atheists and other skeptics who call themselves Pastafarians.

4   The cover of Time magazine on April 8, 1966, asked a question that many Americans had not considered: "Is God Dead?" The cover attracted considerable attention, and a scene in the child-of-Satan film "Rosemary's Baby" shows Rosemary reading that famous issue of Time.

5   Books rejecting the existence of God have had a major impact in recent years. Christopher Hitchens'" God Is Not Great" was a finalist for the 2007 National Book Award. Richard Dawkins' website says his 2006 book "The God Delusion" has sold 1.5 million copies. But not everyone is impressed. Turkey banned his website in 2008.

6   A USA Today/Gallup poll in 2007 found that Americans would sooner have a gay president than an atheist one. Gays were rejected by 42 percent, atheists by 48 percent.

7   Ron Reagan, son of the former president, says he can never win elective office because he is an atheist. But attitudes may be changing. In 2007, U.S. Rep. Fortney "Pete" Stark Jr. (D-Calif.) declared his disbelief in God. He was thought to be the first member of Congress ever to make that declaration.

8   Until a U.S. Supreme Court ruling in 1961, some states banned atheists from holding public office.

9   Katharine Hepburn, who portrayed a missionary in "The African Queen," was an atheist.

10   The expression "There are no atheists in foxholes" asserts that even disbelievers come to God in their most needful moments. But a group called the Military Association of Atheists and Freethinkers would disagree. Author James Morrow once wrote that the expression about no atheists in foxholes is "not an argument against atheism—it's an argument against foxholes."

SOURCES: *"Atheists, Agnostics, and Deists in America" by Peter M. Rinaldo; New York Sun; cnn. com; Tribune archives and news services.*

BIRTHDAYS

1 A "leapling" or "leaper" is a person born on Feb. 29, with a birthday every four years. Among those born on Leap Day: actor Dennis Farina and serial killer Aileen Wuornos. It's also the fictional birthday of a mighty leaper known as Superman.

2 On March 30, 1852, the son of Anna and Theodorus van Gogh was stillborn. His parents named him Vincent and buried him near the Dutch church where Theodorus preached. Exactly a year later—on March 30, 1853—Anna gave birth to another son, whom they also named Vincent and who became one of the world's most famous artists.

3 William Shakespeare is said to have died on his birthday. But like many other purported details about the Bard, this one is unconfirmed. We know for certain that the following people had the ultimate bummer on their birthday: actress Ingrid Bergman, Cubs greats Joe Tinker and Gabby Hartnett, Holocaust heroine Corrie ten Boom, feminist Betty Friedan, talk-show host Mike Douglas and actor John Banner, who played Sgt. Schultz on "Hogan's Heroes."

4 President Lyndon Johnson's birthday cake in 1965 featured a plastic hypodermic needle on top of it, symbolizing the passage of the Medicare Act.

5 Christo, the artist who has decorated such sites as Germany's Reichstag and New York's Central Park, was born on the same day in the same year as his wife and project partner, Jeanne-Claude de Guillebon.

6 It's well known that Marilyn Monroe sang a sultry "Happy Birthday" to President John Kennedy in front of a Madison Square Garden crowd of 15,000 while wearing a dress so tight that she had to be sewn into it. Less remembered is that Kennedy's brother-in-law, actor Peter Lawford, made a joke about Monroe's belated entrance at the 1962 birthday gala. He called her "the late Marilyn Monroe," a quip that took on an eerie tinge when she died less than three months later.

7 In 1984, the Hentzel family of Palo Alto, Calif., received a draft registration notice for a fictitious person named Johnny Klomberg. Years earlier, the family's two boys, Eric and Greg, had made up the names of Johnny and others to get extra helpings of the free birthday ice cream offered by the Farrell's restaurant chain. The draft sign-up notice exposed the fact that the government was using the ice cream list to track down 18-year-old men. Farrell's said it was "outraged" to learn that a mailing-list broker had sold the names without permission, and the government dumped the 167,000 customers from its files.

8 New Jersey authorities seized the children of Heath and Deborah Campbell in January 2009 in a dispute that began over a birthday cake. Heath Campbell went into a ShopRite store and asked for a cake decorated to say, "Happy birthday, Adolf Hitler," in honor of his 3-yearold son, Adolf Hitler Campbell. The store refused. Amid heavy publicity, authorities examined the treatment of young Adolf and his younger sisters, Joyce Lynn Aryan Nation Campbell and Honszlynn Hinler Jeannie Campbell, and took all three away.

9 About 5 percent of babies are born on their due date.

10 The Museum of Birthday Party Excess might feature a special room for the June 2001 festivities honoring the wife of then-Tyco International Chairman Dennis Kozlowski. Held in Sardinia, the party cost $2 million, half of which was billed to the publicly held company. The party's centerpiece was an ice sculpture based on Michelangelo's David, with Stolichnaya vodka pouring out of David's most private appendage. Kozlowski couldn't be prosecuted for bad taste, but he was later imprisoned for misusing company funds.

SOURCES: *National Gallery of Art; snopes.com; "Van Gogh: His Life and His Art," by David Sweetman; "Sons and Brothers: The Days of Jack and Bobby Kennedy" by Richard D. Mahoney; "Creating Your Birth Plan" by Marsden Wagner and Stephanie Gunning; Tribune news services.*

DECEMBER HOLIDAYS

1 The traditional Christmas plant we call a poinsettia was known by the Aztecs as cuetlaxochitl. Its current name came from the first U.S. envoy to Mexico, Joel R. Poinsett, who noticed the plant being used for holiday celebrations and sent a few north to the United States in the 1820s.

2 Hanukkah, which is the same day every year on the Jewish calendar, is a wandering holiday on the Gregorian calendar. In 2011, the eight-day celebration began at sunset Dec. 20. In 2016, it starts on Christmas Eve. In 2013, it's Thanksgiving eve, Nov. 27.

3 Rudolph, who now resides at the North Pole, was born in Chicago in 1939. The Montgomery Ward department store chain assigned ad copywriter Robert May to compose a Christmas poem that could be distributed to customers nationwide. He wrote "Rollo the Red-Nosed Reindeer," but execs didn't like that name. They vetoed Reginald too. May's third name, Rudolph, was accepted, and the poem was shared with millions of customers.

4 Kwanzaa, which is observed Dec. 26 through Jan. 1, is a nonreligious holiday that celebrates African-American culture. The weeklong event highlights seven principles, including Nia, which is Swahili for "purpose." That's where actress Nia Long got her name.

5 Abraham Lincoln's youngest son, Thomas, nicknamed Tad, was known as a sensitive youngster. On Christmas 1864, Tad, then 10, took the spirit of the season to heart and invited some street urchins into the White House for a meal. The cooks refused to feed the kids until Tad took up the issue with the president, who ordered that the children be fed.

6 Among the holiday traditions on a decline are tinsel and spray cans of fake snow, according to an article by Marc Levy on TheStreet.com. Already declared dead are aluminum trees, which became uncool when they were denounced on TV's "A Charlie Brown Christmas."

7   Boxing Day is a weird holiday. No one is sure when it started or how it got its name. Celebrated in many British-influenced lands, Boxing Day is traditionally the day after Christmas. It may be an offshoot of St. Stephen's Day, which is what the Irish call it. In Canada and England, it has turned into a shopping frenzy like America's Black Friday. The "box" in Boxing Day may be the donation bins of the Anglican church that were opened for the poor Dec. 26. Or the name may come from the boxed presents that British aristocrats gave to the help the day after Christmas.

8   The Christmas tradition of kissing someone under the mistletoe took on a decidedly Chicago bent in 1975. The first Mayor Richard Daley was fiercely protective of his family. Responding to criticism that he funneled city business to a company that employed his son, he responded, "There's a mistletoe hanging from my coattail."

9   St. Francis of Assisi is credited with making the nativity scene part of the Christmas tradition. In 1223, he organized a live creche to emphasize Jesus' humble beginnings.

IU   We were all told that the poem "The Night Before Christmas" was written by Clement Clarke Moore, a Manhattan scholar. But the facts are squishier. For starters, the poem was first published as "A Visit From St. Nicholas." For another thing, Moore may not have written it. Literary sleuth Donald Foster investigated the Christmas poem and concluded that Moore was lying. Foster thinks the author was amateur poet Henry Livingston Jr. of Poughkeepsie, N.Y. Foster says the poem bears the style, outlook and cultural references of Livingston, not Moore. Moore didn't claim ownership until 1844, 19 years after the poem's anonymous appearance in a Troy, N.Y., newspaper. By that time, Livingston was dead. Before coming forward as the author, Moore wrote to the Troy newspaper and asked whether anyone remembered the poem's author. The answer came back that anyone who might have known was dead and gone.

SOURCES: *"Panati's Extraordinary Origins of Everyday Things" by Charles Panati; "A Christmas Compendium" by J. John; "Handbook to Life in the Medieval World, Vol. 3" by Madeleine Pelner Cosman and Linda Gale Jones; "Author Unknown" by Donald Foster; "The Upside-Down Christmas Tree" by Delilah Scott and Emma Troy; "Baby Names for Dummies" by Margaret Rose; "Baby Names Now" by Linda Rosenkrantz and Pamela Redmond Satran; "Christmas in the White House" by Albert J. Menendez; "Chase's Calendar of Events"; Claire Suddath in time.com; thestreet.com; chabad.org; holidays.net; literarytraveler.com; Cincinnati Post; Tribune archives.*

FAMOUS EVANGELISTS

1   Zion, a city north of Chicago founded by Scottish evangelist John Alexander Dowie in 1902, at various times banned circuses, theaters, alcohol, gambling, tobacco, pork, politicians, doctors, drugstores, jazz, oysters, chop suey, tan-colored shoes, flirting, dancing, swearing, spitting and whistling on Sunday.

2   British preacher Gipsy Smith's visit to Chicago in 1909 was a textbook example of the danger of spotlighting sin. Smith invaded Chicago's vortex of vice, the Levee District on the Near South Side, to conduct a prayer rally. The event attracted thousands of the pious and the curious, and many of the latter stayed around after prayers to conduct their own fact-finding tours.

3   Billy Sunday was a ballplayer for the Chicago White Stockings who became a well-known preacher. One of his most famous sermons was called "Get on the Water Wagon." A water wagon was a vehicle used to dampen dirt roads to keep the dust down. When a person gave up alcohol, it was said that he had gotten "on the water wagon"—a slang term that was later shortened to "on the wagon."

4   When Prohibition ended in 1933, Rev. Billy Graham's father bought a case of beer and forced the teenage Billy and his sister Catherine to drink bottle after bottle until they threw up, as a lesson on the evils of drink.

5   One of six tax-exempt ministries targeted for scrutiny in 2007 by Sen. Charles Grassley was led by Georgia's Rev. Creflo Dollar, whose ownership of a Rolls-Royce harks back to the quintessential "prosperity preacher" of the 1970s, Rev. Ike. The man born Frederick Eikerenkoetter II turned himself into the charismatic Ike and helped define TV preaching before his death in 2009. Owner of a fleet of mink-appointed Rolls-Royces, Rev. Ike said, "The best thing you can do for the poor is not to be one of them."

6 Missouri evangelist Joyce Meyer's early life story is excruciating. Sexually molested by her father, she married a ne'erdo-well. ("One night I caught him trying to get my wedding ring off me in the middle of the night.") She divorced, remarried and became an evangelist, sometimes sleeping in her car because she had no money for hotels. Eventually, she wrote 70 books and became such a financial success that Grassley asked her about reports that her ministry paid $23,000 for a marble-topped commode.

7 Meyer gets a grade of C and Dollar gets an F in MinistryWatch.com's ratings of "transparency"—the ministries' disclosure of finances and other information. The watchdog website also issues "donor alerts" about preachers it deems especially suspicious, such as faith healer Benny Hinn. In addition, MinistryWatch.com highlights 30 "Shining Light Ministries" as worthy stewards of their followers' donations.

8 Oral Roberts' most famous fundraising effort came in 1987, when he said God would "take me home" if he didn't raise $8 million for medical scholarships. Less well-known was another life-threatening experience he revealed the same year. Roberts said Satan had entered his bedroom and tried to strangle him, only to be chased away by Roberts' wife, Evelyn.

9 Televangelist Tammy Faye Messner (formerly Bakker), who died in 2007, had eye liner, lip liner and eyebrows tattooed onto her face."This way, when you wake up you don't feel faceless," she said. "You can wake up and already have a face."

10 GodTube, an alternative to YouTube, officially debuted on the Internet in 2007. While YouTube's slogan is "Broadcast Yourself," GodTube's is "Broadcast Him." Among the videos: a parody of Sir Mixa-Lot's "Baby Got Back" called "Baby Got Book."

SOURCES: *St. Louis Post-Dispatch; Jet magazine; Time magazine; Memphis Flyer; Patriot-News of Harrisburg, Pa.; Encyclopedia of Chicago.*

HALLOWEEN

1 The idea that strangers try to poison trick-or-treaters with Halloween candy is a myth. Experts say no such incident has been documented in recent decades. But the myth spawned a real-life horror story on Halloween night 1974. Eight-year-old Timothy O'Bryan died after eating Pixie Stix laced with cyanide by his own father to collect life insurance money. As part of his horrific plan to divert suspicion, Ronald O'Bryan also sprinkled poison on candy he gave his daughter and three other children, but luckily none ate it. He was executed in Texas in 1985.

2 In 1972, John Fitzgerald, the mayor of southwest suburban Burbank, contended that trick-or-treating was a violation of the city's solicitation ordinance. He tried to ban it, but cooler heads on the City Council prevailed and the good kids of Burbank got their candy.

3 Many have heard of the Celtic festival of Samhain, a precursor to Halloween. But few know how to pronounce Samhain. It's SOW-win.

4 When Dwight D. Eisenhower turned 10 in 1900, he told his parents he was old enough to go out with his older brothers on Halloween. His father said no, and young Ike flew into a rage. He ran outside and beat the stump of an old apple tree until his fists were bleeding. His dad wasn't amused. He paddled the future president and sent him to his room.

5 The first jack o' lanterns were carved out of turnips and beets. (Pumpkins weren't native to Europe.)

6 The phrase "trick or treat" is neither ancient nor European. Historians have traced its origin to the United States in the 1930s.

7 Halloween Martin was a pioneer in Chicago radio—some say the city's first disc jockey. Host of a morning program called "The Musical Clock" from 1929 to 1946, she got the name Halloween because she was born on that day.

8 The "Halloween" movie franchise is one of the oldest and longest-running in the genre. The first installment appeared in 1978 and featured Jamie Lee Curtis in her feature film debut. She earned just $8,000. For "Halloween: Resurrection" in 2002, she got $3 million. The original "Halloween" was set in the fictional town of Haddonfield, Ill., but the film shows mountains, palm trees and cars with California license plates.

9 Halloween pranksters of the 1880s and '90s stole signs—apparently barber poles were a high-value target—and pulled up wooden sidewalks. According to Tribune reports from the time, gates were also highly prized. Less innocent were the arson, the beatings with bags of soot and the obstructions of the trolley lines. In 1902, a 10-year-old with a peashooter — literally a straw and a pea — hit a motorman on the Fulton Street electric car in the eye. He lost control and crashed into a horse and wagon. Eight people were injured.

10 The night before Halloween has its own, nastier tradition in some U.S. cities. In Detroit, it is called Devil's Night and has been marked by arson. In 1984, at its worst, the three days of Oct. 29-31 saw more than 800 cases of arson that left dozens homeless.

SOURCES: *"Death Makes a Holiday" by David J. Skal; "The Halloween Encyclopedia" by Lisa Morton; "Eisenhower: A Soldier's Life" by Carlo D'Este; "Rockin' Out," by Reebee Garafalo; "Encyclopedia of Chicago," edited by Janice L. Reiff, Ann Durkin Keating and James R. Grossman; "Invisible Stars: A Social History of Women in American Broadcasting" by Donna L. Halper; the-numbers.com; movietome.com; boxofficemojo.com; imdb.com; ABC News; snopes.com; historychannel.com; Austin American-Statesman; Detroit News; Tribune archives.*

SAINTS

1   The Catholic Church recognizes two types of saints: Confessors and martyrs. Confessors show their purity through their extreme virtue; martyrs prove their piety by dying for the faith. Early Christians considered martyrs to be saints automatically.

2   The first U.S. citizen canonized was Frances Xavier Cabrini, a native Italian who is the patron saint of immigrants. The nun who helped found schools, hospitals and orphanages died in 1917 in one of the places she had built — Columbus Hospital in Chicago.

3   A first-class relic is a piece of a saint's remains. While a relic's authenticity is usually difficult to prove, it's ability to capture the imagination of the faithful throughout history is undeniable. You can see relics — usually very small splinters of bone or pieces of cloth — in many Chicago churches, including Holy Name Cathedral, Queen of All Saints Basilica in Sauganash and Our Lady of Sorrows Basilica on West Jackson Boulevard.

4   Clare of Assisi, a 13th-century saint, was in her sickbed, away from church. But she reported a vision in which she was able to see and hear the Mass anyway. Because of that skill, Pope Pius XII in 1958 declared her the patron saint of television.

5   St. Anthony of Padua's reputation as a great speaker is reflected in a tale about the transfer of his remains to a new vault in 1263, three decades after his death. St. Bonaventure reported that Anthony's tongue was undecayed and still red in color, so Bonaventure picked it up and kissed it.

6   Santeria, a religion that originated among slaves in Cuba, is Spanish for "the worship of saints." It's so named because the religion's first followers hid their reverence for African gods (orishas) under the guise of worshipping Catholic saints. Today, Santeria is an African-Catholic hybrid that serves as an example of syncretism, a combination of religions.

7   There was no Great Saint Purge in 1969. Word that many saints would no longer be remembered at Mass on their traditional day was misunderstood to mean they were no longer saints. Not true. Pope Paul VI was cleaning up the church calendar, demoting saints of which very little was known or who lacked worldwide significance. But the confusion and hurt were very real for believers of St. Christopher, the patron saint of travelers, whose statue rode shotgun in many an American's car.

8   In medieval France, a cult developed over a dog known as St. Guinefort. As the story went, Guinefort was guarding his owner's infant and killed a snake to protect the child. But the owner saw blood on the baby and the greyhound, assumed the worst and killed the dog. For centuries, a well that held Guinefort's remains was a pilgrimage site for people who considered the dog a saint. But Catholic officials banned such veneration.

9   Saints are often depicted in Christian art with telltale symbols related to their lives or manner of death. For example, St. Stephen, the first martyr, usually holds a basket of rocks, signifying how he was stoned to death. St. Bartholomew carries his own skin because he was flayed alive. St. Luke is often depicted with an ox because of the Gospel writer's emphasis on sacrifice.

10   You may know that the New Orleans Saints were named after the famous song "When the Saints Go Marching In." But did you know the birth of the team was announced on All Saints' Day, Nov. 1, 1966? The name was cleared with local Catholic Archbishop Philip Hannan, who gave his blessing, and then added: "Besides, I have this terrible premonition we might need all the help we can get."

SOURCES: *"101 Questions and Answers on Saints" by George P. Evans; "Martyrs and Martyrdom in England, c. 1400-1700," edited by Thomas S. Freeman and Thomas Frederick Mayer; "In the Company of Animals: A Study of Human-Animal Relationships" by James Serpell; "The Encyclopedia of Saints" by Rosemary Guiley; "This Saint's for You!" by Thomas J. Craughwell; "Saints Preserve Us!" by Sean Kelly and Rosemary Rogers; "The Dictionary of Saints" by Annette Sandoval; "Santeria: The Religion, Faith, Rites, Magic" by Migene Gonzalez-Wippler; "The Rough Guide to Unexplained Phenomena" by Bob Rickard and John Michell; "Saints and Their Symbols: Recognizing Saints in Art and in Popular Images" by Fernando Lanzi, Gioia Lanzi; "Dictionary of Saints" by John J. Delaney; "The Saints, the Superdome, and the Scandal" by Dave Dixon, Peter Finney; Chicago magazine; New York Times; National Post (Canada); newadvent.org.*

SATAN

1 Satan goes by many names, including Beelzebub, the devil, the deuce, the Great Deceiver, the Father of Lies, the Prince of Darkness, Old Mr. Grim, Old Ned, Old Nick, Old Sam, Old Scratch, the Old One, Old Rip, Old Poker, Old Splitfoot, the Black Spy, the Gentleman in Black and bogey.

2 Many people are certain the devil plays an active role in current events. Pat Robertson said Haiti suffered an earthquake in 2010 because its people "swore a pact to the devil" to gain independence from France two centuries earlier. And Miss California USA 2009 Carrie Prejean said that when she was asked about gay marriage at the Miss USA Pageant, "I felt as though Satan was trying to tempt me in asking me this question."

3 Buddhism also has many names for the devil. As Mara, he represents temptation and death and sin. But as Varsavarti, he is a hedonistic evil, who fulfills the thirsts for existence, pleasure and power.

4 Despite the rumors, KISS does not stand for Knights in Satan's Service. In fact, it doesn't stand for anything. But the rock band's bassist Gene Simmons wrote: "When I was asked whether I worshiped the devil, I simply refused to answer for a number of reasons: The first reason, of course, was that it was good press."

5 When Malcolm X was in prison, he denounced God so vigorously that his fellow inmates nicknamed him "Satan." American ballplayer Brian Warren's misbehavior in Japan earned him the label "Devil Man." And in the film "The Proposal," Sandra Bullock's character is so annoying that her office nickname is "Satan's Mistress."

6 One of the most significant events in American history occurred at Kill Devil Hills, N.C. That's where the Wright Brothers made their groundbreaking flight. "Kill devil" is a slang term for rum, and the place may have gotten its name because rum-carrying ships ran aground in that area along the Outer Banks.

7 Americans' belief in the devil is growing, according to Gallup polls. In 1990, 55 percent of Americans said they believed in the devil. In 2001, it was 68 percent and in 2007, it was 70 percent.

8 Playing Lucifer in the 1997 film "The Devil's Advocate," Al Pacino cursed God with a fury. Asked if that made him nervous, the actor replied, "Of course, naturally. But I thought, you know, it's about something. ...There is an immunity an actor has, right? I hope, I hope."

9 The dramatic rock formation in Wyoming known as Devils Tower was named by an Army colonel who thought the Native Americans called it "Bad God's Tower." Not so much. It went by many names, most related to bears, such as Bear's House, Bear Tipi or Bear Lodge.

10 In 2002, the Devils Lake, N.D., school board banished its high school sports nickname: the Satans. And a few years ago, the Tampa Bay Major League Baseball team changed its name from Devil Rays to simply Rays. In 2005, a New Jersey legislator who was a Baptist deacon took issue with the hockey team being called the New Jersey Devils, but no change was made. In fact, that name does not refer to Satan but instead is a nod to the Jersey Devil, a mythical creature with bat wings and a forked tail that is said to haunt southern New Jersey.

SOURCES: *"Cassell's Dictionary of Slang" by Jonathon Green; "The Autobiography of Malcolm X," as told to Alex Haley; "The History of the Devil and the Idea of Evil" by Paul Carus; "The Jersey Devil" by James F. McCloy and Ray Miller; baseball-reference.com; snopes.com; kdhnc.com; The Baltimore Sun; Los Angeles Times; Gallup.com; National Park Service, Tribune archives and news services.*

10 THINGS YOU MIGHT NOT KNOW ABOUT

LANGUAGE

ACRONYMS

1 WWILF stands for "What was I looking for?" It's not the queen's English, but it is the basis for a British slang word, "wilfing," which means aimless Internet searching, especially at work.

2 DFAC is a "dining facility" in the military. It's pronounced dee-fak. If you call it a "chow hall" or "mess hall," you're old school. Another military term is TRATS, for tin-tray rations that the Army sometimes uses in the field.

3 OTM is used by U.S. border control officials for "other than Mexican."

4 KGOY means "kids getting older younger." This is used by both social scientists and toymakers to describe the perception that children are embracing more mature interests earlier, which is bad news for dollmakers, among others. Some people believe it's also bad for society, and they blame the advertising industry for turning young girls into sexual objects.

5 BSOs are "bright, shiny objects"—anything new and intriguing, especially in technology. The acronym is often used negatively, with the suggestion that BSOs distract a person from what is truly important.

6 "Get Smart," the classic television series from the 1960s that inspired the 2008 Steve Carell movie, has two fake acronyms: The good-guy spy agency, CONTROL, and the evil agency, KAOS, appear to be acronyms but don't stand for anything.

7 EGR is a Christian term for a sinful or difficult person. It stands for "extra grace required."

8 You've heard of NIMBYs ("not in my backyard") and LULU ("locally unwanted land use"). Well, NOTEs go a step beyond: "not over there either." There's also NOPE ("not on planet Earth").

9 An anachronym is a word that started out as an acronym but no longer is thought of that way. Examples include laser (light amplification by stimulated emission of radiation) and scuba (self-contained underwater breathing apparatus), even when worn by dogs such as Hooch the Daredevil.

10 There's also the opposite—a backronym, a word that didn't start out as an acronym but was given such a meaning on the back end. Wiki, the word for media created and edited by users, comes from a Hawaiian word for quick, but some people have alleged that it stands for "what I know is." Another example is bimbo, which most likely comes from the Italian word for baby but has been turned into a backronym: "body impressive, brain optional." Potential picks: Kate Hudson and Matthew McConaughey.

SOURCES: *wordspy.com; doubletongued.org; langmaker.com; reference.com; globalsecurity. org; Computer Weekly; The News & Observer of Raleigh, N.C.*

DOUBLE TALK

1 During the George W. Bush administration, homeland security adviser Frances Townsend rejected the idea that the United States' inability to capture Osama bin Laden was a "failure." Instead, she said, it was "a success that hasn't occurred yet."

2 Trying to take the sting out of the recession, employers shy away from the word "layoff." The alternatives: smartsizing, decruitment, involuntary attrition, employee simplification, corporate outplacing, negative employee retention and career-change opportunity. In 2009, Nokia Siemens Networks announced a "synergy-related head count restructuring."

3 The U.S. War Department ceased to exist in the late 1940s and was absorbed into a new agency called the Defense Department. Since then, not a single American military engagement has begun with a formal declaration of war. More than 100,000 Americans have died in warfare since the War Department disappeared, many of them in a "police action" in Korea and a "conflict" in Vietnam. Most recently, President Barack Obama dumped the George W. Bush-era phrase "global war on terror" in favor of the more bureaucratic and less warlike "overseas contingency operations."

4 Warfare is prime time for euphemists. The accidental killing of comrades is known as "friendly fire." Dead soldiers are "nonoperative personnel." A retreat is a "redeployment." The simple act of reinforcement is a "surge." During World War II, U.S. airmen lost in action assumed the acronym of NYR—not yet returned.

5 In polite company after the American Civil War, the bitter conflict that left about 620,000 people dead was referred to as "The Late Unpleasantness."

6 When leaders of the anti-war demonstrations during the 1968 Democratic National Convention were tried in Chicago two years later, defendant David Dellinger uttered an eight-letter word in court that likened a police officer's testimony to the waste product of a bull. Dellinger was reprimanded and his bail was revoked. New York Times reporter J. Anthony Lukas called his editor, urging that the Times print the word. The editor suggested that it simply be called an obscenity, but Lukas worried that readers would imagine even worse words than the one that was spoken. "Why don't we call it a barnyard epithet?" the editor suggested. And so they did.

7 Let's hope that the marketing person who rebranded adult diapers as "discreet active wear" got a nice bonus.

8 Because of South Carolina Gov. Mark Sanford and his secret trip to Argentina in June 2009 for an extramarital affair, the phrase "hiking the Appalachian Trail" means much more than enjoying the great outdoors.

9 Remember when you were a kid and went to "phys ed" or "gym"? In some school districts, they're extinct. The preferred term now is "kinetic wellness."

10 On the Internet, retailers tout their "wooden interdental stimulators." Also known as toothpicks.

SOURCES: *"A Dictionary of Euphemisms & Other Doubletalk" by Hugh Rawson; "How Not to Say What You Mean: A Dictionary of Euphemisms" by R.W. Holder; "Propaganda and the Ethics of Persuasion" by Randal Marlin; wordspy.com, buzzwhack.com; globalsecurity.org; euphemismlist.com; networkworld.com; pbs.com; bnet.com; businessweek.com; bobsutton.typepad.com; Guardian; Imperial War Museum; Universal Press Syndicate; Tribune news services.*

MIDDLE NAMES

1 Middle names are a somewhat recent tradition in Western civilization. No person aboard the Mayflower had a middle name. Only three of the first 17 U.S. presidents had one.

2 The T in educator Booker T. Washington's name stood for Taliaferro. The former slave added the middle name in his later years after learning that his mother had once called him Booker Taliaferro. Even today, the significance of Taliaferro is not known. Washington's father was a white man whom he did not know, leading some to speculate that the father might have been from a nearby family named Taliaferro. But there is no evidence of that, and Washington seemed to believe that it was simply a name his mother liked.

3 Retailer J.C. Penney had an appropriate middle name: Cash.

4 Cal McLish, who pitched for the Cubs, White Sox and five other major league baseball teams from 1944 to 1964, was named Calvin Coolidge Julius Caesar Tuskahoma McLish. He once wrote: "The only thing I was ever told [by my mother] was that of six previous children my dad was not involved in naming any of them — so he supposedly tried to catch up, using me. He named me after a president, a Roman emperor and an Indian chief. Being part Indian, I guess he felt he had to get an Indian name in there some-where— I've always claimed he had to be in the firewater to give a kid a name like that." So what did McLish's family call him? Buster.

5 Tom Cruise's middle name is Cruise. His birth name was Thomas Cruise Mapother IV. When he moved to New York to pursue acting after high school, he adopted the last name of Cruise, which was the name of an ances-tral family matriarch.

6 When Reginald Kenneth Dwight changed his name to Elton John, he took the middle name Hercules.

7 Frances Bean Cobain, daughter of rockers Kurt Cobain and Courtney Love, got her middle name because her late father thought she looked like a kidney bean. While serving as an intern in 2008 at Rolling Stone magazine, she was the victim of a leak to the New York Post's gossip page. An unnamed source accused her of calling in sick too often, failing to get coffee for employees and wearing "funny outfits."

8 When readers of The New York Times began seeing a byline of "Jennifer 8. Lee," they might have thought it was an attention-getting career gimmick. In fact, Lee took the name in her youth to distinguish herself from other Jennifer Lees and to celebrate her Chinese heritage. The number 8 stands for prosperity in China—witness the starting date for the Beijing Olympics: 8-8-08. Lee's friends call her "Jenny 8."

9 Tennessee politician Byron Anthony Looper legally renamed himself Byron (Low Tax) Looper and ran against state Sen. Tommy Burks in 1998. Then he murdered Burks two weeks before Election Day. Sentenced to life in prison, Looper has fought his conviction. But the evidence was solid. A former high school classmate testified that Looper declared a few hours after the murder: "I did it, man! I did it! I killed that guy I was running against!"

10 In 2005, comedian/magician Penn Jillette named his daughter Moxie Crime- Fighter Jillette, joking that if she ever got stopped for speeding, she could say, "But officer, we're on the same side. My middle name is CrimeFighter." To those who criticize such wacky baby-naming, Jillette declared: "Everyone I know with an unusual name loves it. It's only the losers named Dave that think having an unusual name is bad, and who cares what they think? They're named Dave."

SOURCES: *"Treasury of Name Lore," by Elsdon C. Smith; "Booker T. Washington: The Making of a Black Leader 1856-1901," by Louis R. Harlan; "Kurt Cobain," by Christopher Sandford; "Tom Cruise Unauthorized," by Wensley Clarkson; Orange County Register; Ventura County Star; "Baseball Letters: A Fan's Correspondence with His Heroes," by Seth Swirsky; Sports Illustrated; and Tribune news services.*

PUNCTUATION

1 First of all, let's explain why the serial comma is important to some people. A blog on economist.com cites an apocryphal example: "I'd like to thank my parents, Ayn Rand and God." Without a comma after "Rand," the writer has a mighty unusual parentage.

2 Maybe it's not surprising that New York City, capital of the U.S. publishing industry, has plenty of lore about semicolons. When former Mayor Fiorello LaGuardia was annoyed by an overeducated bureaucrat, he used the insult "semicolon boy." When the Son of Sam killer put a semicolon in a note, police speculated he might be a freelance journalist. (Killer David Berkowitz was a security guard and cabdriver.)

3 Union Gen. Joe Hooker got his nickname because a newspaper printer left out a dash. The label headline that was supposed to read "Fighting—Joe Hooker" became "Fighting Joe Hooker." He hated it, but it stuck.

4 It could be said that the first blow that led to the Russian Revolution was over punctuation. Moscow printers went on strike in 1905, insisting they be paid for typing punctuation marks as well as letters. That led to a general strike across the country and to Czar Nicholas II granting Russia its first constitution.

5 Punctuation marks arranged to form smiley faces or sad faces may be common in today's digital communication, but emoticons predate texting and the Internet. Puck magazine published such typographical art in 1881.

6 The most rudimentary punctuation is the dot between words. Romans' ancient texts often ran together without spaces using all capital letters, which meant readers had to start decoding from the first line every time. The introduction of the dot suddenly rendered a block of text legible. The dot between words and numbers engraved on buildings is a legacy of this.

7 Playwright George Bernard Shaw hated apostrophes, writing: "There is not the faintest reason for persisting in the ugly and silly trick of peppering pages with these uncouth bacilli."

8 Unnecessary use of quotation marks drives some people so "batty" that they have "posted" more than 1,000 examples of "quotation mark abuse" on the photo sharing site Flickr. Our favorites are signs reading: "Cleaning lady 'available' " and "Best 'food' on 'Route 66.'"

9 People get awfully philosophical about punctuation. Said author Kurt Vonnegut: "When Hemingway killed himself he put a period at the end of his life; old age is more like a semicolon." Comedian Gracie Allen is credited with the aphorism "Never place a period where God has placed a comma."

10 In 1899, French poet Alcanter de Brahm proposed an "irony mark" (point d'ironie) that would signal that a statement was ironic. The proposed punctuation looked like a question mark facing backward at the end of a sentence. But it didn't catch on. No one seemed to get the point of it, ironically.

SOURCES: *"The Civil War: A Narrative" by Shelby Foote; "Memoirs of Nikita Khrushchev: Statesman, 1953-64" by Nikita Khrushchev, Sergei Khrushchev, George Shriver, Stephen Shenfield; "Encyclopedia of Emotion" by Gretchen Reevy, Yvette Malamud Ozer, Yuri Ito; "A Rhetoric of Irony" by Wayne C. Booth; "Eats, Shoots & Leaves" by Lynne Truss; "Has modern life killed the semicolon?" by Paul Collins in slate.com; editorandpublisher.com; The Author; Tribune news services.*

SPEECHES

1   Sometimes a long speech can be a good thing. In 1912, presidential candidate Teddy Roosevelt was about to talk in Milwaukee when a would-be assassin shot him. The bullet went through TR's coat, his eyeglass case and the speech itself —50 pages on heavy paper, folded once. The slowed-down bullet cracked one of TR's ribs but wounded him only slightly. Making sure the audience saw his bloodied shirt, Roosevelt gave the entire speech.

2   Bughouse Square on Chicago's Near North Side was a place where even the down-and-out could commit oratory. The late author Studs Terkel recalled a speaker named One-Arm Cholly Wendorf raising the stub of his right arm and declaring, "You know where the rest of this is? Somewhere in France. Somewhere in a trench...Cholly Wendorf's arm is enrichin' the soil that grows the grapes that bring you the best Cognac money can buy."

3   President John F. Kennedy's chief speechwriter, Ted Sorensen, knew his boss' speaking style so well that Kennedy sometimes arranged for Sorensen to impersonate him in phone calls.

4   Rep. Felix Walker, whose North Carolina district included Buncombe County, addressed Congress in 1820 during a debate over slavery. But when fellow lawmakers complained that his speech had little to do with the issue, he said he was making "a speech for Buncombe." That's how "buncombe" came to mean annoying and disingenuous language—leading to the words "bunk" and "debunk."

5   Glossophobia is the fear of public speaking. According to Toastmasters International, a nonprofit education group that helps people improve their communication skills, it is the most commonly cited fear in the U.S.

6   Sojourner Truth, the former slave who fought for emancipation and women's rights, was known for her "Ain't I a Woman?" speech in 1851. But early accounts of her talk did not include that phrase. It was more than a decade later when versions start showing up with "Ain't I a woman?" or "Ar'n't l a woman?" quoted four times. Casting further doubt on whether she was quoted accurately, the latter versions were in a standard Southern slave dialect, even though Truth grew up in New York state, first learned to speak Dutch rather than English, and was said to have an accent similar to uneducated white Northerners.

7 Statesman Henry Clay of Kentucky once gave an hourlong speech on the U.S. Senate floor about his dead bull Orozimbo.

8 When Adolf Hitler attended a meeting of the German Workers Party in 1919, it provided one of the earliest hints of his power as a political orator. Hitler was about to leave the event when a speaker argued to split off a part of Germany. Outraged, Hitler rose to rail passionately against the idea. The speech impressed one of the party's founders, Anton Drexler, who told a companion: "He has a big mouth; we could use him." Shortly after Hitler joined the group, it changed its name to the National Socialist German Workers Party, the Nazis.

9 The original teleprompter, built in 1950, was just a roll of butcher paper on two tubes that was hand-cranked to advance the speech. TelePrompTer Corp., which built an electronic version, found success after former President Herbert Hoover used one to address the Republican National Convention in 1952. In 2010, President Barack Obama was criticized for using the device too much.

10 Dec. 7, 1941, was originally a "date which will live in world history." Not a great opening line. Fortunately, Franklin D. Roosevelt revised that to "a date which will live in infamy" before his address to Congress and the nation the day after the Japanese attack on Pearl Harbor.

SOURCES: *"Touch and Go: A Memoir" by Studs Terkel; "White House Ghosts" by Robert Schlesinger; "One-Night Stands With American History" by Richard Shenkman and Kurt Reiger; "The Merriam-Webster New Book of Word Histories"; "History of World War II, Vol. 1," by Marshall Cavendish; "Hitler" by Joachim C. Fest; "Sojourner Truth: A Life, a Symbol" by Nell Irvin Painter; "Sojourner Truth: Slave, Prophet, Legend" by Carleton Mabee with Susan Mabee Newhouse; Popular Science magazine, July 1960; Peggy Noonan White House exit interview from presidentialtimeline.org; bbc.co.uk; archives.gov.*

MADE-UP WORDS

1 An idiot's journey through life can be called an "idiodyssey."

2 "Hasbian" is a term for a former lesbian.

3 When two words are blended to form one — such as "bromance" or "mocku-mentary" or "spork" — it's called a portmanteau or a portmanteau word. A port-manteau is also a type of suitcase that opens into two halves. (And the plural of portmanteau is correctly written two ways: portmanteaus and portmanteaux.)

4 "Hatriot" is used to describe an extremist member of a militia group, a per-son who greatly distrusts the current government, or a liberal who is always critical of the country. It is also used by football fans who don't like the team from New England.

5 If you've been "dixie-chicked," your own fans or customers have turned on you, as the country music group Dixie Chicks discovered in 2003 when they denounced then-President George W. Bush and the invasion of Iraq.

6 "Anticipointment" is a television and marketing term that was popular circa 1990, describing the feeling of consumers when a product is hyped but doesn't deliver.

7 The word "gerrymander" was invented in 1812 to describe a legislative dis-trict whose contours were grossly manipulated to favor one side. One such dis-trict in Massachusetts resembled a salamander, and the governor at the time was Elbridge Gerry. Thus, gerrymandering had occurred.

8 A "nagivator" is an auto passenger who nags instead of navigates.

9 Without the cell phone, "approximeeting" wouldn't work. That's when you make plans to meet someone but don't firm up the details until later, when you're on the move.

10 A college student who dates only people in his residence hall commits "dormcest."

SOURCES: *wharton.universia.net; urbandictionary.com; dictionary.reference.com; double-tongued.org; wordspy.com; "American Government and Politics Today: The Essentials" by Barbara A. Bardes, Mack C. Shelley and Steffen W. Schmidt.*

10 THINGS YOU MIGHT NOT KNOW ABOUT
HISTORY

THE DEATH PENALTY

1 Nearly 75 percent of all countries have abolished the death penalty or haven't executed anybody for at least 10 years, according to Amnesty International. But eight of the 10 most populous countries (China, India, the U.S. and Indonesia leading the way) allow capital punishment. They account for 53 percent of the world's people.

2 If the ghost of "Terrible" Tommy O'Connor ever shows up, his gallows are waiting for him. The convicted cop killer escaped from the old Cook County jail in 1921, just days before he was to be hanged. Officials kept the gallows around for decades just in case he was ever recaptured. He wasn't. But not until 1977 did a judge rule the county could get rid of them. They went first to Donley's Wild West Town in Union, then in 2006, Ripley's Believe It or Not outbid the Chicago History Museum at an auction. Now the gallows sit in a warehouse in Florida, waiting to be displayed.

3 The first person to die in the electric chair was William Kemmler in 1890. His death was a gruesome event that saw New York officials declare him dead, then hook him up again to finish the job when he started breathing. No less a personage than Thomas Edison, whose direct current technology was in a losing battle with alternating current, had lobbied New York to drop the noose and adopt the electric chair—powered by rival George Westinghouse's AC technology. To further associate his competitor's product with death, Edison suggested the best verb for such executions would be "Westinghoused."

4 How many people were burned at the stake during the witch trials in Salem, Mass.? None. Nineteen were hanged, and one was crushed to death by heavy stones.

5 Joseph Cadotte admitted killing his hunting partner in the 1890s in Montana but insisted it was self-defense. Nevertheless, Cadotte was executed after a prosecutor found a novel argument. Pointing to a birthmark on the suspect's neck that resembled a rope burn, the prosecutor declared: "Nature evidently intended the man to die. He was born to be hung."

6 The third president of the United States once committed a crime punishable by death. Fourteen years before he moved into the White House, Thomas Jefferson was touring the Piedmont region of northern Italy. Encountering a special type of rice, he took it out of Italy even though such smuggling was a capital offense.

7 In ancient Egypt, killing a cat, even accidentally, could be punished by death.

8 Thomas Grasso, who was executed in Oklahoma in 1995 for strangling an 85-year-old woman on Christmas Eve with the wiring of her holiday lights, was picky about his final meal. His request: 24 steamed mussels, 24 steamed clams, a Burger King double cheeseburger, six barbecued spare ribs, two milkshakes, a can of SpaghettiOs with meatballs, half a pumpkin pie and strawberries and cream. He got almost everything he asked for, issuing a last statement reading: "I didn't get my SpaghettiOs, I got spaghetti. I want the press to know this."

9 In parts of Asia, elephants were executioners. If the condemned person were lucky, he would be allowed to place his head on a pedestal to be crushed quickly. In other cases, he died more slowly, with the animal stepping on his limbs one by one and then pressing on his chest until he was dead.

10 When thieves were hanged in old England, their thumb and finger bones were sometimes sold as good luck charms. Likewise, spectators took the perspiration of the executed—known as "death sweat"—and rubbed it on their skin to treat warts and other skin problems.

SOURCES: *"The A-Z of Punishment and Torture" by Irene Thompson;"Last Words of the Executed" by Robert K. Elder (lastwordsoftheexecuted.com); "Thomas Jefferson: A Life" by Willard Sterne Randall; "The Book of Useless Information" by Noel Botham; New York Correction History Society; "Executioner's Current: Thomas Edison, George Westinghouse, and the Invention of the Electric Chair" by Richard Moran; "Empires of Light: Edison, Tesla, Westinghouse, and the Race to Electrify the World" by Jill Jonnes; "The Ancient Egyptian World" by Eric H. Cline and Jill Rubalcaba; Ripley's Believe It or Not!; Amnesty International; Tribune news services; salemwitchmuseum.com.*

DESPERADOES

1 A Wyoming ne'er-do-well known as "Big Nose George" Parrot tried to derail a payroll train by removing rail spikes. When a posse went after him, he and an accomplice killed two pursuers. Finally captured, Parrot was lynched in 1881. Dr. John Osborne, a local physician, skinned Parrot's body and arranged for the hide to be tanned and made into a pair of shoes.

2 In many books, a photo shows William Bonney, a.k.a. Billy the Kid, with a Winchester carbine in his right hand and a Colt single-action pistol holstered on his left hip. That has led people to assume that the gunslinger was left-handed. A 1958 film in which Paul Newman played Billy the Kid was titled "The Left-Handed Gun." But the photo of Billy the Kid was a tintype, which means the image was reversed. In fact, the kid fired his pistol with his right hand.

3 A desperado is defined as a "bold, reckless criminal or outlaw." But it's also slang for a chess piece that behaves in a kamikaze fashion, destined to be captured but doing as much damage to the opponent as possible. And it was a member of Dallas' team in the Arena Football League. And it's a beverage featuring beer, limeade and tequila.

4 "The Lady in Red" didn't wear red. Anna Sage, who helped FBI agents ambush John Dillinger outside Chicago's Biograph Theater, was wearing an orange skirt that appeared red under the theater's marquee lights.

5 The movie "Butch Cassidy and the Sundance Kid" embraced the story that the two desperadoes died in a 1908 shootout in Bolivia. But it's not a certainty that Cassidy met his end there. Cassidy's sister, Lula Parker Betenson, said he visited her in Utah in 1925. Others suspect Cassidy was a man known as William Phillips who died in Spokane, Wash., in the 1930s.

6   Convicted of killing a police officer, "Terrible" Tommy O'Connor awaited the hangman in Chicago's Criminal Court Building in 1921. But he got hold of a gun—some said it was smuggled in a pork chop sandwich—and he managed to escape. After a series of carjackings, he disappeared for good, or for bad. In 1977, Cook County finally sold off the wooden gallows it intended to use on O'Connor if he had ever been caught.

7   The modern equivalent of Robin Hood was India's "bandit queen," Phoolan Devi. Forced into an arranged marriage at age 11 to a man three times her age, she repudiated the marriage and took up a life of crime. She joined a band of dacoits (bandits), and led them in raids, including a notorious massacre of about 20 high-caste men in 1981. After spending more than a decade in prison, she was elected to parliament in 1996. Five years later, she was assassinated by masked gunmen.

8   Nat Turner was a desperado, but he also was a freedom fighter. Guided by messianic visions, Turner led a Virginia slave rebellion that massacred 55 whites before he was captured and hanged in 1831. A decade earlier, Turner had escaped from slavery, but voluntarily came back after 30 days, explaining that a spirit had told him to return to bondage.

9   Desperadoes routinely come to a bad end. Sixteenth Century Japanese outlaw Ishikawa Goemon was captured and boiled in oil. Virgulino Ferreira da Silva, the bespectacled Brazilian bandit leader known as Lampiao, was killed with 10 members of his gang in 1938, and their heads were cut off and displayed in public.

10   Dillinger was behind bars when Bonnie Parker and Clyde Barrow were grabbing headlines. Annoyed that they were knocking off only small-time banks, Dillinger complained that they were "giving bank-robbing a bad name."

SOURCES: *"In Search of Butch Cassidy" by Larry Pointer, "Digging Up Butch and Sundance" by Anne Meadows, "Dillinger: The Untold Story" by G. Russell Girardin and William J. Helmer, "To Serve and Collect" by Richard C. Lindberg, "To Inherit the Earth" by Angus Wright and Wendy Wolford, "Encyclopedia of Chess Wisdom" by Eric Schiller, "The Arkansas Journey" by Trey Berry, Time magazine, Americas magazine, Spokesman-Review of Spokane, Toronto Sun, New Zealand Herald, drinksmixer.com, britannica.com, news.bbc.co.uk, pbs.org, dictionary.reference.com and imdb.com.*

FOUNDING FATHERS (AND MOTHERS)

1   Paul Revere did not shout "The British are coming!" Stop and think about it—he was a British subject at the time. In fact, he said the "regulars" were coming—regular uniformed troops. But regulars had one too many syllables for poet Henry Wadsworth Longfellow.

2   Before President Josiah "Jed" Bartlet on "The West Wing," there was Josiah Bartlett, a signer of the Declaration of Independence. The New Hampshire physician is credited with saving the lives of people suffering from diphtheria by breaking with the common practice of bloodletting or sweating and treating them with Peruvian bark, which contains quinine.

3   The phrase "Founding Father" is widely credited to President Warren Harding, who said it at the 1916 Republican National Convention in Chicago when he was still a senator. (And by Harding, we mean Judson Welliver, a campaign aide who wrote his speeches.)

4   Phillis Wheatley, whose first name came from the slave ship that brought her from Africa as a child, was too frail for housework but brilliant at poetry. She wrote patriotic verse honoring George Washington and was welcomed at his headquarters—a remarkable meeting considering she was a slave and he a slaveowner. (Four of the first five U.S. presidents owned slaves, the exception being John Adams.)

5   You probably haven't heard of Button Gwinnett unless you're an avid autograph collector. The Georgia politician, a signer of the Declaration of Independence, died violently during the Revolutionary War — but in a duel, not while fighting the British. That early demise makes his signature quite rare, and some say it's the most valuable of any American's. A Gwinnett letter fetched $722,500 at auction in 2010.

6 Francis Hopkinson, another signer, most likely designed the U.S. flag, the Stars and Stripes. He was never paid, though, and in 1780 he asked the government for "a quarter cask of the public wine" as a "reasonable reward." He never got it.

7 Speaking of American flags, there's little reason to think Betsy Ross sewed the first one. Her legend gained popularity long after the purported events, when her grandson addressed a Philadelphia historical group in 1870 and presented relatives' sworn statements that they had heard Ross tell the story.

8 Like the Ross legend, the Molly Pitcher story was popularized many decades after the fact. But the tale of a woman operating a cannon in place of her fallen husband matches the real exploits of at least two women: Mary Ludwig Hays at the battle of Monmouth and Margaret Corbin at the battle of Fort Washington. The badly wounded Corbin was the first woman to earn a U.S. military pension.

9 Samuel Adams wasn't such a good brewer (he ran his family's business into the ground), but he was a tireless revolutionary. One of the earliest colonists to argue for independence, he wrote hundreds of letters to newspapers promoting the cause. And he signed the letters with myriad fake names so it appeared the countryside was teeming with rebels.

10 What battlefield commander was most vital to American victory in the Revolution? Probably Benedict Arnold. His audacious attacks in upstate New York and Canada protected New England early in the war, and the victory at Saratoga (in which he suffered a grievous leg wound) led to the alliance with the French that made all the difference. OK, so Arnold later committed treason. Nobody's perfect.

SOURCES: *"Politics: Observations & Arguments; 1966-2004" by Hendrik Hertzberg; "For You They Signed" by Marilyn Boyer; "Flag: An American Biography" by Marc Leepson; "Signing Their Lives Away: The Fame and Misfortune of the Men Who Signed the Declaration of Independence" by Denise Kiernan and Joseph D'Agnese; "Stupid History" by Leland Gregory; "Washington: A Life" by Ron Chernow; "Molly Pitcher: Heroine of the War for Independence" by Rachel A. Koestler-Grack; Gleaves Whitney of the Hauenstein Center for Presidential Studies at gvsu. edu; poetryfoundation.org; betsyrosshouse.org; snopes.com; britannica.com; San Diego Union Tribune.*

THE SUMMER OF LOVE

1   The Summer of Love started in the winter. An acknowledged jumping-off point was the Human Be-In at San Francisco's Golden Gate Park, which attracted about 35,000 people in January 1967 and featured a speech by LSD guru Timothy Leary. According to Leary, philosopher Marshall McLuhan urged him to invent a catchy slogan, and as an example, McLuhan offered a jingle: "Lysergic acid hits the spot / Forty billion neurons, that's a lot." Later, while in the shower, Leary came up with his own motto to deliver at the Be-In: "Turn on, tune in, drop out."

2   In 1967, artists, musicians such as Joan Baez, and tens of thousands of young people descended on San Francisco's Haight-Ashbury neighborhood, named for the intersecting streets of Haight and Ashbury. The area was perfect for communal living because of its Victorian rooming houses, originally built for Irish workers.

3   A classified ad in the San Francisco Oracle newspaper offered "Hippi-Kits" that included "flowers, bells, flute, headbands, incense, feathers" for $4.50.

4   A young woman called Mountain Girl lived in Haight-Ashbury with her boyfriend, Jerry Garcia, and his band, the Grateful Dead. She later married him and was known as Carolyn Garcia. Recalling 1967, she told the San Francisco Chronicle recently: "It was sort of like a farmer unloading a truckload of onions—once the onions start to move, there's no stopping them. That's kind of how it felt, that the streets were just filling up with people, vegetables yearning to be free."

5   When the summer of 1967 began, LSD had been illegal in California for only eight months.

6   The musical event of the summer—and a model for rock concerts ever since—was the Monterey International Pop Festival near San Francisco, featuring the Grateful Dead, the Animals, Simon and Garfunkel, Jefferson Airplane, The Who, Jimi Hendrix and Janis Joplin. After the Dead played, its roadies made off with some of the festival's Fender amps, using them for free "guerrilla concerts" in Golden Gate Park before returning them a month later.

7   The anthem of the Summer of Love, "San Francisco (Be Sure to Wear Flowers in Your Hair)," promoted an outlook that was mellow and peaceful, but the song's creation was anything but. John Phillips wrote the tune for his friend, Scott McKenzie, instead of giving it to his own group, The Mamas and the Papas, which infuriated executives at his record label. The drug-using Phillips played guitar on the recording but later wrote that it was difficult "because I was speeding my brains out."

8   An article by Times of London critic Kenneth Tynan referred to "a decisive moment in the history of Western civilization." Was he talking about Gutenberg's breakthrough in printing? The discovery of penicillin? No, the June 1967 release of the Beatles' "Sgt. Pepper's Lonely Hearts Club Band," the perfect theme music for a psychedelic summer.

9   It took a letter from the Beatles to persuade actress Mae West to let her picture be used on the "Sgt. Pepper's" album cover. At first, West refused, saying, "What would I be doing in a lonely hearts club?"

10   During the Summer of Love, the uptight but curious could take an antiseptic tour of Haight-Ashbury from inside a Gray Line bus. It was called the "Hippie Hop." Flower children reacted by holding up mirrors at the gawkers. But eventually, the use of methamphetamines and other drugs fueled a crime wave and ugly street scenes. As the summer faded, many of the hippie elite picked up and moved across the Golden Gate Bridge to Marin County.

SOURCES: *San Francisco Chronicle, Monterey County Herald, "Papa John" by John Phillips, "Timothy Leary: A Biography" by Robert Greenfield.*

WOMEN AT WAR

1 Historians believe hundreds of women, disguised as men, fought on both sides of the American Civil War. Among them was Loreta Velazquez, a Confederate soldier who reportedly wore a specially padded uniform and fake facial hair. According to her memoir, she fought in the first battle of Bull Run and at Shiloh. Her disguise was discovered when she was treated for shrapnel wounds.

2 Soviet sniper Lyudmila Pavlichenko was credited with killing 309 Germans in World War II. Forced out of action by her wounds, she went on a publicity tour in 1942 and boasted about her exploits. "Dead Germans," she said, "are harmless."

3 Israel's compulsory military service includes women. But after the nation's initial war in 1948, they were barred from close combat. Retired U.S. Lt. Col. Dave Grossman, in his book "On Killing," cites two problems the Israelis encountered with women in combat: The sight of a female soldier being killed or wounded seemed to trigger "uncontrolled violence" among her male comrades. Also, Arab fighters were reluctant to surrender to a woman. Since the 1990s, Israel has liberalized its policies on women in combat.

4 In modern times, Vietnamese women have been especially fierce fighters, according to David E. Jones in his book "Women Warriors." A unit of markswomen supporting the South Vietnamese government had a policy of wounding Viet Cong fighters with a single shot, then beating them to death with their rifle butts to save bullets. Ming Khai, an anti-French Vietnamese fighter in the 1940s, wrote a poem in blood on her prison cell wall. The last lines were: "The sword is my child, the gun is my husband."

5 Joyce Mujuru, who is one of the two vice presidents of Zimbabwe under the autocratic Robert Mugabe, commanded guerrillas in the fight against white rule in the 1970s and claimed that she single-handedly shot down a helicopter with an AK-47. She was given the nickname Teurai Ropa, which means "Spill Blood."

6 Women's contributions to America's military numbers have soared since 1973, when the U.S. went to an all-volunteer force. Back then, women represented 2 percent of enlisted personnel and 4 percent of officers. Now it's 14 percent of enlisted personnel and 16 percent of officers.

7 Black Hawk pilot Tammy Duckworth lost both legs when her helicopter was hit by a rocket-propelled grenade north of Baghdad in 2004. She's a two-time congressional candidate, and her public image is well-known. Her private pain after her wounds was described by husband Bryan Bowlsbey: "It was necessary to tell her that she had lost her legs, as she felt the phantom pain in the appendages, and didn't understand why the pain meds weren't taking that away."

8 An Iraq war veteran, former Army Sgt. Kayla Williams, wrote a racy 2005 memoir called "Love My Rifle More Than You" that was frank about sexual activity between male and female soldiers. "The Army is not a monastery," she wrote. "More like a fraternity. Or a massive frat party. With weapons."

9 The problem of sexual assault against female soldiers has gained great notice. On salon.com in March 2006, journalist Helen Benedict quoted Spec. Mickiela Montoya as saying that she kept a knife with her at all times: "The knife wasn't for the Iraqis. It was for the guys on my own side."

10 A 1999 study found that 5 percent to 6 percent of Army women were pregnant at any one time. And yes, the military has maternity uniforms.

SOURCES: *pewsocialtrends.org; Tribune archives and news services.*

WORLD WAR II

1   On May 5, 1945, Elsie Mitchell took five neighborhood children on an outing to Gearhart Mountain, Ore., where they encountered a strange object. One of them touched it, and suddenly all six were dead. It was one of at least 6,000 "balloon bombs" launched by the Japanese to drift toward the U.S., and that single bomb caused the only known American war deaths on the U.S. mainland.

2   U.S. Gen. George Patton was nearly sent stateside because he slapped a hospitalized soldier suffering from shell shock in Sicily. But another action by Patton—unreported at the time—was far worse. Before the Sicily fighting, Patton told his troops that enemy soldiers who continued to fight as Allied forces drew within 200 yards of them should not be taken prisoner and should instead be killed even if they surrendered. This, of course, was a violation of international law, but such killings happened several times in areas of Sicily controlled by Patton.

3   According to British Field Marshal Bernard Montgomery, the biggest quarrel he ever had with Prime Minister Winston Churchill was over two dentist chairs delivered to Normandy shortly after D-Day. Churchill thought the delivery was frivolous; Monty believed that a soldier with a toothache could not fight effectively.

4   After the Germans were driven from Paris, French authorities detained fashion diva Coco Chanel because of her affair with a German official a dozen years younger than her. Chanel, in her early 60s, told a French interrogator, "Really, sir, a woman of my age cannot be expected to look at his passport if she has a chance of a lover." She was freed.

5   The German 6th Army, encircled by the Russians at Stalingrad, was starving and freezing to death in the winter of 1942-43. Food, clothing and fuel were desperately needed. But an airlift was badly disorganized. Thousands of right shoes arrived without left shoes. Four tons of spices were delivered. And when soldiers opened one shipment, they were stunned to discover millions of condoms.

6   The British showed impressive courage and common purpose, but there were exceptions. In 1943, a stampede at a London air raid shelter killed 173 people in 90 seconds.

7   Poison gas is associated with World War I. But during World War II, neither side trusted the other to resist using gas, so both kept stockpiles. When German bombers attacked the port of Bari, Italy, in December 1943, they struck an Allied ship loaded with 100 tons of mustard gas, fatally poisoning scores if not hundreds of Allied troops. Doctors who treated victims of the gas noticed it had a specific effect on white blood cells, and they realized it might be useful to treat some cancers. After the war, doctors at the University of Chicago and two other universities produced the world's first cancer chemotherapy, based on mustard gas.

8   Alan Magee was a ball turret gunner on an American B-17 bomber that was shot up and began spinning out of control over France on Jan. 3, 1943. Magee's parachute was unusable, but he jumped anyway, losing consciousness as he fell about 20,000 feet. He crashed through the glass skylight of the St. Nazaire train station and suffered severe injuries. Yet Magee recovered, enjoying backpacking until his death at age 84. Magee's 4-mile plunge was well-documented, but it's not clear how he survived. Some believe the angle of the skylight deflected his fall.

9   Few human beings saw as much history as Mitsuo Fuchida. The Japanese flight commander led the first wave at Pearl Harbor and sent the signal "Tora! Tora! Tora!" that indicated his pilots had achieved complete surprise. Six months later, before the battle of Midway, Fuchida underwent an emergency appendectomy aboard the carrier Akagi. Unable to fly, he was on the ship when U.S. planes attacked. An explosion broke both of his legs, and the Akagi was so badly damaged it had to be sunk. Later in the war, Fuchida visited Hiroshima but left the city a day before the atomic bomb fell. After the war, he raised chickens, supplying eggs for a U.S. artillery unit that was part of the force occupying Japan.

10   An American-Canadian force attacked the Aleutian island of Kiska in 1943 to root out Japanese occupiers. Amid confused combat in the fog, at least 28 Allied troops were killed and 50 wounded. But the attackers later realized that every casualty was caused by booby traps or friendly fire. The Japanese had left the island weeks earlier.

SOURCES: *"Chanel: A Woman of Her Own" by Axel Madsen; "The Greatest War Stories Never Told" by Rick Beyer; "God's Samurai" by Gordon W. Prange with Donald M. Goldstein and Katherine V. Dillon; "Warlord: A Life of Winston Churchill at War, 1874-1945" by Carlo D'Este; "General Patton: A Soldier's Life" by Stanley P. Hirshson; "199 Days: The Battle for Stalingrad" by Edwin P. Hoyt; "Whistling in the Dark: Memory and Culture in Wartime London" by Jean R. Freedman; "1942" by Winston Groom; "The U.S. Home Front, 1941-45" by Alejandro de Quesada; "What Every Person Should Know About War" by Chris Hedges; "Eurekas and Euphorias" by Walter Gratzer; Albuquerque Journal; Smithsonian magazine.*

D-DAY

1 War photographer Robert Capa, who said, "If your pictures aren't good enough, you aren't close enough," landed at Omaha Beach on D-Day. He took more than 100 pictures, but when the film was sent to London, a darkroom technician dried it too quickly and melted the emulsion, leaving fewer than a dozen pictures usable. Even so, those shaky and chaotic photos tell the story of Omaha Beach. A decade later, Capa got too close: He died in 1954 after stepping on a land mine in Indochina.

2 In the weeks before D-Day, British intelligence was highly concerned about crossword puzzles. The London Daily Telegraph's recent puzzle answers had included Overlord and Neptune (the code names for the over-all operation and the landing operation), Utah and Omaha (the two American invasion beaches) and Mulberry (the code name for the artificial harbors planned after the invasion). Agents interrogated the puzzle-maker, a Surrey school headmaster named Leonard Dawe. Turns out, it was just a coincidence.

3 The people who planned D-Day were bigots. That was the code word — bigot — for anyone who knew the time and place of the invasion. It was a reversal of a designation — "to Gib" — that was used on the papers of those traveling to Gibraltar for the invasion of North Africa in 1942.

4 The Allied effort to hoodwink Adolf Hitler about the invasion was code-named Fortitude, and it was nearly as elaborate and detailed as the invasion itself. The Allies went so far as to parachute dummies, outfitted with firecrackers that exploded on impact, behind enemy lines as a diversion. Under an effort code-named Window, Allied airplanes dropped strips of aluminum foil cut to a length that corresponded to German radar waves. The effect created two phantom fleets of bombers out of thin air — and ingenuity.

5   Among those who landed at Normandy on D-Day were J.D. Salinger (who went on to write "Catcher in the Rye"), Theodore Roosevelt Jr. (the president's son, who died of a heart attack a month later) and Elliot Richardson (attorney general under President Richard Nixon).

6   D-Day secrets were almost exposed in Chicago. A package from Supreme Headquarters in London arrived at a Chicago mail-sorting office a few months before D-Day and was accidentally opened. Its contents — including the timetable and location of the invasion — may have been seen by more than a dozen unauthorized people. The FBI found that a U.S. general's aide of German descent had sent the package to "The Ordnance Division, G-4" but had added the address of his sister in Chicago. The FBI concluded that the aide was overtired and had been thinking about his sister, who was ill. But just to be safe, the Chicago postal workers were put under surveillance and the aide was confined to quarters.

7   In a 1964 interview, Dwight Eisenhower said a single person "won the war for us." Was he referring to Gen. George Patton? Gen. Douglas MacArthur? No — Andrew Higgins, who designed and built the amphibious assault crafts that allowed the Allies to storm the beaches of Normandy. The eccentric boat builder foresaw not only the Navy's acute need for small military crafts early on, but also the shortage of steel, so he gambled and bought the entire 1939 crop of mahogany from the Philippines. His New Orleans company produced thousands of the unimpressive-looking — but vital — boats for the war effort.

8   While U.S. forces were conducting a training exercise off the southwestern English coast to prepare for the landing on Utah Beach, German torpedo boats ambushed them. More than 700 Americans were killed — a toll far worse than when U.S. forces actually took Utah Beach a few months later.

9   Woe be unto a politician who commits a gaffe during a D-Day remembrance. In 2004, Canadian Prime Minister Paul Martin referred to the "invasion of Norway" when he meant Normandy. Last year at an event with President Barack Obama, British Prime Minister Gordon Brown cited "Obama Beach" when he meant "Omaha Beach."

10   France wasn't the only theater of action in early June 1944. On June 5, the B-29 Superfortress flew its first combat mission; the target: Bangkok.

The day before that, U.S. forces were able to capture a German submarine off the African coast because they had broken the Enigma code and learned a sub was in the vicinity. On the eve of D-Day, the U.S. couldn't risk that the Germans would realize the code was cracked. So they hid away the sub and its captured crew until the end of the war, and the Germans assumed the vessel was lost at sea. But the U-505 would survive to become one of the most popular attractions at Chicago's Museum of Science and Industry.

SOURCES: *"D-Day: Operation Overlord Day by Day" by Anthony Hall; "Bodyguard of Lies: The Extraordinary True Story Behind D-Day" by Anthony Cave Brown; "Soldiers Lost at Sea" by James E. Wise and Scott Baron; "Slightly Out of Focus" by Robert Capa; "Voices from D-Day" by Jonathan Bastable; "Fortitude: The D-Day Deception Campaign" by Roger Hesketh; "Andrew Jackson Higgins and the Boats That Won World War II" by Jerry E. Strahan; skylighters.org; U.S. Navy; Museum of Science and Industry.*

10 THINGS YOU MIGHT NOT KNOW ABOUT

PEOPLE

HUGO CHAVEZ

1 Venezuela President Hugo Chavez's parents were teachers, and he was raised in a dirt-floor adobe that was later bulldozed and replaced with a hamburger stand. But his family has come a long way. His father served as governor of the state of Barinas, a post now held by a brother who had been the country's education minister. Another brother is mayor of the town of Sabaneta. Critics cry nepotism.

2 Arrested for plotting a coup in 1992, he insisted on wearing his lieutenant colonel's uniform during his two years in prison, he has said.

3 In beauty pageant-obsessed Venezuela, Chavez once defeated Miss Universe. Irene Saez, a Venezuelan who captured the 1981 world title and later became a politician, finished far behind in the 1998 presidential election won by Chavez.

4 Chavez's television and radio talk show, "Alo, Presidente" ("Hello, President"), sometimes has lasted six hours. He might announce tax and oil policies or sing songs such as "Guantanamera." The children-hugging host has interviewed such celebrities as actor Danny Glover and baseball's Ozzie Guillen. In 2007, Chavez showed his audience a newspaper photo of him looking at a bikini-clad Brazilian dancer during a summit in Rio de Janeiro, and joked: "I didn't know where to look."

5 Venezuela's leader ordered his government to distribute 1 million copies of "Don Quixote," Miguel de Cervantes' novel about a mad, idealistic knight.

6 In 2005, evangelist Pat Robertson called for Chavez's assassination, saying it would be "a whole lot cheaper than starting a war." He later apologized. But in June 2007, he said: "Well, a couple of years ago I made a comment or two about Mr. Chavez. Nobody even knew who Hugo Chavez was. They thought he was some grape picker from out in California. And all of a sudden my comments put him on the front page, and now we've begun to see the kind of person he is, and more and more people are saying to me, 'I think you were right.'"

7 Chavez drinks at least 26 cups of coffee a day, according to ABC's Barbara Walters, who interviewed him in 2007.

8 Chavez visited Iran in July 2007 to support Iranian President Mahmoud Ahmadinejad in his confrontation with the U.S. But Chavez's people weren't so sure. A Pew survey found that 56 percent of Venezuelans have a favorable view of the United States, while only 33 percent were pro-Iran. And a mere 16 percent of Venezuelans expressed confidence in Ahmadinejad's foreign policies.

9 Chavez suffered a rare electoral defeat in 2007 when he tried to push through a series of constitutional amendments. He tried to impose term limits on governors and mayors, but not on El Presidente, because the other officials "have governing methods that don't have anything to do with revolution."

10 Chavez has labeled former President George W. Bush "the devil," "donkey," "drunkard," "Mr. Danger" and a "political corpse." But his statements about former U.S. Secretary of State Condoleezza Rice are downright strange. He has called her "illiterate" and nicknamed her "Condolencia," which is Spanish for "condolence." He also has suggested she was sexually frustrated and had a crush on him, declaring in a speech a few years ago: "I cannot marry Condolencia, because I am much too busy."

SOURCES: *Tribune news services; the National Post; Media Matters for America; The Independent; "Chavez, Venezuela and the New Latin America" by Aleida Guevara.*

DICK CHENEY

1   We've been pronouncing former Vice President Dick Cheney's name wrong all these years. The Cheney family's preferred pronunciation rhymes with genie, not zany. Cheney told the Chicago Sun-Times' Lynn Sweet in 2000 that people got it right when he was growing up out West, but when he moved East, they pronounced it differently. "I'll respond to either," he said. "It really doesn't matter."

2   Cheney has often been depicted as the elder regent presiding over the reign of a boy king named Dubya. But Cheney is only 5½ years older than former President George W. Bush. And Bush has a better academic record. Bush earned his undergraduate degree from Yale; Cheney flunked out of Yale. Bush earned a master's degree in business administration at Harvard; Cheney got his bachelor's and master's at the University of Wyoming, but left the University of Wisconsin without completing his doctoral studies.

3   Cheney has suffered four heart attacks — a fact so well known that it's fodder for comedians. It's less well known how Cheney battled back from his first heart attack at age 37 while making his first run for Congress. He sent a letter to every registered Republican in Wyoming announcing that he was staying in the race and would quit smoking. (He was a three-pack-a-day man.) It worked. In March 2012, at the age of 71, he received a heart transplant.

4   When Bush chose Cheney as his running mate in 2000, there was one problem: They both lived in Texas. The Constitution prohibits a state's electors from voting for both a president and vice president from their state. So four days before the announcement, Cheney changed his official residency back to Wyoming — an action later challenged in court but upheld.

5   His middle name is Bruce.

6   Cheney's parents were New Deal Democrats. As Joan Didion recalled in the New York Review of Books, Cheney's father told him during his first run for Congress as a Republican, "You can't take my vote for granted."

7   In her book "Now It's My Turn," Mary Cheney says she told her parents she was gay when she was a high school junior. After breaking up with her first girlfriend, she was so upset that she wrecked the family car, then told her parents the whole story. At first, she says, her mother thought it might just be "the world's most creative excuse for a car accident." But both parents quickly accepted her sexual orientation.

8   For a couple of hours, Cheney was leader of the free world. While Bush underwent a colonoscopy from 6:09 a.m. to 8:24 a.m. Central time on June 29, 2002, Cheney served as "acting president."

9   He met his wife, Lynne, at age 14. She is the author or co-author of 10 books, holds a doctorate in 19th Century British literature and is former chairwoman of the National Endowment for the Humanities. Her mother was a deputy sheriff in Casper, Wyoming.

10   Cheney uttered the F-word on the Senate floor on June 22, 2004. He was annoyed by comments from Sen. Patrick Leahy (D-Vt.) about Halliburton's no-bid contracts in Iraq. A Cheney spokesman called it a "frank exchange of views."

SOURCES: *"Now It's My Turn" by Mary Cheney; Tribune archives and news services.*

RAHM EMANUEL

1   Chicago Mayor Rahm Emanuel's father, Benjamin, was born in Jerusalem with the last name of Auerbach. But Benjamin changed his last name to honor his brother, Emanuel Auerbach, a Jew killed in the Arab insurrection in 1936. The renamed Benjamin Emanuel settled in Chicago, where he became a pediatrician.

2   One of the best-known stories about Rahm Emanuel is that he sent a dead fish to a political enemy in 1998. But it wasn't that simple. Emanuel and two Democratic colleagues got into a dispute with a pollster. One of the colleagues read a USA Today story about a company that could be hired to send a dead fish in a handsome mahogany box, and he suggested that the three send the fish to the pollster. Which they did. Emanuel later claimed not to know that such a gesture carried Mafia overtones of "you will sleep with the fishes."

3   Emanuel, who has built a take-no-prisoners macho image, was once a ballet dancer. He studied at the Evanston School of Ballet, and at Sarah Lawrence College, where he graduated with a B.A. in liberal arts.

4   In "The Thumpin'," a book by former Tribune reporter Naftali Bendavid, Emanuel is quoted as using the F-word more than three dozen times. House Speaker Nancy Pelosi said she had found a way to finance the stimulus program: "Put a quarter in a jar every time Rahm uses a swear word."

5   Emanuel lost part of the middle finger on his right hand as a high school senior working on a meat slicer at Arby's. He avoided treatment because he didn't want to miss the prom, but was hospitalized when the finger became infected. He has been known to flip the middle half-finger at people to great effect, though President Barack Obama has joked that the injury "rendered him practically mute."

6 In three years after he left the Clinton administration, Emanuel made $16 million in investment banking, including at least $320,000 after he was appointed by President Bill Clinton to a 14-month stint on the board of mortgage giant Freddie Mac. The Tribune sought minutes of Freddie Mac's meetings from Emanuel's tenure, but the Obama administration denied the request, saying it was "commercial information" exempt from the Freedom of Information Act.

7 When Richard Daley won the mayor's office in 1989, Emanuel was his chief fundraiser, helping the campaign collect $13 million in seven weeks. In 2002, Daley's political organization — including patronage workers whose hiring was later found illegal — helped Emanuel win election to Congress.

8 Emanuel has two accomplished brothers. Ezekiel, a physician who is a leading figure in medical ethics, served as an adviser to Obama. He is now a professor at the University of Pennsylvania. Ari is a Hollywood agent, one of the inspirations for the Ari Gold character in HBO's "Entourage," played by Jeremy Piven.

9 Emanuel's friendship with White House adviser David Axelrod dates to 1982, when Axelrod was a Tribune reporter and Emanuel sought publicity for a political group, Illinois Public Action. Axelrod told The New Yorker: "He was just relentless. Rahm chased me down to the recovery room after my second child was born. He says, 'What is it, a boy or a girl?' I said, 'It's a boy.' He said, 'Mazel tov,' and then a little pause. Then he says, 'When do you think you'll be back at work?'"

10 The president, whose middle name is Hussein, had a chief of staff whose middle name is Israel. What a country.

SOURCES: *"The Thumpin'" by Naftali Bendavid; The New Yorker; The Washington Post; washingtonian.com; Tribune archives; and Tribune news services.*

THE DALAI LAMA

1 "Dalai" is a Mongolian word for ocean, and "lama" is a Tibetan word for a monk of high rank. The Dalai Lama's wisdom is said to be as broad as an ocean.

2 The boy who would become known as the Dalai Lama (and as Kundun, meaning "The Presence") was born on the floor of a cowshed on his family's farm in the northeastern Tibetan village of Taktser in 1935. He was named Lhamo Dhondrub. His parents, who met for the first time at their wedding ceremony, had 16 children, but only seven survived past infancy.

3 The leadership of Tibetan Buddhism is transferred through reincarnation, adherents believe. When a dalai lama dies — as the 13th one did in 1933 — monks begin the search for a boy who is his new embodiment. According to various accounts, including the book "Kundun" by Mary Craig, the discovery of the 14th Dalai Lama occurred like this: Members of a Buddhist search party arrived in Taktser disguised as traders. The group's leader was dressed as a servant but was wearing a rosary that had belonged to the 13th Dalai Lama. Two-year-old Lhamo Dhondrub asked for the rosary and was told he could have it if he guessed who he was talking to. The boy said correctly that the man dressed as a servant was a "Sera aga," a lama from the Sera monastery. The boy also impressed the visitors by knowing other details about them, and he later identified more possessions of the 13th lama.

4 In the film "Caddyshack," the golf course groundskeeper played by Bill Murray describes how he caddied for the Dalai Lama. An excerpt: "I give him the driver. He hauls off and whacks one — big hitter, the Lama — long, into a 10,000-foot crevice, right at the base of this glacier...So we finish the 18th and he's gonna stiff me. And I say, 'Hey, Lama, hey, how about a little something, you know, for the effort, you know.' And he says, 'Oh, uh, there won't be any money, but when you die, on your deathbed, you will receive total consciousness.' So I got that goin' for me, which is nice."

5   The great monk has plenty of celebrity admirers, including Richard Gere, Steven Seagal and Carmen Electra. Model-actress Elle Macpherson said last year that she was considering a lawsuit against model Heidi Klum for allegedly appropriating her nickname, "The Body," but after meeting with the Dalai Lama, she dropped any plans to sue. "A few people have made me stop in my tracks, and the Dalai Lama would be one of them," Macpherson said.

6   The Dalai Lama is fascinated by science and has said that if he had not become a monk, he would have become an engineer. He is especially interested in neuroplasticity, the study of how the brain rewires itself. The Dalai Lama spoke to the Society for Neuroscience in 2005 despite some members' objections about mixing religion and science. The Dalai Lama declared that "if a surgery of the brain could provide the same benefits as hours of meditation daily, I would do it," according to the Agence France-Presse news service.

7   Rock star Patti Smith was keenly interested in the Dalai Lama when she was 12. She studied Tibet for a yearlong school project, and she prayed that it would become newsworthy. When China's oppression became so severe that the Dalai Lama fled in 1959, "I felt tremendously guilty," she told the Shambhala Sun, a Buddhist magazine. "I felt that somehow my prayers had interfered with Tibetan history. I worried about the Dalai Lama. It was rumored that his family had been killed by the Chinese. I was quite relieved when he reached India safely." (The Dalai Lama has been based in Dharamsala, India, since then.)

8   He served as a guest editor for an issue of French Vogue magazine in 1992.

9   Tibetans often change their names after major events, such as recovery from illness or the visit of a great lama. When the boy named Lhamo Dhondrub was recognized as the reincarnated leader of his people, he was renamed Jetsun Jamphel Ngawang Lobsang Yeshe Tenzin Gyatso (meaning Holy Lord, Gentle Glory, Compassionate, Defender of the Faith, Ocean of Wisdom). His people sometimes call him Yeshe Norbu (the Wish-fulfilling Gem).

10   What will happen when the 71-year-old Dalai Lama dies? He has left open the possibility that the tradition of the dalai lama will end. But more likely, he says, there will be rival dalai lamas — one found among the Tibetan exile community, and another appointed by the Chinese.

SOURCES: *"Kundun" by Mary Craig; Shambhala Sun; Tribune archives and news services.*

THE KENNEDYS

1   The Kennedys' matriarch, Rose, was the daughter of a Boston mayor and visited President William McKinley at the White House as a child. But raising nine children might have been more intimidating. She maintained a system of index cards listing her children's weights, shoe sizes and medical conditions. She scheduled meals in two shifts: one for the young children and another for the older children and adults. The family sometimes went through 20 quarts of milk in a day.

2   Considering the liberal reputation of the Kennedy family, some might be surprised that the patriarch of the family, Joseph Kennedy Sr., was friends with red-baiting Sen. Joseph McCarthy of Wisconsin. McCarthy was a guest at the Kennedys' home, hired Robert as a Senate staffer, and even dated two Kennedy sisters, Patricia and Eunice.

3   President John F. Kennedy commonly went through three or four shirts a day.

4   When John F. Kennedy received the Roman Catholic sacrament of confession, he attempted anonymity. Visiting a church, he would line up with a group of Secret Service agents who were Catholic and would try to slip into the confessional unrecognized. That sometimes worked, but on one occasion Kennedy entered the booth and the priest greeted him with "Good evening, Mr. President." Kennedy answered, "Good evening, Father," and quickly left.

5   Chicago's Northwest Expressway was renamed the Kennedy Expressway a week after President John F. Kennedy's assassination in 1963. Chicago's Wilson College was renamed Kennedy-King College in 1969 in the wake of the assassinations of Robert Kennedy and Martin Luther King Jr.

6 Benjamin Smith was the ultimate seat warmer. When John F. Kennedy was elected president in 1960, his replacement in the Senate was his old college pal — Smith, the mayor of Gloucester, Mass. Two years later, Smith chose not to run for the seat, clearing the way for JFK's brother Ted, who had just reached the minimum age of 30.

7 When the Kennedys played touch football, Eunice was a quarterback. The four Kennedy men all played football at Harvard. Joe Jr. and John were not outstanding, nor was Robert, who broke his leg crashing into an equipment cart during practice. Ted was the best, a tight end who received a smattering of interest from the Green Bay Packers but chose politics instead.

8 The last of Robert Kennedy's 11 children, Rory, was born six months after her father's 1968 assassination.

9 Air travel has always been a curse for the Kennedys. The most recent incident — the death of John Kennedy Jr. in 1999 — is well-remembered. But there are other major accidents that are less well-known. Ted Kennedy broke two ribs and three vertebrae in a 1964 crash. His sister Kathleen died in a 1948 plane crash in France. The first-born son, Joe Jr., volunteered for a World War II mission called Operation Aphrodite in which he flew a bomber laden with 21,170 pounds of high explosives. The idea was for the crew to bail out and for the bomber to be directed by radio controls to its target in France. But it exploded prematurely, killing the first great hope among the Kennedy brothers.

10 In her elder years, Rose Kennedy sometimes played golf all by herself at the Hyannisport Club, carrying her own clubs for nine holes.

SOURCES: *"The Kennedy White House: Family Life and Pictures, 1961-1963" by Carl Sferrazza Anthony; "John F. Kennedy on Leadership: The Lessons and Legacy of a President" by John A. Barnes; "Grace and Power: The Private World of the Kennedy White House" by Sally Bedell Smith; "Joseph McCarthy: Re-examining the Life and Legacy of America's Most Hated Senator" by Arthur Herman; "John F. Kennedy: A biography" by Michael O'Brien; "Football: The Ivy League Origins of an American Obsession" by Mark F. Bernstein; jfklibrary.org; Tribune archives.*

MICHAEL MOORE

1 As a teenager, Michael Moore attended a seminary for a year. One of the main reasons he dropped out was that he wasn't allowed to watch the Detroit Tigers, who went to the World Series that year.

2 What does Moore have in common with former President Gerald Ford and businessman Ross Perot? All were Eagle Scouts. For his Eagle project, Moore put together a slide show on pollution by local businesses.

3 Moore grew up in the middle-class suburb of Davison, Mich., outside Flint. At age 18 he was elected to the school board on a platform of removing the principal and assistant principal at his high school. Both eventually left.

4 Moore quit college because he couldn't find a parking space. As he told the Tribune's Julie Deardorff: "The first semester of sophomore year of college I was at a commuter campus at the University of Michigan, Flint. I drove around for what seemed to be an hour, looking for a parking space. After an hour, I said, 'The hell with it!' and gave up and drove home...and I haven't been back since."

5 One of Moore's early benefactors was singer Harry Chapin, who held benefit concerts to help finance a youth hot line and alternative newspaper run by Moore in the Flint area.

6 Moore got his start in filmmaking when he was hired by documentary director Kevin Rafferty to interview Ku Klux Klan members. Rafferty, who was cinematographer for Moore's first film, "Roger & Me," is the cousin of former President George W. Bush.

7 Moore was fired twice within two months in 1986. After less than half a year as editor of Mother Jones magazine, he was dismissed. He took a job as a writer for a Ralph Nader newsletter but was fired again.

8 Staff Sgt. Raymond Plouhar, one of the Marine recruiters in Moore's "Fahrenheit 9/11," was killed in 2006 by a roadside bomb in Iraq.

9 Moore's interview with actor and gun advocate Charlton Heston in "Bowling for Columbine" prompted criticism that the filmmaker was taking advantage of a sick man. (After the interview, but before the film's general release, Heston announced he had Alzheimer's-like symptoms.) Moore once considered — and rejected — the idea of running against Heston for the presidency of the National Rifle Association.

10 Move over, David Hasselhoff — Germany's in love with Michael Moore. At least two of Moore's books — "Downsize This!" and "Stupid White Men" — have sold more than 1 million copies each in Germany, and Moore's following there has been compared to comedian Jerry Lewis' fame in France.

SOURCES: *Tribune news services, "Michael Moore" by Emily Schultz, The New Yorker, Rolling Stone.*

OPRAH

1 Oprah Winfrey's mother intended to name her Orpah, after the sister-in-law of Ruth in the Bible. But the "P" and the "R" got switched. Biographers have described it as a paperwork error, but Winfrey has said that the people around her in Kosciusko, Miss., simply pronounced it wrong.

2 As a teen, Winfrey was Miss Fire Prevention of Nashville.

3 Winfrey, hired as a news anchor in Baltimore at age 22, was a disaster. She cried while reporting on a fatal house fire. She annoyed the news writers by ad-libbing. She mispronounced "Canada" three times in the same newscast. Her hair fell out after a bad perm. The station yanked her off the nightly news and assigned her to co-host a morning show, "People Are Talking." It was not a disaster.

4 Movie critics Gene Siskel of the Tribune and Roger Ebert of the Sun-Times appeared on Winfrey's Baltimore show. The guest ahead of them was a chef demonstrating how to make zucchini bread. He knocked over a blender, spraying pureed zucchini on the interview couch. During a commercial break, Winfrey turned over the couch cushions and wiped off the back of the couch with a copy of the Baltimore Sun. Then she told Siskel and Ebert: "OK, boys, sit down and don't mention the zucchini."

5 Winfrey once dated Ebert.

6 For a 1984 episode on blindness during her first year as host of "A.M. Chicago," Winfrey wore a blindfold for most of a day. That included dinner at Yvette's. The Tribune's Inc. column noted that "she didn't try soup."

7   Oh, to be a fly on the wall of a Southern California restaurant on Jan. 28, 1985, when Winfrey dined with Maria Shriver and her boyfriend, Arnold Schwarzenegger. Winfrey, a growing force in Chicago, was in California to make her first appearance on NBC's "Tonight Show," hosted by Joan Rivers. Her friend Shriver was on the "CBS Morning News" at the time. Schwarzenegger's first "Terminator" movie had recently debuted. As they sat in a booth, Schwarzenegger pretended he was Rivers and interviewed Winfrey. She recalled: "He kept pumping me. 'Why are you successful?' 'Why did you gain weight?'"

8   The idea of casting Winfrey in "The Color Purple" came from a TV set in a Chicago hotel room in 1984. Quincy Jones, co-producer of the film, was in Chicago to testify for Michael Jackson in a lawsuit over his song "The Girl Is Mine." While eating a room-service breakfast, Jones saw the talk show hosted by Winfrey, whom he already knew. He realized immediately that she should be Sofia.

9   In the audience of Winfrey's TV show, women outnumbered men 19 to 1.

10   Oprah.com may be the only website that gives advice on tax deductions while also featuring a detailed map of female private parts and recommending three William Faulkner novels.

SOURCE: *oprah.com, Chicago magazine, Tribune news services, International Directory of Business Biographies, "Oprah: The Real Story," by George Mair, "Roger Ebert's Movie Yearbook," by Roger Ebert.*

SARAH PALIN

1   Former Alaska Gov. Sarah Palin inspires both positive and negative nicknames like few other people in modern history. The names include Sarah Barracuda, Caribou Barbie, Disasta from Alaska, Wasilla Godzilla, Thrilla from Wasilla, Moosealini, Dick Cheney in Lipstick, Dan Quayle with an Up-do, Snowjob Squareglasses, June Cleavage, the Pit Bull with Lipstick, Hockey Mom and the Quitter on Twitter.

2   Sarah Heath (later to be Palin) learned to shoot a firearm at age 8 and hunted for rabbits and ptarmigans. What's a ptarmigan? It's a type of grouse whose name comes from Scottish Gaelic and is pronounced TAR-migan, with the "P" silent.

3   Much has been made of Palin leading her Wasilla High School basketball team to the state championship. Though she was certainly an important part of that team, her state tournament performance was limited. Suffering from an ankle injury, she scored only nine of her team's 170 points in the three tournament games.

4   Part of Palin's popular appeal is her willingness to risk humor in public. While campaigning for vice president at a North Carolina bar in October 2008, a patron handed her his cell phone and urged her to say hello to his wife. Palin asked the wife: "Libby, why is your husband here drinking beer without you?"

5   At the 2008 Republican National Convention in St. Paul, Minn., Palin accepted the vice presidential nomination with a speech declaring, "I told the Congress, 'Thanks, but no thanks,' for that Bridge to Nowhere. If our state wanted a bridge, we'd build it ourselves." But Palin was once a solid supporter of spending more than $200 million in federal funds for the bridge linking Gravina Island with the town of Ketchikan. Like others, Palin backed off when the political heat got intense.

6 Palin never tried to establish her foreign policy credentials by saying, "I can see Russia from my house!" That was actress Tina Fey, doing a parody of Palin on "Saturday Night Live." Palin had merely cited Alaska's proximity to Russia — and trade missions between them — in a discussion about foreign policy experience. But Fey's impersonation was so spot-on that some people attribute the remark to Palin.

7 When Sarah and Todd Palin eloped, they forgot to bring any witnesses to the courthouse in Palmer. So two witnesses were recruited from the nursing home next door, one in a wheelchair and another using a walker.

8 A few years ago, Palin set up a marketing and consulting firm, but it hasn't done business. She called it Rouge Cou — playfully using the French words for "red" and "neck." But in proper French, "red neck" would have been cou rouge, with the adjective coming after the noun.

9 Palin does not particularly like cats but is fond of dogs. While governor, she named her pet bloodhound AGIA, an acronym for the Alaska Gasoline Inducement Act.

10 The Palins picked unusual names for their five children — Track, Bristol, Willow, Piper and Trig. Their first-born, Track, got his name because it was track season. Palin joked that if it were basketball season, he would've been Hoop, and if it were wrestling season, he would've been Mat.

SOURCES: *"Trailblazer: An Intimate Biography of Sarah Palin" by Lorenzo Benet, "Sarah" by Kaylene Johnson, "Going Rogue" by Sarah Palin, wickedlocal.com and Tribune news services.*

ELVIS PRESLEY

1   Elvis liked to shoot things. Famously, he shot out his own TV because Robert Goulet was on the screen. Less famously, he sat beside his pool and ate watermelon while squeezing off rounds with his .22-caliber pistol to blast light bulbs floating in the water.

2   Elvis used to speak sentences backward as a code with his friends.

3   Elvis' manager, who called himself Col. Tom Parker, was a Dutch illegal immigrant born Andreas Cornelis van Kuijk. He served in the U.S. Army, but "colonel" was an honorary title conferred by Louisiana Gov. Jimmie Davis. Before meeting Elvis, Parker operated a carnival act in which chickens danced because Parker hid a hot plate under the sawdust in their cage. Parker was known for charging Presley extraordinary fees. British journalist Chris Hutchins said he once asked Parker, "Is it true that you take 50 percent of everything Elvis earns?" Parker's answer: "No, that's not true at all. He takes 50 percent of everything I earn."

4   Elvis liked his meat well-done. One of his favorite expressions was "That's burnt, man." Whether he was talking about a steak or a song, something "burnt" was good.

5   When John Lennon heard Elvis had died, he caustically remarked: "Elvis died the day he went into the Army."

6   Was Elvis' middle name Aaron or Aron? The answer: both. The King's middle name was in honor of his father's friend Aaron Kennedy, but the Presleys used the Aron spelling to match the middle name of Elvis' stillborn identical-twin brother, Jesse Garon Presley. Even so, Aaron is the spelling on the Graceland grave site. Either spelling is OK, according to the official elvis. com website.

7   Elvis salted his food before he even tasted it.

8   Elvis got his first name from his father, Vernon Elvis Presley. But it's unclear where Vernon got it. The name of a 6th Century Irish saint was variously spelled Elvis, Elwyn, Elwin, Elian and Allan. Wherever the name came from, it has caught on. Modern-day Elvii include singer Elvis Costello (originally Declan Patrick McManus), film critic Elvis Mitchell, salsa star Elvis Crespo and Canadian skater Elvis Stojko.

9   The "catfish incident" occurred at a concert in Norfolk, Va., on July 20, 1975. The apparently drug-addled Elvis insulted his audience by complaining that the 11,000 people in the crowd were breathing on him. Then he said he smelled green peppers and onions and suggested that his quartet of black female backup singers, the Sweet Inspirations, had been eating catfish. Two of the "Sweets" walked offstage in disgust. Some took Elvis' comment as a racial insult, but it was more likely the culmination of bizarre remarks Elvis had made to his female backup singers — both black and white — during the tour. The offended Sweets returned the next night, and Presley publicly apologized.

10   The last food that Elvis Presley ate was four scoops of ice cream and six chocolate chip cookies. The last book that Elvis read — and may have been reading on the toilet when he died — was "A Scientific Search for the Face of Jesus" by Frank O. Adams, a slim volume about the Shroud of Turin.

SOURCES: *"All Shook Up: Elvis Day by Day, 1954-1977" by Lee Cotton; "The Inner Elvis" by Peter Whitmer; "The Life and Cuisine of Elvis Presley" by David Adler; "The Death of Elvis: What Really Happened" by Charles C. Thompson II and James P. Cole; "Baby Names Now" by Linda Rosenkrantz and Pamela Redmond Satran; the Memphis Commercial Appeal; and Tribune news services.*

ABOUT THE AUTHORS

Mark Jacob is first deputy metro editor at the Chicago Tribune and has co-authored five other books, including "What the Great Ate: A Curious History of Food and Fame" and "Treacherous Beauty: Peggy Shippen, the Woman Behind Benedict Arnold's Plot to Betray America." He started the Tribune's "10 Things" feature in February 2007.

Stephan Benzkofer is the weekend editor at the Chicago Tribune. He also edits the newspaper's history feature, called Chicago Flashback. Benzkofer joined the "10 Things" team in February 2010.

ACKNOWLEDGMENTS

The authors wish to thank their Tribune editors, especially Marcia Lythcott, Steve Mills, Colin McMahon, Saleema Syed and Pam Becker. Graphic artist Mike Miner has provided years of solid support to "10 Things." The Tribune's photo desk also as been a key resource, especially photo editors Robin Daughtridge, Andrew Johnston, and Erin Mystkowski. Our gratitude to John McCormick for contributing amazing facts about Iowa and to David Jahntz as a co-author of the "10 Things" on presidential inaugurations.

SOURCES

By order of appearance

Jacob, Mark. "10 Things You Might Not Know About Best-sellers." Sunday, November 15, 2009.

Jacob, Mark, and Stephan Benzkofer. "10 Things You Might Not Know About Blonds." Sunday, January 9, 2011.

Jacob, Mark. "10 Things You Might Not Know About Bridges." Sunday, August 12, 2007.

Jacob, Mark, and Stephan Benzkofer. "10 Things You Might Not Know About Fictional Fathers." Sunday, June 9, 2011.

Jacob, Mark. "10 Things You Might Not Know About Modern Art." Sunday, May 10, 2009.

Jacob, Mark, and Stephan Benzkofer. "10 Things You Might Not Know About Music Festivals." Sunday, July 31, 2011.

Jacob, Mark. "10 Things You Might Not Know About Screenwriters." Sunday, November 11, 2007.

Jacob, Mark. "10 Things You Might Not Know About Stanleys." Sunday, March 13, 2010.

Jacob, Mark, and Stephan Benzkofer. "10 Things You Might Not Know About Teachers." Sunday, August 28, 2011.

Jacob, Mark, and Stephan Benzkofer. "10 Things You Might Not Know About TV Ads." Sunday, February 6, 2011.

Jacob, Mark, and Stephan Benzkofer. "10 Things You Might Not Know About...Underwear." Sunday, December 12, 2010.

Jacob, Mark, and Stephan Benzkofer. "10 Things You Might Not Know About the Unhinged." Sunday, April 3, 2011.

Jacob, Mark, and Stephan Benzkofer. "10 Things You Might Not Know About Leaks." Sunday, February 26, 2012.

Jacob, Mark. "History Lesson: 10 Things You Might Not Know About Chicago's Ballparks." Sunday, April 1, 2007.

Jacob, Mark, and Stephan Benzkofer. "10 Things You Might Not Know About the Chicago Bears." Sunday, September 5, 2010.

Jacob, Mark. "10 Things You Might Not Know About College Football." Sunday, January 6, 2008.

Jacob, Mark. "10 Things You Might Not Know About Sports Gambling." Sunday, January 27, 2008.

Jacob, Mark. "10 Things You Might Not Know About the Olympics." Sunday, September 27, 2009.

Jacob, Mark. "10 Things You Might Not Know About the Olympic Torch." Sunday, May 4, 2008.

Jacob, Mark, and Stephan Benzkofer. "10 Things You Might Not Know About Running." Sunday, October 9, 2011.

Jacob, Mark. "10 Things You Might Not Know About: Stadiums." Sunday, April 11, 2010.

Jacob, Mark, and Stephan Benzkofer. "10 Things You Might Not Know About Chicago Authors." Sunday, May 29, 2011.

Jacob, Mark. "10 Things You Might Not Know About The Chicago City Council." Sunday, May 20, 2007.

Jacob, Mark, and Stephan Benzkofer. "10 Things You Might Not Know About Chicago Elections." Sunday, February 20, 2011.

Jacob, Mark, and Stephan Benzkofer. "10 Things You Might Not Know About Chicago Mayors Not Named Daley." Sunday, September 19, 2010.

Jacob, Mark. "10 Things You Might Not Know About Chicago Murders." Sunday, December 21, 2008.

Jacob, Mark. "10 Things You Might Not Know About The Outfit." Sunday, August 26, 2007.

Jacob, Mark, and Stephan Benzkofer. "10 Things You Might Not Know About Chicago Protests." Sunday, November 6, 2011.

Jacob, Mark. "10 Things You Might Not Know About Chicago Radio." Sunday, September 14, 2008.

Jacob, Mark, and Stephan Benzkofer. "10 Things You Might Not Know About the North Side." Sunday, July 25, 2010.

Jacob, Mark, and Stephan Benzkofer. "10 Things You Might Not Know About the South Side." Sunday, July 18, 2010.

Jacob, Mark, and Stephan Benzkofer. "10 Things You Might Not Know About the West Side." Sunday, August 1, 2010.

Jacob, Mark, and Stephan Benzkofer. "10 Things You Might Not Know About Chicago's Northern Suburbs." Sunday, August 8, 2010.

Jacob, Mark, and Stephan Benzkofer. "10 Things You Might Not Know About Chicago's South Suburbs." Sunday, August 22, 2010.

Jacob, Mark. "10 Things You Might Not Know About Chicago Transit." Sunday, April 29, 2007.

Jacob, Mark, and Stephan Benzkofer. "10 Things You Might Not Know About Chicago's Western Suburbs." Sunday, August 15, 2010.

Jacob, Mark. "10 Things You Might Not Know About Divorce." Sunday, March 23, 2008.

Jacob, Mark. "10 Things You Might Not Know About Gay Rights." Sunday, June 1, 2008.

Jacob, Mark. "10 Things You Might Not Know About...Lovers." Sunday, February 14, 2010.

Jacob, Mark. "10 Things You Might Not Know About Marriage." Sunday, April 19, 2009.

Jacob, Mark, and Stephan Benzkofer. "10 Things You Might Not Know About Tipping." Sunday, December 4, 2011.

Jacob, Mark, and Stephan Benzkofer. "10 Things You Might Not Know About Class Warfare." Sunday, October 23, 2011.

Jacob, Mark, and Stephan Benzkofer. "10 Things You Might Not Know About Royal Weddings." Sunday, April 17, 2011.

Jacob, Mark. "10 Things You Might Not Know About Racism." Sunday, January 17, 2010.

Jacob, Mark. "10 Things You Might Not Know About the Color Green." Sunday, March 15, 2009.

Jacob, Mark, and Stephan Benzkofer. "10 Things You Might Not Know About CONTRACEPTIVES." Sunday, March 25, 2012.

Jacob, Mark, and Stephan Benzkofer. "10 Things You Might Not Know About Elephants." Sunday, May 15, 2011.

Jacob, Mark, and Stephan Benzkofer. "10 Things You Might Not Know About Epidemics." Sunday, September 25, 2011.

Jacob, Mark. "10 Things You Might Not Know About Gasoline." Sunday, May 18, 2008.

Jacob, Mark. "10 Things You Might Not Know About HAIR." Sunday, October 18, 2009.

Jacob, Mark, and Stephan Benzkofer. "10 Things You Might Not Know About Height." Sunday, December 26, 2010.

Jacob, Mark, and Stephan Benzkofer. "10 Things You Might Not Know About Hurricanes." Sunday, September 18, 2011.

Jacob, Mark. "10 Things You Might Not Know About the Nobel Prize." Sunday, October 14, 2007.

Jacob, Mark. "10 Things You Might Not Know About...Numbers." Sunday, November 30, 2008.

Jacob, Mark. "10 Things You Might Not Know About Robots." Sunday, July 6, 2008.

Jacob, Mark, and Stephan Benzkofer. "10 Things You Might Not Know About Skin Color." Sunday, February 12, 2012.

Jacob, Mark. "10 Things You Might Not Know About Snow." Sunday, February 10, 2008.

Jacob, Mark, and Stephan Benzkofer. "10 Things You Might Not Know About Space." Sunday, January 15, 2012.

Jacob, Mark. "10 Things You Might Not Know About TV Technology." Sunday, June 14, 2009.

Jacob, Mark. "10 Things You Might Not Know About Twins." Sunday, July 20, 2008.

Jacob, Mark. "10 Things You Might Not Know About Air Travel." Sunday December 13, 2009.

Jacob, Mark. "10 Things You Might Not Know About Beer." Sunday, September 16, 2007.

Jacob, Mark. "10 Things You Might Not Know About Candy." October 28, 2007.

Jacob, Mark. "10 Things You Might Not Know About Drunkenness." Sunday, October 5, 2008.

Jacob, Mark. "10 Things You Might Not Know About Eggs." Sunday, April 5, 2009.

Jacob, Mark, and Stephan Benzkofer. "10 Things You Might Not Know About Chicago Food." Sunday, June 20, 2010.

Jacob, Mark. "10 Things You Might Not Know About Ice Cream." Sunday, July 19, 2009.

Jacob, Mark. "10 Things You Might Not Know About Marijuana." Sunday, April 20, 2008.

Jacob, Mark. "10 Things You Might Not Know About Meat." Sunday, August 24, 2008.

Jacob, Mark, and Stephan Benzkofer. "10 Things You Might Not Know About Salt." Sunday, January 29, 2012.

Jacob, Mark, and Stephan Benzkofer. "10 Things You Might Not Know About Tomatoes." Sunday, March 20, 2011.

Jacob, Mark. "10 Things You Might Not Know About Toys." Sunday, December 23, 2007.

Jacob, Mark, and Stephan Benzkofer. "10 Things You Might Not Know About Turkey." Sunday, November 20, 2011."

Jacob, Mark. "10 Things You Might Not Know About France." Sunday, April 6, 2008.

Jacob, Mark. "10 Things You Might Not Know About Iran." Sunday, February 25, 2007.

Jacob, Mark. "10 Things You Might Not Know About Ohio." Sunday, February 24, 2008.

Jacob, Mark. "10 Things You Might Not Know About Texas." Sunday, March 2, 2008.

Jacob, Mark, and Stephan Benzkofer. "10 Things You Might Not Know About Wisconsin." Sunday, August 14, 2011.

Jacob, Mark, and Stephan Benzkofer. "10 Things You Might Not Know About Iowa." Sunday, January 1, 2012."

Jacob, Mark. "10 Things You Might Not Know About Michigan." Sunday, January 24, 2010.

Jacob, Mark. "10 Things You Might Not Know About Dirty Politics." Sunday, October 19, 2008.

Jacob, Mark. "10 Things You Might Not Know About Election Day." Sunday, November 2, 2008.

Jacob, Mark. "10 Things You Might Not Know About the G-8." Sunday, June 3, 2007.

Jacob, Mark, and David Jahntz. "10 Things You Might Not Know About Inaugurations." Sunday, January 18, 2009.

Jacob, Mark. "10 Things You Might Not Know About Lieutenant Governors." Sunday, February 7, 2010.

Jacob, Mark. "10 Things You Might Not Know About Philandering Politicians." Sunday, July, 15, 2007.

Jacob, Mark, and Stephan Benzkofer. "10 Things You Might Not Know About Politicians' Kids." Sunday, October 17, 2010.

Jacob, Mark, and Stephan Benzkofer. "10 Things You Might Not Know About Republicans." Sunday, November 14, 2010.

Jacob, Mark. "10 Things You Might Not Know About Taxes." Sunday, February 28, 2010.

Jacob, Mark, and Stephan Benzkofer. "10 Things You Might Not Know About Third Parties." Sunday, October 3, 2010.

Jacob, Mark. "10 Things You Might Not Know About the U.S. Supreme Court." Sunday, May 9, 2010.

Jacob, Mark, and Stephan Benzkofer. "10 Things You Might Not Know About April Fools' Day." Sunday, March 28, 2010.

Jacob, Mark. "10 Things You Might Not Know About Atheists." Sunday, December 9, 2007.

Jacob, Mark. "10 Things You Might Not Know About Birthdays." Sunday, February 15, 2009.

Jacob, Mark, and Stephan Benzkofer. "10 Things You Might Not Know About December Holidays." Sunday, December 18, 2011.

Jacob, Mark. "10 Things You Might Not Know About Famous Evangelists." Sunday, November 25, 2007.

Jacob, Mark, and Stephan Benzkofer. "10 Things You Might Not Know About Halloween." Sunday, October 31, 2010.

Jacob, Mark, and Stephan Benzkofer. "10 Things You Might Not Know About Saints." Sunday, May 1, 2011.

Jacob, Mark, and Stephan Benzkofer. "10 Things You Might Not Know About Satan." Sunday, March 11, 2012.

Jacob, Mark. "10 Things You Might Not Know About Acronyms." Sunday, June 22, 2008.

Jacob, Mark. "10 Things You Might Not Know About Double Talk." Sunday, January 3, 2010.

Jacob, Mark. "10 Things You Might Not Know About Middle Names." Sunday, August 10, 2008.

Jacob, Mark, and Stephen Benzkofer. "10 Things You Might Not Know About Punctuation." Sunday, July 18, 2011.

Jacob, Mark, and Stephan Benzkofer. "10 Things You Might Not Know About Speeches." Sunday, January 23, 2011.

Jacob, Mark, and Stephan Benzkofer. "10 Things You Might Not Know About Made-up Words." Sunday, November 28, 2010.

Jacob, Mark, and Stephan Benzkofer. "10 Things You Might Not Know About the Death Penalty." Sunday, March 6, 2011.

Jacob, Mark. "10 Things You Might Not Know About Desperadoes." Sunday, June 28, 2009.

Jacob, Mark, and Stephan Benzkofer. "10 Things You Might Not Know About the Founding Fathers (and Mothers)." Sunday, July 3, 2011.

Jacob, Mark. "10 Things You Might Not Know About the Summer of Love." Sunday, June 17, 2007.

Jacob, Mark. "10 Things You Might Not Know About Women at War." Sunday, April 15, 2007.

Jacob, Mark. "10 Things You Might Not Know About World War II." Sunday, Mary 24, 2009.

Jacob, Mark, and Stephan Benzkofer. "10 Things You Might Not Know About D-Day." Sunday, June 6, 2010.

Jacob, Mark. "10 Things You Might Not Know About Hugo Chavez." Sunday, July 29, 2007.

Jacob, Mark. "10 Things You Might Not Know About Dick Cheney." Sunday, March 11, 2007.

Jacob, Mark. "10 Things You Might Not Know About Rahm Emanuel." Sunday, April 25, 2010.

Jacob, Mark. "10 Things You Might Not Know About the Dalai Lama." Sunday, May 6, 2007.

Jacob, Mark. "10 Things You Might Not Know About the Kennedys." Sunday, August 30, 2009.

Jacob, Mark. "10 Things You Might Not Know About Michael Moore." Sunday, July 1, 2007.

Jacob, Mark. "10 Things You Might Not Know About Oprah." Sunday, January 4, 2009.

Jacob, Mark. "10 Things You Might Not Know About Sarah Palin." Sunday, March 14, 2010.

Jacob, Mark. "10 Things You Might Not Know About Elvis Presley." Sunday, November 16, 2008.